The Foreign Policies
of the Taft Administration

The Foreign Policies
of the Taft Administration

By Walter V. Scholes and Marie V. Scholes

University of Missouri Press
Columbia

ISBN 0-8262-0094-X
Library of Congress Catalog Card Number 70-122310
University of Missouri Press, Columbia, Missouri 65201
Printed and bound in the United States of America
Copyright © 1970 by The Curators of the University of Missouri

For
Lillith Ainsley Scholes

Acknowledgments

We thank the American Philosophical Society and particularly the University of Missouri Research Council for financial help; various individuals for giving us permission to use personal papers; and librarians and staff at Ursinus College, Cornell, Harvard, Yale, and Oxford universities, the Manuscript Room of the Library of Congress, and the Public Record Office for efficient service. We are especially indebted to Mrs. Judy Carroll, Mrs. Pat Dowling, and Mr. Ronald Heise of the National Archives for help far beyond the call of duty.

From Dr. Ralph Parker and his staff at the Library of the University of Missouri we received the greatest cooperation and consideration, for which we are deeply grateful. We also thank Professors David Pletcher and Raymond O'Connor whose criticisms of the manuscript were of the greatest assistance.

W. V. S.
M. V. S.

University of Missouri–Columbia
June, 1970

Contents

Of Men and Methods, 1

Of Men and Methods

Of Men and Methods

William Howard Taft's family background, his abilities and training, and his long experience in public administration seemed to justify the assumption that he was well-equipped for the Presidency of the United States. His father Alphonso Taft was prominent in Ohio politics, served in President Grant's Cabinet, and held diplomatic posts in Vienna and St. Petersburg. The younger Taft, after graduating from Yale as salutatorian of the Class of '78, continued his excellent academic record at Cincinnati Law School, this time sharing with a classmate honors for first place. His appointment in 1886 to the Ohio Superior Court was certainly a considerable and seemingly a premature plum for a man only twenty-nine years old, but he had worked for the party and, helped along by his father's political influence, had held several lesser appointments before reaching the court. In 1887 he won his first—and next-to-last—victory at the polls by being confirmed on the bench. Later he became Solicitor General of the United States and then, in 1892, a judge of the federal circuit court. This last judiciary appointment apparently ended any thought he had entertained of a political career; indeed, his ambition now looked toward an appointment to the United States Supreme Court.

The Spanish-American War changed the direction of his career. Initially unsympathetic to the jingoes' clamor, once war was declared, Taft concluded that President McKinley could not have avoided hostilities. It never entered his mind, however, to emulate Theodore Roosevelt, his junior by one year, by volunteering for active service. His turn to serve the country in this international crisis came in the postwar period when, much to his astonishment, McKinley asked him to head the commission that was to govern the Philippine Islands. His sense of civic duty, his family's urging that this appointment might well be the gateway to greater honors, and McKinley's assurance that he need not stay in the Islands more than nine months overcame his initial reluctance to accept the post. Taft landed in the Philippines in June 1900 to take up a task that, ultimately, he did not surrender—and then only unwillingly—until February 1904.

Taft's first reaction to the Filipinos was typical of that of most Americans of the time: He regarded them as light-fingered, light-hearted liars who were thoroughly unfit for independence. Yet this judgment did not blind him to their sensitivities; from the first he drew no color line at social functions, an atypical approach that won the Filipinos' hearts. In many ways Taft's attitude toward his charges is reminiscent of the sixteenth-century Spaniards' treatment of Indians as irresponsible children and the later Western concept of Orientals as the white man's burden. He thought of the natives as children who needed direction and whose guidance was a sacred trust laid upon the United States for civilization.

By the turn of the century Roosevelt, as McKinley's Vice President, had developed a high opinion of Taft, and Taft's successes in the Philippines greatly increased his admiration. After assuming the Presidency, Roosevelt began urging Taft to come home because he wanted him available as an adviser and counselor. In October 1902 Roosevelt offered Taft an appointment to the Supreme Court, but although strongly tempted, Taft felt duty-bound to continue his work in the Islands. In 1904, however, when Elihu Root resigned as Secretary of War, Taft agreed to accept the vacated post, since its duties included responsibility for the administration of the Philippines. Soon afterward Root returned to the Cabinet as Secretary of State, and such mutual respect and camaraderie grew up among the three men that they sometimes referred to themselves (incorrectly, to be sure) as the Three Musketeers. Roosevelt, naturally, was D'Artagnan; Root was Athos; Taft was Porthos.

As Secretary of War, Taft continued to exercise his skills as administrator. He served the President well, and Roosevelt in his turn demonstrated his confidence in Taft's ability by entrusting to him a number of important tasks, several of them in the diplomatic field. In the fall of 1906, when the president of Cuba, faced with a revolt, asked for American intervention, Roosevelt was loath to comply. He dispatched Taft and Robert Bacon of the State Department on a mission to unravel the tangle of Cuban politics by peaceful means, but the task proved impossible and American military authorities took over.

During his service in the Philippines Taft had developed what was to be a lasting interest in the Orient and particularly in China. He came to realize that the Islands' location and the United States' commitments there placed this country in an awkward strategic position. Yet he never accepted the idea, as did practically all the military men who served in the area, that Japan contemplated invading the Philippines. As Secretary of War, Taft's responsibility toward the Islands continued and he thereby had the opportunity to keep his hand in Far Eastern politics. Two missions allowed him to gather firsthand impressions of the situation there, for in 1905 Roosevelt sent him on an inspection tour of the Philippines with instructions to stop in Japan for talks on the Far Eastern situation. Taft returned to the Islands again in 1907, and Roosevelt used the opportunity to have him visit Tokyo, this time to soothe Japanese feelings aroused by Japanese-American frictions in California.

While in the Cabinet, Taft received assurances from Roosevelt that he would support Taft for the presidential nomination in 1908. The Supreme Court—not the Presidency—was Taft's great ambition, but, driven by his admiring family and by an ambitious wife who never faltered in her determination to keep him from "decay" in the judiciary, he at last consented reluctantly to run for the office. After an uninspired campaign during which he regularly consulted Roosevelt—one wit had it that TAFT stood for "Take Advice From Theodore"—the returns gave Taft 321 electoral votes to William Jennings Bryan's 162. His plurality was 1,269,606, which, although large, was less than half Roosevelt's lead in 1904.

In spite of the impressive qualifications he brought to the office, Taft made an indifferent record as President, and for some obvious reasons. When Taft became a candidate his supporters claimed that his executive experience in the Philippines qualified him for the White House. The President of the United States is, however, not merely an executive. He is his party's and his country's leader, and his success in office depends upon his political skill in these roles. As president of the Philippine Commission and later, as governor-general of the Islands, Taft had no need for these skills; his word was law. His tenure of these positions and his record of achievement in them did not depend on hard work on the hustings, on a grasp of the political facts of life, or on the subtle exercise of that intangible known as "power." In the Islands he was free to administer his office without subtle political overtones. But the President of the United States is no proconsul. He must be acutely conscious of the political effects of his acts, and Taft disliked politics; he stated flatly that when he got involved in them, they made him sick—a fact that his more political associates recognized. Senator Henry Cabot Lodge admitted that Taft lacked political *savoir-faire,* especially in his appointments, while "Uncle Joe" Cannon, sempiternal member of the House, putting it more colorfully, declared that the trouble with Taft was that if he were Pope he would think it necessary to appoint a few Protestant cardinals.[1]

Ideally, the President is the leader not only of his own political party but of the whole nation in their efforts to adjust to social and economic changes. Taft assumed office at a time when many such problems, both old and new, were demanding solutions, but he was incapable of moving toward the necessary changes. First of all, despite the fact that he had gone along with Roosevelt's reforms, Taft remained a conservative. He revered the law and the judicial process; he respected the past and its institutions; he disliked change, especially if the impetus came from below.[2] In addition, he was inept in projecting his own ideas, since he lacked the capacity and taste for popular leadership. He disliked the limelight and he disliked crowds; he got no exhilaration from the masses of people who came to see and hear him, and as a result, they in turn did not respond to him. Taft's press relations were badly handled—an important factor at a time when newspapers and magazines were the only means of communication between the White House and the public.[3] But poor press relations were not the only negative factor; Taft himself was in large measure responsible for his situation because he reacted sharply and tactlessly to criticism.

Although Taft worked hard and dutifully, he lacked imaginative drive. Rather than pushing his ideas with congressmen either personally or through aides or with the public by holding press conferences in which he could match wits with the newspapermen, he preferred to nap, to chat with old cronies, to play bridge,

1. Henry Cabot Lodge, ed., *Selections from the Correspondence of Theodore Roosevelt and Henry Cabot Lodge,* II, 335; Mark Sullivan, *Our Times,* IV, 410.
2. G. E. Mowry, *The Era of Theodore Roosevelt, 1900-1912,* 234.
3. Taft got off to a bad start when, in contrast to the old days at the War Department, he did not let members of the press corps drop in and see him on Inauguration Day.

and, on warm nights, to sit on the porch of the White House listening to records on the "music machine." He never spent much time or thought in preparing his speeches; he put off writing them until the last moment and, consequently, made remarks that later caused him much embarrassment. As he himself confessed, he liked the comfort, dignity, and power of the Presidency without its worries. Had Mrs. Taft kept her health she might have been able to force her husband to greater activity, but on May 17, 1909, she suffered what was probably a cerebral hemorrhage that left her partially paralyzed. For some time afterward she was unable to speak, and although her health gradually improved, she never fully recovered.

Perhaps most important in reducing Taft's effectiveness as President was his break with Roosevelt. A slight misunderstanding between them developed early in Taft's incumbency over the appointment of new members of the Cabinet and the dismissal of Henry White from the diplomatic service. Then came the Pinchot-Ballinger controversy over public lands, which led Roosevelt to think that Taft was undoing all the previous work on conservation. The families of both men widened the breach. Mrs. Taft had long distrusted Roosevelt, and she pressed her doubts on her husband, while Alice Roosevelt Longworth, a good mimic, delighted a wide circle with her performances, especially her barbed imitations of Mrs. Taft.[4] Taft himself let his differences with Roosevelt grow by not stopping the conservatives' persistent verbal sniping at Roosevelt, remarks that became more and more personal and that Taft, as a matter of fact, came to enjoy. On the other hand, Roosevelt was a politician, a breed that is unhappy out of office. In any case the alienation between the two old friends cost Taft much valuable support in the Congress and in the country.

Taft's reasoning in this break with his former friend had its roots in the conviction that Roosevelt had aroused public opinion to demand reforms for which no legal basis existed, and Taft considered it his duty to provide such a foundation by changes in the laws. The people best fitted to help him carry through this program "without injury to the business interests of the country, are those lawyers who understand corporate wealth, the present combination, its evils, and the method by which they can properly be restrained." Taft believed further that the men who led Congress would be more apt to reject recommendations made by a

4. Alice Roosevelt Longworth, *Crowded Hours,* 164-65.

Cabinet composed of "the more radical members of the party."[5] He was aware, as he wrote Roosevelt, that he would probably be attacked for choosing more lawyers for his Cabinet than he ought to and for those lawyers to have had corporate connections. Nevertheless, he wanted the best talent available; he did not believe that he could get it without calling on men with Big Business connections.[6] As a result of this reasoning, five of the nine Cabinet members, in addition to the President, were members of the bar.

Elihu Root refused Taft's invitation to serve as Secretary of State and Henry Cabot Lodge also declined. Apparently on Root's recommendation, Taft then offered the post to Senator Philander Chase Knox, a wealthy conservative lawyer who had served in the Cabinet earlier. After considering the matter for a few weeks, Knox accepted appointment as Secretary of State in mid-December 1908, and from this time on he gradually became one of Taft's most trusted advisers. Taft consulted him not merely on foreign affairs, which was natural, but also on domestic policy, an area in which Taft grew to rely heavily on Knox's advice as well as on that of Root and George W. Wickersham, his Attorney General.

In this consideration of the foreign policy of the United States during the Presidency of William Howard Taft, the personality and background of the man who helped to shape and implement it are of paramount interest. Knox's attitudes toward his office and subordinates and his methods of work are also notable for complete understanding of the nation's international relations during his tenure of office. Born on May 6, 1853, in Brownsville, a small community about fifty miles south of Pittsburgh, Knox was the son of a banker and the grandson of a Methodist Episcopal minister. After attending the local public schools, he matriculated at Mount Union College in Ohio and received his B.A. degree in 1872. He then read law in Pittsburgh, and shortly after his admission to the bar of Allegheny County in 1875 he was appointed assistant district attorney of the Western District of Pennsylvania. After a year he resigned from this office to begin in earnest building his private practice, which he did with noteworthy success. Although his cases were varied and not confined to any one branch of the law, he came to be regarded as a corporation lawyer. One of his best-known legal efforts, and one of the

5. Henry R. Pringle, *The Life and Times of William Howard Taft; A Biography,* I, 382.
6. Theodore Roosevelt Papers.

more remunerative, was his work in helping to reorganize the Carnegie Steel Corporation. The connection brought returns far beyond his retainer, since it introduced him to Henry C. Frick, who gave him good advice on how to invest his money.

Knox's engagement in private practice would seem, in an overview of his career, as simply an interruption to his political life. As one of McKinley's early backers, he raised $6,000 among his friends for campaign expenses for McKinley's nomination. In 1899 McKinley asked him to become Attorney General, but Knox was not ready to abandon his practice. While there is no positive evidence, it would seem that Knox wanted to be in sound financial condition before giving up the private practice of law for public service. When McKinley repeated his request two years later, Knox accepted, but his service to his old friend was of short duration. Five months later McKinley was assassinated.

When Roosevelt assumed the Presidency on September 14, 1901, he took over McKinley's Cabinet, and until Knox resigned three years later he was a man of importance in the Roosevelt Administration. Roosevelt in fact held Knox in such high esteem that it was with obvious reluctance that he agreed to let Knox resign from the Cabinet and accept appointment as Senator from Pennsylvania. The President assured Knox that the United States had never had an Attorney General who set so high a standard and one who brought such keen insight, resolute fairness, and statesmanlike grasp of affairs to the office.[7] When Knox's credentials were presented to the Senate in December 1904, the Senators discovered that Governor Samuel Pennypacker had written that Knox could hold office only "if he behaves himself well." This characteristic bit of Pennypackery nearly convulsed Knox's new colleagues. Subsequently, in January 1905, Knox was elected to a full term in the Senate.

Some talk developed of pushing Knox for the presidential nomination of 1908, and in June he received the endorsement of the Pennsylvania Republican State Convention. There is at least a hint that he was interested, for in 1916 he wrote Francis M. Huntington-Wilson that Roosevelt forced Taft on the party in 1908 when no one else wanted him, and Taft paid the penalty in 1912 when the bosses forced him on the people, who wanted Roosevelt.[8] But in 1908 Roosevelt of course was committed to Taft, and

7. Philander C. Knox Papers.
8. Francis M. Huntington-Wilson Papers.

Knox had no chance of winning his party's nomination.

The new Secretary of State was only five feet five inches tall; Roosevelt often referred to him affectionately as "Little Phil" or "a sawed-off cherub." To his nieces and nephews he was "Uncle Cupid." He was always carefully and expensively dressed. A stand-up collar, with points slightly turned down, combined with the jowl it supported to serve as a foundation for the face and head, made them look the more impressive.[9] Most people who met him were struck by the massive dome of his well-shaped head; others by his dignity and by the grave wisdom of his face. Others thought that he looked far more like a French or Italian churchman whose avocation was diplomacy and statecraft, rather than an American politician.[10] The *Nation* called him a political cardinal.[11]

Knox gave the impression of being a cold man and one hard to know. At times his face became an immobile mask that effectually concealed his thoughts, which might well account for his success at poker, a game he thoroughly enjoyed. Certainly he was not a gregarious man, and neither he nor his wife could be called society people. Yet his friends knew that he enjoyed huge Partaga Invincible cigars, good wine, and good conversation.[12] Indeed, Mitchell Innes of the British embassy described the Secretary as "short, fat and benevolent."[13]

To get away from the capital, Knox tried to spend part of his summers in New England. If this were not possible he went to the home that he had bought while a senator, at Valley Forge, close to Philadelphia. During the winter he enjoyed a short vacation in Florida. In Washington his three-story home on K Street was his headquarters. Knox did some of his work in the first-floor library, which was lined with shelves of handsome volumes and furnished with pieces that included a huge French desk with brass trimmings, a bust of Napoleon, and a portrait of himself. He did a great deal of work early in the morning in a small library next

9. Francis M. Huntington-Wilson, *Memoirs of an Ex-Diplomat,* 175.
10. *Bankers Magazine,* September, 1909.
11. *Nation,* May 22, 1920.
12. On his tour of the Caribbean in 1912 Knox took with him 30 dozen quarts of Pol Roger Brut 1900 and the same numer of Roeder Carte Blanche, three dozen quarts of Chambertin, three dozen quarts of Château Margaux, and six dozen quarts of Château Latour Blanche. His supplies also included Pall Mall and Philip Morris cigarettes and plenty of cigars. Knox Papers.
13. Innes to Alston, November 2, 1910, Foreign Office, 800/248. Henceforth cited as FO.

to his bedroom. He liked to get up around five, when his butler would bring him a thermos flask of coffee, and then, with the morning paper, State Department material, and other pertinent information at hand, he considered the problems of his department.[14] He arrived at his office in the old State Department Building at about ten or ten-thirty and seldom returned there after luncheon except on Thursdays, the regular calling day for foreign representatives who had business with him, or on days when he had special appointments.

About three times a week Knox took his first assistant secretary, Francis Huntington-Wilson, to lunch at either the Metropolitan Club or the Shoreham Hotel. After a cocktail or two, they would settle down to either terrapin and a bottle of champagne or canvasback duck, done very rare, with a bottle of red wine. The ritual luncheons were a combination of business and pleasure. Huntington-Wilson always briefed himself carefully and during the meal would draw from his pocket a list of the matters in the department that were too important to go forward without the approval of the Secretary. He would explain each item and make recommendations, which Knox usually approved.[15] Luncheon over, Knox strolled home for a little nap, and later, if the weather permitted, he would motor out to Chevy Chase for golf.

Apparently Knox's relationships with his subordinates in the department were good; his relationships with the United States Senate, the press, and certain foreign diplomats were not. In spite of the fact that Knox had served in the Senate, he rarely showed any appreciation of that body's notorious sensitivities. In the one instance when Knox did take the trouble to prepare the ground, the Senate approved the proposed treaty—the commercial treaty with Japan in 1911. This was not, of course, the only treaty approved by the Senate during the Taft Administration. At least two important agreements—those concerning fur seals and Canadian reciprocity—passed without excessive pressure from the Administration.[16] In most cases, however, Knox refused to make the

14. Huntington-Wilson, *Memoirs,* 175, 178.
15. Huntington-Wilson, *Memoirs,* 180, 232.
16. By the late nineteenth century hunters had taken so many seals from the Pacific islands that the herds had practically disappeared except around those in the Bering Sea, notably the American Pribilof group. Congressional attempts to save and increase the herds were frustrated when the Canadians resorted to pelagic sealing—taking the animals on the high seas—which meant, in most cases, females during the breeding season. Since both Russian and American domestic law prohibited pelagic sealing, the problem was to reach an agreement with Great

effort to smooth the way for international agreements, and he
generally ignored the frequent suggestions that he wine and dine
at least the key senators.[17] As a result of his disdain for personal
and social influence on legislators, many treaties he considered
important never became law.[18]

Britain. This was done in 1893 by an arrangement that put an end to pelagic
sealing within a sixty-mile zone around the Pribilof Islands, which in effect gave
the Canadians a virtual monopoly of pelagic sealing in the Bering Sea. In 1901,
however, the Japanese, bound by no domestic or international restrictions, entered
the field and for all practical purposes drove the Canadians out of business. The
United States wanted an international ban on pelagic sealing, because the seals
then could be taken only on American shores and only at the rate set by Congress.
The Administration realized that it would have to compensate Canada and Japan,
and after much involved and tedious negotiation, details of the compensation
were settled. The four governments signed the convention on July 17, 1911. For a
summary, see C. C. Tansill, *Canadian-American Relations, 1875-1911,* Chap. XII,
and Department of State File 711.417.
L. E. Ellis, in his book *Reciprocity, 1911,* discusses in detail the subject of Canadian-American reciprocity and the efforts of the Taft Administration to conclude a
treaty on the subject. The agreement, approved by the Senate, was rejected by
Canada. The Americans expected more from the treaty than just tariff changes.
Taft wrote to Roosevelt that the movement of products from Western Canada
could result in a current of business that would make Canada an adjunct of the
United States. The traffic would transfer all the Canadians' important business to
Chicago and New York (January 10, 1911, William Howard Taft Papers). Charles
Nagel told A. Busch that the real significance of the agreement was in having the
closest possible bond forged between the United States and a vigorous, promising
country like Canada. It was not merely a question of the exchange of products.
Rather, it was a matter of having close ties with a powerful neighbor of our own
kind. In the not far distant future an intimate relationship with Canada would be
of utmost importance and it could be established only by commercial connections;
no political treaty would accomplish this end. The only factor that could cement
the two countries together permanently was to have the arteries of commerce run
north and south, making the people so commercially interdependent that they
would in no circumstance agree to have the bonds severed. Nagel to Busch, February 20, 1911. Charles Nagel Papers.
17. In a long letter to his government, Ambassador Jean Jusserand recounted his
difficulties in trying to get Knox to approach the members of the Senate committee
with regard to the Franco-German arrangement on Morocco. Finally, when Jusserand realized that Knox did not intend to act, the Ambassador asked the Secretary
if he had any objection to Jusserand's discussing the question with senators whom
he knew. To Jusserand's satisfaction Knox made no objection whatsoever. Jusserand to De Selves, December 16, 1911. *Documents diplomatiques français,* Ser. 3,
I, No. 353, 347-50. Henceforth cited as *DDF.*
18. The arbitration treaty with England is a good example. Since Taft was devoted
to world peace and believed in man's ability to shape society toward a better life,
he thought that the Anglo-Saxon countries should take the leadership in making
peace possible. If the United States and England set an example through a treaty
of arbitration, other nations might well follow and wars could be avoided. Moreover, Taft and others had doubts about the Anglo-Japanese Alliance. Should the
United States and Japan differ critically, would England, under the requirements
of the alliance, support the Japanese? A properly worded arbitration treaty might
eliminate this potential threat. Not until February 15, 1911, however, did the
United States make a definite proposal. On that date the department sent Bryce
a draft treaty.
The British, looking for some way to convince the United States that England was

Although on certain issues, such as the arbitration treaty with England, most of the press applauded the Secretary, its responses to his efforts were usually lukewarm or hostile. The *New York Tribune,* owned by the Ambassador to Great Britain, Whitelaw Reid, consistently supported the Administration's policies. The *Pittsburgh Dispatch* was also behind Knox, and journals such as *World's Work* and the *Nation* had some good things to say about American foreign policy, but the over-all reaction of the press was unfavorable. It was a case of tit for tat: Knox remarked that "the reason the newspapers attack our foreign policies so frequently

not bound to support Japan in case of an American-Japanese conflict, welcomed the overture. Sir Edward Grey discussed the matter with the Japanese ambassador and the two men agreed that whenever the British reached a satisfactory treaty of general arbitration with the United States, Japan and England would then revise that article of the treaty of alliance, making it inapplicable to any country with which Great Britain had a treaty of general arbitration. On March 29 Grey reported to the Cabinet on his conversations with Kato. After considerable discussion the Cabinet decided to propose to the Japanese Government, in addition to revision of the pertinent article, a renewal of the alliance, which was to expire in 1915, for a further term of ten years, to date from 1911.

On March 30 Grey informed Bryce of the Cabinet's decision. On April 13 Reid talked to Grey about the effect of the arbitration treaty on the Anglo-Japanese Alliance. Grey told him—but Reid was not to repeat it to his government—that the matter had already been arranged. Without giving any details, Reid cabled Knox to assure him that there would be no obstacles to the treaty, and finally, on April 21, he sent the Secretary a complete account of the British position.

By mid-May Knox and Bryce were discussing the draft. Although Bryce was irritated by what he considered the Secretary's niggling demands, eventually the final treaty was ready for signature. At the same time Knox was dickering with England, he was haggling with France over an arbitration treaty, also annoying that country by his demands. Here too, however, a solution was finally found. On August 3, 1911, the treaties were signed with England and France, the first in Washington, the second in Paris.

Although the arbitration treaty with England was Taft's most popular venture in foreign affairs and the President campaigned ardently in its favor, the support given it by public opinion and a good part of the press was not sufficient to overcome senatorial opposition. It was another case in which the Secretary showed that he did not understand the importance of "domestic diplomacy." Knox did not consult with the members of the Senate Foreign Relations Committee while the treaty was being drafted. Lodge, a committee member, went to the department on June 15 to try to find out what terms the treaty would include. Knox was not at his office, "which is not infrequently the case." But Lodge had a more fundamental complaint against the treaty—it was not, in his opinion, in the national interest. In January, when it was obvious that the Administration did not have the votes needed for approval, it accepted Lodge's proposal for a modification that, the Senator believed, would leave the international situation exactly as if the treaty did not exist. In addition, opposition arose from the fact that many senators believed that the arbitration arrangement deprived the Senate of one of its most important prerogatives. Eventually, in March, the Senate passed an emasculated version of the treaty, which the Administration refused to accept. Taft and Knox considered reopening negotiations with England but realized that it was a hopeless course. The above is based on Department of State (henceforth cited as DS) 711.4112; Herbert Asquith Papers; James Bryce Papers; Whitelaw Reid Papers; Taft Papers; Knox Papers; and Roosevelt Papers.

and violently is because they make it a point to attack whatever they don't understand and the violence of the assault depends upon the depth of the ignorance." Or again: "You can safely take large liberties in attack upon a public officer whose hands are tied by the reserves incident to the nature of his duties."[19] Knox never acquired the knack, as many public officials do, of using the press to his advantage.

The *New York Tribune*'s reporter George G. Hill cited some specific reasons for the unfavorable comments on Knox's actions. As early as December 1909 he pointed out that popular criticism arose in part from the fact that Knox was determined not to ruin his health by working so hard as some of his predecessors. But the adverse criticism was also attributable to Knox's extreme reticence in dealing with the press, toward whose mistakes he was disposed to be somewhat intolerant, despite the fact that neither he nor any of his associates was willing to give any intimation as to the truth or error of current rumors until after they had appeared in print; they were then denied with some acerbity.[20] By early 1910 the *New York Times* was observing that the unfavorable criticism of the department was so loud, it drove out most favorable comment. It is interesting that practically all the criticism concerned methods rather than policies.

In dealing with foreign diplomats, Knox was at his worst with the Latin-American representatives. Root might think of them as "dagos" and express such sentiments to friends, but he was able to convince the Latin-American diplomats that he regarded them as equals. Knox did not conceal the fact that he considered them inferior and as representing inferior peoples. He made no effort to establish a real rapport, and the Latin Americans, on their part, did not consider him *simpático*. After the Pan-American Conference in Buenos Aires in 1910, Henry White suggested that Knox receive the ministers from the various countries more frequently, since they had the feeling that he was difficult to reach. A little personal interchange, White stressed, was most effective with the Latin Americans; it was, as a matter of fact, the whole secret of diplomatic success in that part of the world. White also encouraged Knox to attend some of the meetings of the Pan American Union, tiresome as they were.[21] Knox was not amenable; he found

19. Knox Papers.
20. Hill, Washington, December 22, 1909, to Reid, Reid Papers.
21. Apparently Huntington-Wilson did not show the letter to the Secretary. White

it difficult to cultivate "the delicate entente with the Latins which had been nourished and maintained largely in the past upon champagne and other alcoholic preservatives."[22]

When Taft appointed Knox as his Secretary of State, Roosevelt, Lodge, and Whitelaw Reid approved of the choice: Although Knox knew little about foreign policy, he was a well-trained public servant and a lawyer of exceptional ability; therefore he would be a good Secretary. Henry Adams dissented and prophesied gloomily that four years of Taft plus Knox would make a nightmare such as Sinbad never dreamed.[23] Root revised his early opinion of the suitability of Knox for the post—to which he had recommended him—chiefly on the basis of the change in relationships between the United States and the Latin-American states, for he now saw that Knox rekindled all the suspicions and fears Root had done so much to dampen. Further, Knox's temperament was no help in diplomatic exchanges. According to Root's description, "Knox was a peppery sort of fellow. He got mad very easily. He did mix into things too much." Root commented later, "Knox was an awfully good fellow, and very able and it was a delight to have anything to do with him in any matter that came within the training and experience of an American lawyer. He was, however, absolutely antipathetic to all Spanish-American modes of thought and feeling and action."[24]

Roosevelt, too, changed his mind about Knox, only his complaint was with Knox's management of the Taft Administration's Far Eastern policy. After several exchanges of views with Roosevelt on the subject, the Secretary reported to Taft that in Roosevelt's opinion the situation in the Far East should be dealt with as a fact and not on theories of interest based on treaties. With Lord Grey, the governor-general of Canada, Roosevelt was more candid. Knox was a lawyer and, Roosevelt asserted, the Oriental policy of the United States was a matter for statesmen, not lawyers.[25] Mitchell Innes of the British embassy, who did not doubt Knox's sincerity and his friendly feeling toward England, agreed in regarding Knox's legal training as a handicap to his success as a diplomat. A shrewd lawyer, Knox brought to the department the

to Knox, October 22, 1910, DS Conf., 710.11/46. Bears stamp of Assistant Secretary but not of the Secretary.
22. Knox to Taft, March 14, 1911, Taft Papers.
23. *Henry Adams and His Friends. A Collection of His Unpublished Letters,* Harold D. Cater, ed., 637-40.
24. Philip C. Jessup, *Elihu Root,* II, 250-51.
25. Grey to Bryce, January 20, 1911, Bryce Papers.

lawyer's tendency to consider his country as his client, whose commercial interests he meant to fight for as hard as he could, without the slightest consideration for his opponents' welfare or dignity. This viewpoint was Knox's greatest difficulty, in Innes' opinion—he was too much a lawyer and too little a student of man. "To him a treaty is a contract, diplomacy is litigation and the countries interested are parties to a suit."[26] As Edmund Burke observed long ago about the law: It is a profession which may quicken the intellect, but it does not enlarge the understanding, save in those happily born.

In formulating over-all policy, Knox of course consulted the President and at times men outside the executive branch such as Roosevelt and Root; Lodge had lost his former influence. But the man on whom he relied most heavily was his luncheon companion, the first assistant secretary, Francis M. Huntington-Wilson.[27] He was the hardest-working man in the department, the one who made the day-by-day decisions and directed the formulation of major policy decisions. Even a cursory glance at the files of the department for 1909–1913 shows an astonishing number of items bearing his comments. One is perplexed, on the other hand, to see how few bear the stamp of the Secretary of State. When a problem developed, Huntington-Wilson asked for a memorandum, which was then sent for comment either to an area desk or to Alvey A. Adee, third assistant secretary of state, and finally to Huntington-Wilson. If the subject was important enough, he commented on it and passed it on to Knox or discussed it orally with him.

There is no doubt, however, that Knox kept final control in his own hands and that the members of the department understood where the power lay, although on occasion he found it necessary to remind them. In a handwritten note he once asked why Huntington-Wilson had signed certain telegrams after Knox had given directions that when he was in the city, all telegrams of major importance were to be submitted to him and the remainder were to be signed with his name by the Assistant Secretary.[28] As in the past, most of the negotiations were conducted in Washington, since trained diplomats in the field were rare. The department

26. Innes to Campbell, November 2, 1910, FO 800/248; Innes to Grey, November 11, 1910, FO 405/200/152.
27. Although he was known as Wilson during the Knox era, he preferred and eventually legally adopted the hyphenated form, which is the one that will be used in this book.
28. Huntington-Wilson Papers.

usually preferred to keep the high-level work, such as the formulation of treaties and agreements, in its own hands and at its headquarters.

The man on whom Knox relied so heavily and through whom he carried out most of his responsibilities as Secretary of State was an officer of considerable ambition and the abilities to achieve it. Francis M. Huntington-Wilson was a member of a Chicago family wealthy enough to provide him with a private income of approximately $10,000 a year. After graduating from Yale in the Class of '97, he became interested in a diplomatic career, and through influence he received an appointment as second secretary in Tokyo, where he remained for nine years. He was extremely fortunate in his choice of a wife. Colonel T. Bentley Mott, the knowing military attaché who had served many years in France, described Lucy Huntington-Wilson as one of the most beautiful and intelligent women the United States had ever produced. She proved to be a true helpmate to her ambitious husband.[29] While Taft was visiting in Tokyo, he saw that Mrs. Huntington-Wilson worked hard to discharge the duties of a diplomat's wife. Her efforts did much to advance her husband's career, for Taft referred her to Root, and the Secretary, not one to deny beauty, saw to it that Huntington-Wilson was recalled to Washington, where he became third assistant secretary in June 1906. Root was soon unhappy with him for personal reasons; to get him out of the Secretary's way, Roosevelt, in January 1909 appointed him Minister to Argentina.[30] Huntington-Wilson never left Washington to take up his post; instead, much to everyone's surprise, he received an important appointment in the new Administration.

Taft and Knox had agreed that in order to implement policy more effectively the department must be reorganized, and in all probability it was Huntington-Wilson's plan for concrete reforms that saved him from Argentina. Knox, strongly impressed by Huntington-Wilson's exposition of needed reforms, picked him for the department's number-two post. He was an excellent choice, in the sense that he was well qualified to carry through the reorganization of the department. Moreover, he devoted himself to the cause of improving both the quality of men in the service and the terms of their employment. He was most kind to new

29. Later there was a divorce.
30. Previous paragraphs based on Huntington-Wilson, *Memoirs*; Huntington-Wilson, *The Peril of Hifalutin*; G. H. Stuart, *The Department of State*.

members of the department, and the career men held him in high regard because they knew he would defend them whenever possible.[31]

In spite of his abilities and his kindness to subordinates, however, Huntington-Wilson was no diplomat; he had an almost limitless capacity for antagonizing people. Root drew up a lengthy indictment: Huntington-Wilson was of a mean disposition, ungenerous, rather formal and quite lacking in a sense of humor, suspicious, egotistical, and ready to take offense.[32] Sir Claude MacDonald, the British ambassador to Japan who had known Huntington-Wilson in Tokyo, described him as much more preoccupied with whether he had been assigned his proper place at diplomatic functions than in promoting friendly relations with the Japanese and his colleagues. Indeed, that Huntington-Wilson's voice or views could carry weight anywhere seemed remarkable to this British diplomat.[33]

Others noticed Huntington-Wilson's suspicious nature. After accompanying Huntington-Wilson on a special mission to Turkey in 1910, Colonel Mott stated that, except for General Hugh Scott, Huntington-Wilson was the most suspicious person he had ever served under. The Assistant Secretary habitually glanced over his shoulder to see who was behind him before making the simplest remark, and he ordered blue paper pasted on the panes of the glass door of his room at the legation.[34] Apparently Huntington-Wilson inculcated this feeling, or at least the observance of it, upon the rest of the department. After a week in the Washington offices, Joseph Grew declared that he would have greeted the Sphinx with shouts of joy at finding something really human again. Everyone, from the mail clerk up, wore a continual expression of "Hush! the very walls have ears!"[35]

Many congressmen regarded the department's number-two man as a bit too precious, for Huntington-Wilson disliked the crude and enjoyed the exquisite. A bon mot was important and so was good tailoring. Foreign representatives found him very difficult to deal with. His objective was always to get the best of any bargain, and in the process he could be as hard as nails. He was little inclined to make even the obviously necessary concessions,

31. Hugh Wilson, *The Education of a Diplomat,* 10; Huntington-Wilson Papers.
32. Jessup, *Root,* I, 457.
33. MacDonald to Grey, December 9, 1910, FO 405/200/212.
34. T. B. Mott, *Twenty Years as Military Attaché,* 172.
35. Joseph C. Grew, *Turbulent Era,* I, 76-77.

and if he did offer any, they were put in terse and insolent terms. Many of Huntington-Wilson's mistakes were due to his lack of tact and knowledge of men.[36]

Since Huntington-Wilson delighted in twisting the Lion's tail, both Lord Bryce and Innes understandably regarded him with antipathy. Innes bitterly referred to him as "that pestilential beast."[37] Bryce, more restrained, described him as "sometimes rather unmeasured in his utterances" and considered his press statements as frequently lacking in judgment. Although Huntington-Wilson was a subordinate whose voice carried little weight with Americans and, in Bryce's opinion, none at all with the President, he probably had influence in the department, owing to Knox's "not very keen interest in the Department's affairs."[38]

Among the men who were shaping and transacting the nation's foreign affairs in Taft's Presidency was Alvey A. Adee, a key member of the Department of State, for he provided continuity in addition to valuable skills. After serving for eight years as secretary of legation in Madrid, Adee in 1877 agreed to accept a temporary appointment in Washington; there he remained until his death in 1924 at the age of eighty-two. John Hay called him "Semper Paratus," while to Huntington-Wilson he was "the Nestor" of the department. Besides being a man of some depth and original judgment, Adee was an accomplished linguist, a distinguished Shakespearean, and an expert in the composition of state papers. His deafness allowed him to hear only what he wanted to through his ear trumpet, and his salty character made him a memorable personality. To this day many of his remarks and suggestions in red ink on diplomatic correspondence are a delight to read. Once Adee called Fred M. Dearing into his office to confer on a Mexican problem and thrust a little piece of yellow paper before Dearing's startled eyes: "Shall Mexico be recognized or wreckognized?"[39]

Adee could range knowledgeably over surprisingly wide geographic and political fields, and his comments and suggestions cover practically all areas of the world. Yet he was not a man to take the intitiative. Knox learned very early that if he wanted

36. Wilson, *Education,* 10; Stuart, *State,* 204; Huntington-Wilson, *Memoirs* and *Peril;* Willard Straight Papers; Bryce Papers; Microfilm of the Japanese Foreign Office Archives, Reel 123, Tele. Series. Henceforth cited as JFO.
37. Innes to Campbell, November 2, 1910, FO 800/248.
38. Bryce to Grey, August 24, 1910, FO 405/200/67.
39. Fred Dearing Papers.

Adee's opinion on anything, he had to conceal his own. Once Adee knew that a proposal came from the Secretary, he would not criticize it.[40]

The newly created post of Counselor of the Department went to Henry Hoyt, formerly Solicitor General of the United States, who had worked closely with Knox when the latter was Attorney General. Hoyt held this position from August 1909 until his death in November of the following year. On that occasion Innes reported that the United States had lost a valuable servant, for Hoyt had been Knox's chief adviser and the mainstay of the department.[41] Huntington-Wilson had worked well with Hoyt but did not with his successor, Chandler Anderson. Before accepting the position of counselor, Anderson spelled out for Knox what he understood his duties and status to be. His assignments would involve not just legal work but also diplomatic negotiations, which Anderson would carry on under Knox's direction and without responsibility to or interference by anyone in the department subordinate to the Secretary. Huntington-Wilson was powerless to change this infuriating situation.[42] Had he known of a further arrangement between Knox and Anderson, no doubt he would have been even more overwrought. Knox confided to Anderson that, although nothing had yet been said on the subject, he thought Huntington-Wilson would request a diplomatic appointment in the near future. If a vacancy did occur in the office of the first assistant, Knox promised that he would urge the President to offer it to Anderson. As it was, Huntington-Wilson's resentment over Anderson's status eventually led to a complete break; the two men ceased speaking to one another.[43]

Willard Straight, a holdover from the Roosevelt Adminstration, continued as acting head of the Far Eastern Division. Straight had spent a number of years in the Orient, having worked in China after his graduation from Cornell University in 1901, first with the Imperial Chinese Maritime Customs Service and then, upon the outbreak of the Russo-Japanese War, as a newspaper correspondent in Korea. At the end of the war Straight accepted the post of vice consul general in Seoul, where he remained until his return to Washington in 1905. In June of the following year he

40. Knox Papers.
41. FO 414/219/35.
42. Anderson to Knox, December 15, 1910; Chandler P. Anderson Papers; Huntington-Wilson Papers.
43. Huntington-Wilson Papers.

was appointed consul general at Mukden, and he served there until his recall to the department in the summer of 1908. In June 1909 Straight resigned to accept a position with the group of financiers that was to represent the United States in the China consortium. Although he then severed his official ties with the department, he retained an intimate connection with its China policy, for whose inception he was partly responsible. Replacing Straight was Ransford S. Miller, Jr., who, after going to Japan as a missionary, had served for a decade as interpreter at the legation in Tokyo and then as secretary and interpreter to the embassy. Edward T. Williams, an authority on Chinese affairs, was Miller's chief assistant.

Major responsibility for the new Division of Latin-American Affairs was assigned to Thomas C. Dawson. He began his service in 1897 as secretary of legation at Rio de Janeiro, where he stayed nearly seven years. Then, as minister resident and consul general in the Dominican Republic, in 1904 he negotiated the two conventions providing for the United States' administration of the customs and finances of that country. Appointed minister to Colombia in 1907, he was transferred to Chile two years later. His assistant, W. T. S. Doyle, had served in Central America, and in 1910 he replaced Dawson as chief of the division. This division was the most overworked in the department.[44]

When it came to the department overseas, Taft had a definite idea about who should—or rather, who should not—represent the United States abroad. He was not in sympathy with the practice of rewarding rich supporters with key posts, for he inclined to the belief that the maintenance of elaborate ambassadorial establishments tended to make diplomats unmindful of their obligation to visiting American citizens. He preferred, as he put it, men who could recognize an American when they saw one.[45] Taft apparently had formed this opinion years earlier, when he and Mrs. Taft visited London shortly after their marriage. They asked Henry White, then at the legation, to get them tickets for the House of Commons, but since these were scarce, White instead offered them tickets for the Royal Mews. The Tafts, especially Mrs. Taft, were indignant at what they considered a snub. No doubt White had many of the instincts of a snob; he was a name

44. Stuart, *State*, 215-16; W. Barnes and J. H. Morgan, *The Foreign Service of the United States*, 180-85.
45. Taft Papers; *New York Times*, March 10, 1909.

dropper, constantly boasting of his connections with royalty and influential people. The spiteful called him "Three-in-a-Bed-Harry" because, they said, his idea of ultimate happiness was to sleep three in a bed—between Lord Lansdowne and Prime Minister Balfour.[46] Notwithstanding these pecularities, he was an effective representative. Roosevelt trusted him and used him in delicate negotiations.

The London incident still rankled, however, and White, a career diplomat whom Roosevelt had appointed ambassador to France, was high on the list of Taft's undesirables. Three weeks after his inauguration Taft asked Knox to tell White that his resignation from the service would be accepted, to take effect on January 1, 1910.[47] As a career man, White had every reason to expect a transfer rather than dismissal, and his summary discharge hurt the department's efforts to build a permanent professional corps. White's dismissal demonstrated that even men with "tenure" had to depend upon political connections to stay alive in the Foreign Service. Replacing White was Robert Bacon, Harvard classmate of Roosevelt, member of J. P. Morgan and Company, who became Secretary of State for a short time in 1909.

Another man Taft wanted to get rid of was Whitelaw Reid, ambassador to the Court of St. James's. Taft had the feeling that Reid was carrying on "high-jinks" in London by entertaining royalty, including the King, and upperclass Englishmen at Devonshire House. This high life was all very well, but it did not seem to Taft that such activity added in the slightest degree to Reid's usefulness in representing the nation's interests in London.[48] But Reid wanted to stay, and he was not an easy man to slough off. He had contributed generously to Taft's campaign: $10,000 and the support of his paper, the *New York Tribune,* whose influence the Administration could scarcely ignore. At home he had excellent connections through Root and Lodge.[49] He was popular in England, and Sir Edward Grey went so far as to write Bryce that the report that Reid was disliked was not true. He was a very pleasant and agreeable ambassador.[50]

Taft nonetheless decided to offer the post to Charles W. Eliot of

46. E. Bax, *Miss Bax of the Embassy,* 23; Hardinge to Bryce, March 26, 1909, Bryce Papers.
47. Taft to Knox, March 24, 1909, Taft Papers.
48. Taft to Mrs. Taft, July 11, 1909, Taft Papers.
49. Reid Papers.
50. Grey to Bryce, February 11, 1909, Bryce Papers.

Harvard, but when Eliot declined, Taft postponed a decision.[51] Perhaps the fact that Reid could write gossipy letters softened the President. At any rate both he and Mrs. Taft enjoyed them, a fact Reid tried to use to his advantage.[52] Eventually, Reid stayed in London, where he died in 1912. Although not a great ambassador, he was a good one, more than adequate, and he had excellent connections with influential people. He did not approve of the department's methods and complained especially about its insistence on immediate results in matters that needed time to mature, a reaction shared by Bacon, Oscar Straus in Turkey, and other diplomats in the field. Reid tried to get this idea across to Washington but did not succeed.[53]

Actually, Taft did not attach much importance to the United States' relations with European countries, and he considered the ambassadors had little to do. In the Far East, however—where his greater experience and knowledge lay—the situation was different, and he regarded Peking as the most important of all the Foreign Service posts. He believed that the Chinese were very friendly to the United States and anxious to encourage trade with this country and American capital investment, since they did not distrust our motives. Taft thought the man who represented the United States must have the "force and pluck" to take advantage of the opportunity to pick off these dangling prizes and the energy and ability to negate the aggressive policies of Japan, England, and Russia.[54]

Taft concluded that William W. Rockhill, the incumbent minister, was not the man of strength and vigorous action whom the United States needed in China. He was, in Taft's view, a dilettante who had outlived whatever usefulness he might once have had. But, even more damaging to Rockhill was Taft's impression that he had not the slightest interest in American trade or its expansion. This impression was correct. Not only did Rockhill lack interest; he lacked all conviction that an increase in trade with China was possible.

Rockhill had little respect for the American businessman and not much more for the Chinese people, although he did admire their civilization. He was not an "old China hand," and he was

51. Elihu Root Papers; Reid Papers.
52. Reid Papers.
53. Reid Papers.
54. Taft to H. S. Brown, April 1, 1909; Taft to R. Ogden, April 21, 1909, Taft Papers; *Review of Reviews,* August, 1909.

more interested in keeping the Manchu Empire territorially intact than in preserving equality of economic opportunity for the West. China, he believed, ought to achieve a position from which she could control her own destiny so she need not resort to playing one nation off against another.[55] Therefore Rockhill, an eminent Sinologist and a career diplomat with long experience both in the field and in departmental policy making with regard to the Far East, was "promoted" to Russia. "This is a d——d poor, uninteresting place," he wrote to Henry Fletcher. "There is not a man in the diplomatic corps here who likes it, so far as I can learn. Don't you ever take it if it is offered to you."[56]

It was easier to move Rockhill than to replace him. Ex-Senator Charles Fulton of Oregon and engineer John Hays Hammond refused the post. Hammond, Taft, and Knox were playing golf one afternoon while the appointment was under consideration, and Hammond asked Knox why he did not go to China that summer after Congress adjourned. Hammond suggested that they make the trip together and study the situation at first hand. Knox teed off and while watching the ball in flight remarked: "Hammond, I'm just learning to play this game, and I'm not going to let anything so unimportant as China interfere."[57]

Finally Charles R. Crane of Chicago, a businessman who had knowledge of Europe and the Far East, accepted.[58] After being briefed by the department and told by Taft to talk about the Far East, Crane did just that. He leaked information about his diplomatic mission to Summer Curtis, Washington correspondent of the *Chicago Record Herald,* which carried the story on September 27. Although Crane had reached San Francisco en route to China, Knox was so furious that he called him back to Washington for an explanation. Knox found Crane's answers unsatisfactory, and despite Taft's reluctance, the Secretary insisted on Crane's dismissal.[59]

After further search, the choice fell on William J. Calhoun, a sixty-one-year-old lawyer who had had some diplomatic experience in the Caribbean area. Just before the outbreak of the Span-

55. P. A. Varg, *Open Door Diplomat. The Life of W. W. Rockhill,* 1-46.
56. Rockhill to Fletcher, December 21, 1909, Henry Fletcher Papers.
57. J. H. Hammond, *Autobiography,* II, 545.
58. *New York Tribune,* April 17, May 25, 1909.
59. Huntington-Wilson, *Memoirs,* 205-6; Knox Papers. The *Chicago Record* printed his instructions practically intact; his mission was to stop Japanese encroachments in China and to press hard for favorable opportunities for American trade and investment.

ish-American War McKinley had appointed him special commissioner to investigate conditions in Cuba, and Calhoun's report was a moderate document that showed diplomatic capacity. Later, McKinley asked him to serve on an assignment to Venezuela and Roosevelt sent him on a mission to Cuba. In addition, he had been a member of the Interstate Commerce Commission for two years.[60] After arriving in Peking, Calhoun regretted his acceptance of the post, for he was unwell for many months and openly deplored the fact that at his age he had left the comforts of Chicago for such strange and uncongenial surroundings. But eventually he recovered his health and served in China.

Minister Sir John Jordan and Max Müller of the British legation in Peking both developed a high regard for their American colleague. In spite of the fact that Calhoun had a reputation for reticence and reserve, Jordan generally found him quite frank and open. "Upright," "straight," and "honest" were adjectives that always seemed to crop up when Calhoun was under discussion. In Jordan's opinion Calhoun had just one besetting weakness for which there was no remedy: He was usually late for diplomatic meetings, rarely kept appointments on time, and sometimes forgot them completely.[61]

Calhoun strove to carry out the department's wishes, but he was set an impossible task. When he tried to point out what was wrong with the United States' policy or strategy, the department rarely paid any attention to his views; on occasion his judgment earned him reprimands. Fortunately, however, Calhoun and Straight, who were forced to work closely together in Peking, got along admirably. Straight admired the Minister—"really a corker"—and greatly appreciated his "nice line of profanity."[62]

Of the foreign representatives in Washington the most distinguished was Lord Bryce, who had arrived during the Roosevelt Administration and remained until near the end of the Taft regime. A former cabinet member, Bryce was a well-known political figure in England and had won wide acclaim for his study, *The American Commonwealth.* He spent a good deal of his time touring the United States and making speeches, in the hope of improving England's image in America. At the start of the Taft Administration Bryce was on good terms with its members, but with time

60. Bryce to Grey, December 14, 1909, FO 405/191/163.
61. FO 405/200/64; 405/204/228.
62. H. Croly, *Willard Straight,* 375; Straight Diary; Leonard Wood Papers.

the relationships cooled. Bryce felt that Taft had neither the initiative nor the proper relations with Congress to carry out the
functions of his office successfully. Yet Bryce found the President
very helpful in resolving matters that concerned England and the
United States. It was quite usual and regular, Bryce reported
home, for Taft to take up foreign policy questions personally.
Since Taft was by nature so much more frank and expansive than
Knox, from whom it was difficult to extract anything whatsoever,
Bryce found that an exchange of views with the President was far
more likely to achieve substantial results. The English did not
hold the department generally in high esteem, and Bryce thought
the Secretary too autocratic, too impatient, lacking in consideration for others, and generally useless.[63] The Americans returned
the compliment. Taft considered Bryce a bore and Knox found
him hard to deal with on occasion. But Bryce's own staff liked him
and referred to him affectionately as "the old bunny."[64]

Historians may argue over the merits of the Taft Administration's foreign policy, but no one can deny that the Administration
improved the machinery for formulating and carrying out the
foreign policy of the United States. Roosevelt had taken the first
step in this direction in 1905, when he issued an executive decree
ordering changes in the recruitment of personnel for the diplomatic service.[65] Vacancies were now to be filled either through
transfer or promotion within the service or by appointment of
qualified new personnel. On the basis of satisfactory evidence of
character, responsibility, and capacity, the President recommended the candidates eligible to take a qualifying examination.
The State Department set up its Board of Examiners whose duty
it was to determine fitness to serve. Examinations were both written and oral, and the applicant was required to know at least one
foreign language, preferably French.

Roosevelt's order not only established the principle that a candidate must prove himself qualified to serve. By implication, the
order also provided for security of tenure for, although employment was not guaranteed, the requirement of transfer, promotion, or a qualifying examination eliminated much of the threat
of the spoils system. Since, after 1905, ministers were more fre-

63. Bryce to Grey, March 31, 1910, FO 405/202/157. Jusserand represented France;
Von Bernstorff and Rosen, Germany and Russia.
64. Taft Papers; Knox Papers; H. A. L. Fisher, *Lord Bryce,* II, 1-28; Bryce Papers.
65. In 1906 an order was issued for the reorganization of the Consular Service to
put it on a merit basis, but it resulted in few practical changes.

quently appointed from the ranks of career men, such a procedure suggested an increasing security of office.

Despite its excellences, too much of the new plan remained confined to the paper it was written on. As Post Wheeler and other successful candidates noted, appointments did not come automatically if an applicant passed the examination and met the other requirements. Good political connections continued to be most helpful in getting a job and in enhancing a career man's chances of promotion.

From early in his career in the Foreign Service, Huntington-Wilson had been an advocate of reform and had given much thought to the question of departmental reorganization. On March 3, 1906, *Outlook* magazine published an article in which he put his ideas into concrete form. His list of recommendations was long: an increase of personnel, a more logical division of work, improvement of recruitment procedures, in-service training, rotation of men between Washington and abroad, rotation among posts abroad, promotion based on merit, a pension system, more perquisites so that not only the rich could hold first-rank posts, and better legation buildings abroad.

Immediately after his appointment as first assistant secretary, Huntington-Wilson took steps to remedy a situation that he deplored for personal reasons. On the basis of his own experience, he felt strongly that it was a mistake to throw men into diplomatic life without adequate preparation. Consequently, he set up an in-service training program. Beginning in June 1909, new appointees received a month's instruction at the department before undertaking any duties.[66]

But the thorough overhaul the department needed depended on congressional support. The opportunity to secure such support came in August 1909 when Congress passed a new tariff law that placed a new burden on the department. Knox therefore asked for an additional appropriation of $100,000 to meet the new demands, and Congress complied. In the fall of 1909 Huntington-Wilson carried through the most complete reorganization of the department since 1870.

One of Huntington-Wilson's major reforms increased the specialization of the department's staff. In 1908 he had helped create the Far Eastern Division, and when discussing the department's administrative problems with Knox, he had pointed out that, after

66. W. F. Ilchman, *Professional Diplomacy in the United States,* Chap. III.

the Far East, Latin America was the area in most urgent need of specialized treatment.[67] Now that the opportunity offered itself, Huntington-Wilson added not only a division for Latin-American Affairs but also desks for Western Europe and the Near East as well.

Huntington-Wilson also organized the Division of Information to distribute important current dispatches to the missions abroad so the men in the field would have some idea of events and developing situations in other areas. The division also made digests of current domestic and foreign publications, drew up summaries of current views of political or economic importance, and prepared the volumes of the Foreign Relations series for publication.[68]

The department staff was enlarged by adding new senior positions. The counselor investigated the legal and technical aspects of major problems of foreign policy; the resident diplomatic officer assisted the secretary in formulating and executing policy from the standpoint of a career officer who had had actual experience in the field. After the third assistant secretary became responsible for the administrative direction of the diplomatic service, supervision of the consular service became the responsibility of the new director.[69]

While reorganization led to a greater emphasis on ability and qualifications, it did not mean the elimination of patronage in appointments to either the foreign or consular service. In making appointments to the Foreign Service, the Administration still had to take care of old political friends and to weigh requests from people with political influence. Taft did not always comply with such requests, yet he did the principles of merit and tenure no good by dismissing five professionals, two of whom—John Riddle and Henry White—had held important posts. As for the consular service, although its yardstick was now supposedly jobs-on-merit, jobs-by-geography continued in effect. Each state enjoyed a certain allotment of positions in the service; California's quota, for example, was seven. Since eight Californians were already in the service, applicants from that state had little prospect of place-

67. Huntington-Wilson Papers.
68. Huntington-Wilson was instrumental in putting through a change in the department's filing system. Until Root's time the system was organized on the basis of Instructions, Dispatches, etc. Root replaced this classification by the system he had installed in the War Department. Possibly it was an improvement, but materials are hard to find. Huntington-Wilson's numerical system was a great improvement.
69. Stuart, *State,* 213-17; Barnes and Morgan, *Foreign Service,* 159-60.

ment.[70] In addition, Taft had a personal axe to grind; he wanted Negroes appointed simply because they were Negroes.[71] Since they could be assigned only to Liberia, Haiti, or northeastern Brazil, few were actually brought into the department.

On the whole, the reorganization meant a real advance for the State Department, which is not to say that it became a model of efficiency. Indeed, the British and German ambassadors made pointed remarks to the contrary, and Lord Bryce went so far as to say that the department's inefficiency reminded him of Constantinople.[72] It was not only foreigners who found fault. Henry Davison, liaison between the American group of bankers in New York and the department, expressed amazement at the way State handled its business. After telephoning on an urgent matter that required prompt attention, Davison had to wait a week for the department's reply.[73]

WHEN TAFT succeeded Roosevelt in the Presidency, it was assumed (not least by Roosevelt himself) that he would continue his predecessor's policies. As events proved, the assumption was false not only in domestic but in foreign affairs as well. Because the two men looked at the world from different angles and because their orders of priorities were so different, American foreign policy under Taft inevitably assumed a new orientation. Of course both saw the need for maintaining existing markets and for finding new outlets for American goods and capital. Roosevelt, however, thought of foreign policy in terms of power politics and regarded international relations as an affair for statesmen, not lawyers. Taft, a lawyer, believed that many of the issues between nations could be settled by resort to legal institutions. Believing sincerely that treaties of arbitration could do a great deal to promote peace, he worked hard to encourage their development.

Furthermore, Roosevelt's concept of *Weltpolitik* naturally led him to think of American foreign policy in the context of Europe. Taft, on the other hand, did not envision the United States as having any direct concern in European affairs; he thought of American foreign policy in the context of backward nations and

70. Huntington-Wilson to Taft, May 1, 1909, Taft Papers.
71. Taft Papers.
72. Bryce Papers.
73. Davison to Straight, November 6, 1909, Straight Papers.

their need for trade. For Taft, the two theaters of American involvement were the traditional one, Latin America, and the less
traditional one, in which he had acquired such a great personal
interest during his stay in the Philippines, the Orient. Because the
chief interest of the President and the State Department in negotiating with the Europeans was to further American policy in
these two areas, the title of this book might well be *Diplomacy on
Two Continents.*

While still Secretary of War, Taft had given a speech in Shanghai in 1907 that clearly expressed his convictions.[74] He told his
audience that trade between China and the United States was
important enough to merit protection against diminution or injury resulting from political preference to any of its competitors.
How far the United States would go to defend the China trade, no
one could say. But American merchants, increasingly aware of its
significance, would view political obstacles to its expansion with
deep concern, and Taft believed that the governments would be
likely to reflect their feeling. His Secretary of State repeated the
economic forecast that had become popular: Because of domestic
expansion, American business had in the past concentrated on the
home market; as the population of the United States increased,
however, as its territory filled, and as its vast manufacturing and
agricultural capabilities developed more fully, interest in foreign
trade was sure to grow. Taft felt certain that, as international
trade developed, there would be no reason to complain of official
indifference to it.

The United States and other countries who favored the Open
Door policy would, if they were wise, not only welcome but encourage the Chinese Empire to introduce administrative and governmental reforms, develop her natural resources, and improve
living conditions for her citizens. By strengthening herself internally, China would then become strong enough to resist all foreign aggression that sought undue, exclusive, or proprietary
rights in her territory. She would be able, without help from
abroad, to enforce the Open Door, with equal opportunity for all.

Taft was not of course alone in his conviction that foreign trade
was becoming increasingly important to the American economy.
Many people held that the panic of 1907 was due to the saturation
of the domestic market. Since Americans were now producing
more goods than they could consume, the only way to prevent

74. William Howard Taft, *Present Day Problems*, 45-48.

economic depressions was to increase exports. Furthermore, the pattern of American foreign trade was changing. In the past the United States had been a supplier of raw materials. But the balance between raw materials and finished or semifinished products had been gradually shifting, so that in 1910, for the first time, American exports of manufactured goods exceeded the foreign sales of raw products. The transition seemed to imply the conclusion that in the future the lucrative markets for American trade did not lie primarily in the well-protected European markets, but rather in nonmanufacturing but populous lands such as Latin America and China.[75]

This change in American trade patterns could not have found in office a government more determined to protect and promote American interests. A State Department memorandum dated October 6, 1909, might well have served as the Administration's credo. As a consequence of intense internal development, the memorandum stated, all countries were turning their attention increasingly to foreign trade. To avoid the perils of overproduction and congestion, the United States too must find markets abroad for its surplus products. At the moment foreign outlets were not so important to American prosperity as they would become in the future. But the Administration should not wait until the need was urgent, since the rivalry in this area was steadily growing keener. A government could not carry on a more important service than to search for trade opportunities; Germany, for example, had reaped great rewards by studying and exploiting foreign markets for the benefit of her manufacturers and merchants. It was, therefore, not improper for the United States Government to cooperate in the advancement of trade by finding openings abroad and by insisting that American investment money compete equally with that of other nations. It was just as true now as it had always been in the past that financiers and merchants needed government aid and protection to secure investments abroad and to build up trade with foreign lands. Experience showed that protection for American capital, enterprise, trade, and investments overseas was quite as necessary as tariff protection for domestic industry. Private enterprise was always of first importance, but its ventures were more apt to be successful when backed by government influence. If the United States

75. H. M. Kahler, "Current Misconceptions of Trade with Latin America," *Annals of the American Academy of Political and Social Science,* May, 1911.

wanted its share in the highly competitive world markets, diplomacy must support the efforts of American financiers and merchants.

The memorandum pointed out that diplomacy could only supplement private effort. If Americans wanted foreign trade, a share in foreign investment, and a chance to exploit the wealth of other nations, they must buy those nations' bonds, help float their loans, build their railroads, and establish banks in their chief cities. When these countries wanted money, it was proper that they should come to the United States for it. As a consequence, when railroads were to be built, American mills would furnish the equipment; when mines were to be opened, bridges constructed, great enterprises started, the finished materials and machines would come from American plants. "This is the way others do it and it is to be our way."

This memorandum applied to foreign trade in its broadest meaning. Foreign trade meant more than selling American products in competitive overseas markets or furnishing to other countries those products which met their current needs. Foreign trade meant, in addition, creating new outlets by lending backward nations the money to increase their purchasing power and consequently their demand for goods. In this it differed markedly from the concepts of the 1880's, for in that period Blaine and others thought in terms of exporting surplus commodities, not of exporting surplus capital.

That this memorandum accurately reflected Knox's views was borne out by an article in the *Pittsburgh Dispatch* of November 14, 1909, written by Knox's friend L. W. Strayer. According to Strayer, the objective of Knox's foreign policy was the expansion of American trade, with equal opportunity for American capital and American genius in all lands. The chancelleries of Europe concerned themselves with plans for territorial aggrandizement and military supremacy; the United States devoted itself to providing an outlet for American industry and skill. Knox was aware that American industry and commercial supremacy demanded new opportunities for marketing the products of its factories. Since Knox subscribed to the theory of the glutted home market, he was working to expand foreign trade, especially in China and Latin America. Thus, both Taft and Knox agreed that these areas should be the focal points of American diplomatic attention.[76]

Both men were willing to use direct government intervention in support of American enterprise.[77]

The necessity for an ever-expanding economic frontier was therefore the assumption on which the Taft Administration based its foreign policy. In China the concomitant factor, essential to the policy's success, was maintaining the Open Door policy. In the Caribbean area the Administration struggled to establish American pre-eminence both in political and economic affairs.

76. In 1909 the total exports and imports of the Latin-American republics amounted to more than $2,000,000,000, of which the American share was $600,-000,000 (*Bankers Magazine,* September, 1910). The trade for 1909 represented a 100 per cent increase over the year 1899. With 73,000,000 potential customers in Latin America, it was easy to assume that these statistics represented only the beginning of the flood. Indeed, some optimists thought the Latin-American market might well solve the problem of American overproduction. However, the United States lacked adequate credit facilities and rapid and direct steamship connections. The Taft Administration tried to improve both, but it failed in its attempts.

77. The department used its "friendly advice" in order to prevent Cuba from admitting, free of duty, sugar plantation machinery and unassembled railroad material. Had Cuba put this import policy into effect, American producers would have been unable to compete with German producers (DS 1943/266). In 1909 the American minister advised the President of Panama not to agree to a commercial treaty with England, for such a treaty would contain a most-favored-nation clause. The President accepted the advice (DS 5067/5-7). One of the most spectacular instances of the Government's support of business occurred in the sale of battleships to Argentina. As S. W. Livermore has pointed out in his article, "Battleship Diplomacy in South America, 1905-1925," *Journal of Modern History* (March, 1944), Taft and Knox used every means to persuade Argentina to buy her new ships in the United States, and they were successful.

Latin America

1

Introduction

Taft and Knox were not reactionaries who wanted to turn back the clock. Rather, they were sober men trying to develop policies that would benefit not only the United States but Latin Americans as well. When they referred to "Latin America," they thought in terms of the Caribbean area, where unsettled economic and political conditions might unfavorably affect the national interest of the United States. Therefore, the goals they set themselves were to maintain stable governments and to prevent financial collapse by American intervention in the financial affairs of that area. In Knox's words:

> True stability is best established not by military, but by economic and social forces. . . . The problem of good government is inextricably interwoven with that of economic prosperity and sound finance; financial stability contributes perhaps more than any other one factor to political stability.[1]

In practical terms *dollar diplomacy* meant economic intervention to stave off military intervention or, as the Administration was fond of saying, it meant the use of dollars instead of bullets.[2]

1. Speech given at the University of Pennsylvania, June 15, 1910, Philander C. Knox Papers; *New York Tribune,* June 16, 1910.
2. Advice went with the dollars. Knox instructed the United States Minister in Cuba on May 6, 1911: "You are informed that because of its special treaty relations with Cuba, and of its interest in the welfare of the Cuban Republic, the Department considers that besides the direct protection of American interests you are to endeavor, by friendly representations and advice, to deter the Cuban Government from enacting legislation which appears to you of an undesirable or improvident character, even though it seem improvident or ill advised purely from the Cuban standpoint, especially if it is likely in any degree to jeopardize the future welfare or revenue of Cuba" (DS 14065/42-43). Fear of a revolt in Cuba in 1912 led to the landing of four companies of marines at Guantánamo. One seldom has the opportunity to see what the landing of marines actually means to an American concern in a foreign country. Fortunately, the evidence is available in this specific case. The president of a Cuban sugar company, with headquarters in New York, wrote the department that, just before the marines landed, the company was quoted by

But it did not rule out the use of bullets. The United States was the political, economic, and military power in the Western Hemisphere, and when the need arose, Taft and Knox were not averse to using force, or the threat of force, to maintain order and to protect American interests.[3] Both the United States and the Latins would profit from the successful execution of the policy. For the United States the achievement of these goals meant more trade, increasingly profitable investments, elimination of European intervention, and the security of the Panama Canal. For the locals it meant peace, prosperity, and improved social conditions resulting from the introduction of capitalism and internal peace.

But the obstacles to success were great. The Caribbean governments were republican only on paper. If the president was strong enough, he ruled with asbolute power; otherwise, he served as a figurehead for a military leader or a strongman in the cabinet. In any case the "ins" controlled the elections, and the administration need not pay much attention to public opinion so long as it had the support of the army and the officeholders. The underdeveloped economy furnished little revenue for the government, whose money came chiefly from customs receipts. An inordinate amount of the budget went to maintain the army. "Budget" was actually a misnomer, since there was no real accounting for public funds and graft prevailed on all levels. High officials amassed fortunes, petty bureaucrats extorted petty bribes. Graft among the latter was at least partly due to grossly inadequate salaries that were, in many instances, paid only irregularly.

The economy was tinged with feudalism. Nowhere was there any middle class to speak of, artisans and small farmers accounting for only a tiny fraction of the population. A small, powerful upper class controlled most of the land and employed the great mass of the people to work it. The lower class bore the entire

Lloyd's of London at a rate of 5½ per cent for term war risk covering its property. But since the landing, Lloyd's had accepted the insurance at 1½ per cent for $50,000 and at 1 per cent for $600,000 (DS 033.1137ST5/1). It should be remembered that, by 1912, of the 173 active mills in Cuba, 34 were owned by Americans and these produced 35 per cent of the total sugar output.

3. After 1905 the Joint Board operated on the assumption that any enemy would make the Caribbean its first theater of operations. Washington's strategic and political plans called for the protection of Puerto Rico and Guantánamo; a guarantee of independence for Cuba and Panama; the neutrality of the canal; and the preservation of the republican form of government in all parts of the Western Hemisphere not held by European Powers. The plans indicated that the Joint Board regarded Germany as the potential enemy. Joint Board, War Portfolio, No. 1, Atlantic States; Department of the Navy.

burden of military service and of compulsory labor on roads and other public facilities. Everywhere the peons suffered under heavy, though indirect, taxation. Revolution offered the only release from bondage for the masses and the only hope of power for the upper-class "outs" who led the "reform" movements. But the United States opposed revolution.

Since the customhouses supplied the bulk of the government's revenues, their control naturally became one of the rebels' chief objectives. Knox believed that the only way to improve conditions in any of the Caribbean nations was to place the customs under competent foreign (by which he meant United States) management and to revise the monetary system.[4] Foreign control over collection of revenue would put the customhouses beyond the reach of local leaders, and the increased revenue from honest administration would provide money for desperately needed reforms. The Secretary drew his conclusions from the operation of the arrangement between the United States and the Dominican Republic, which he regarded as a "brilliant" success.

The United States' intervention in the Dominican Republic, to which State Department officials so often pointed with pride, dated back to the Administration of Theodore Roosevelt and represented a concrete application of the Roosevelt corollary to the Monroe Doctrine. Under an arrangement worked out by the United States and the Dominican Republic, the latter refunded its debt by contracting a $20,000,000 American loan and, as a guarantee of repayment, allowed the President of the United States to appoint the receiver general of customs. From the revenues collected each month, this official paid the expenses of the receivership and turned over $100,000 to the bankers' agent for interest and amortization on the loan; the balance went to the Dominican Government. The money received from the sale of the bonds was put into a depository fund earmarked to pay adjusted claims and debts, retire certain monopolies and harbor concessions, and construct various public improvements. Until the bonds were paid off, the Dominican Republic could not increase the public debt or raise import duties without American consent.

Thoroughly dissatisfied with the agreement, the British Council of Foreign Bondholders queried the embassy in Washington concerning the practicality of opening the question to broader discussion. After Mitchell Innes had delved into the matter—an investi-

4. Bryce to Grey, May 21, 1910, FO 420/252/47.

gation that led him to compare the study of Dominican financial history to "raking in a muck-heap"—he defended American intervention. In his opinion all the debts had their origin in the shameless exploitation of an ignorant people by corrupt leaders and rulers, for whose malpractices unscrupulous moneylenders and speculators supplied the funds. As for the bondholders, Innes concluded, they were either simpletons or speculators. Had the United States Government not stepped in, their bonds would still be worthless. Instead, their claims had been paid off at a rate far above what the most sanguine investor might have expected. For this reason Innes believed that the British bondholders had received adequate compensation; indeed, he regarded the settlement as a generous one.[5]

Despite the council's dissatisfaction the agreement solved many of the Dominican Government's worst problems: The public debt was reduced to manageable proportions; customs revenues met the service charges on the new loan and provided the government with more money for current expenses. The management of customs revenues was vitally important, for customs were the chief source of government income, in some years furnishing 75 per cent and others even more.[6] Cash collections generally amounted to over $3,000,000 annually, and even after the service charges on the loan were deducted, the government retained enough to function satisfactorily.

Since the Dominican experiment was working so well, Knox wanted to extend it to the Central American countries. Although the Secretary believed that all the nations in that area, with the exception of Costa Rica, had been retrograding for the past eighty to one hundred years, he regarded Nicaragua and Honduras as the real trouble spots.[7] Knox assumed that intervention in Central America would not be a unilateral venture by the United States, for he expected Mexico's help in keeping the peace among neighboring countries.

Endless disturbances in Central America had earlier led Roosevelt and President Porfirio Díaz of Mexico to invite representatives of the five nations involved—Costa Rica, El Salvador, Guatemala, Honduras, and Nicaragua—to a conference in Washington. Out of these deliberations came the Washington Conven-

5. March 10, 1911, copy to Department of State. DS 839.51/730.
6. DS 839.51/661; Dominican Customs Receivership, *Sixth Annual Report*, October 20, 1913.
7. Bryce to Grey, May 21, 1910, FO 420/252/47.

tions of 1907. A treaty of peace and amity, effective for ten years, provided that any measure tending to alter the constitutional organization of one of the republics should be deemed a menace to the peace of all. In conflicts arising among the other four nations, Honduras would remain neutral territory as long as Honduras herself did not take sides. Each country promised not to allow political refugees to reside near its frontiers. A separate convention established the Central American Court of Justice to adjudicate all future disputes. Finally, the five countries agreed not to recognize any administration that came to power through a revolution against a recognized government. Although neither the United States nor Mexico was a signatory, they both recognized that their intimate involvement in the treaty-making process committed them morally to uphold the principles involved.[8]

Such was the international situation in Latin America with which Taft's Secretary of State needed to deal.

8. Philip C. Jessup, *Elihu Root,* II, 509-12.

2

Dominican Republic

On January 19, 1912, Secretary of State Knox delivered a major address on the Monroe Doctrine before the New York Bar Association.[1] Knox emphasized the "brilliant" success of the Dominican arrangement—a stable government had kept the peace and paid its debts promptly; United States-Dominican trade had increased from $4,000,000 in 1903 to $11,500,000 in 1910. The Secretary predicted that when the Senate approved the then-pending Honduran and Nicaraguan conventions, equally favorable results would ensue, and he talked of a substantial increase in this nation's share of Central America's trade.

Knox picked a bad moment to make his glowing report. The facts were correct, but his assumption that Dominican stability, with its concomitant advantages, flowed from the United States' control of customs was not. In his evaluation the Secretary omitted the human element.

After assuming office in 1905, President Ramón Cáceres had proved to be a strong and popular leader who was able to keep uprisings to a minimum. In 1911, however, when Cáceres was killed by political enemies, the Dominican situation began to deteriorate. General Eladio Victoria took over the presidency, but the *de facto* ruler was his nephew General Alfredo Victoria. Too young to qualify for office, Alfredo arrogantly directed the government through his puppet and soon drove a number of political leaders into armed opposition. The Dominican showcase was badly shattered.

To the Taft Administration the Dominican imbroglio was no mere internal affair to be deplored by all right-thinking people; as the guarantor of Dominican financial stability, the United States

1. *New York Tribune,* January 20, 1912; *Foreign Relations, 1912,* 1083-92.

was deeply involved in the republic's domestic affairs. Even more, the State Department had boasted about the Dominican plan and had used it as a model for the Honduran and Nicaraguan treaties.[2] A revolt in the Dominican Republic would be distinctly embarrassing.

Despite warnings from the United States to the Dominicans to put their house in order, by the summer of 1912 the situation had deteriorated to such a point that an effective government no longer existed. United States Minister W. W. Russell reported in midsummer that, although the revolutionists did not seem strong enough to overthrow the government, the government was not strong enough to subdue the insurgents. The Victoria administration was so corrupt and inefficient that it had little public support. Furthermore, angry with the Dominican Republic over a boundary dispute, sympathetic Haitians gave refuge and aid to the insurgents.[3]

By mid-September the situation had become so acute that the department decided it must take some action to restore peace; it asked Russell to offer suggestions. He replied promptly that the Victoria regime was extremely unpopular and "very detrimental" to the country; on the other hand, a successful revolution would be "disastrous." Only complete control by the United States would restore order and justice, but any degree of control would be beneficial to some extent.[4] In brief, he recommended intervention.

A memorandum drawn up in the department did not, however, advocate such a bold course. Although Alfredo Victoria was recognized as the cause of the discontent, disorder, and financial decline, none of the rebels appeared capable of taking over the government and operating it with order and justice. "We are thus confronted with the wretched Victoria regime on the one hand and a revolution on the other, which, if successful, would supply no remedy." The solution of the problem seemed to require interference by the United States to eliminate Victoria's influence and to initiate reforms. Indeed, if the United States could merely get rid of Alfredo Victoria and neutralize his power, it would have taken a long step in the direction of reform. Settlement of the

2. The United States used the Dominican model when it established control over Liberian customs in 1912. *FR, 1912,* 693-94.
3. *FR, 1912,* 359-64; DS 839.00/659D; 83951/551.
4. *FR, 1912,* 365-66.

continuing Dominican-Haitian boundary dispute would also serve to restore order.[5]

Huntington-Wilson forwarded the department's memorandum to Taft along with his own recommendation, designed to ward off "the disaster which we see impending."[6] To avert such a calamity was of the utmost importance, wrote Huntington-Wilson, for any worsening of the situation would seriously discredit the entire United States policy and would be "a very severe blow to American diplomacy," especially in Nicaragua and Honduras. As a first step he recommended presenting a strong note to President Victoria that would advise him, among other things, to remove his nephew from office and to proclaim a general amnesty. The dispatch of a warship was an indispensable prerequisite to action and was also in accord with the Minister's suggestion; its arrival should coincide with the presentation of the note. As for the border dispute with Haiti, the United States should inform both countries that it was establishing a provisional boundary. The Navy ought to be ready to send a ship if the Haitian attitude required this show of interest.

Should the note fail in its objective, the United States would have two choices. It could stand by and see its whole Dominican policy fail, carrying down with it the broad policy to be pursued in Central America; or the United States could convert its recommendations into demands, enforcing them if necessary by measures short of war. Should the United States be compelled to make such demands, Huntington-Wilson favored sending an emissary to Santo Domingo to persuade the Victoria regime to accept them; if he failed, then measures short of war would ensue. Huntington-Wilson assumed that this "drastic action" would include breaking off diplomatic relations, armed protection of the customhouses, and, conceivably, withholding customs receipts pending the installation of a government responsive to its obligations.

The President invited Huntington-Wilson to the White House to discuss the matter, and as a result of their conference on September 23, Huntington-Wilson's recommendations were in large part adopted. The next day, the department instructed the United States ministers in Haiti and the Dominican Republic to inform those governments that the United States had fixed a provisional

5. Memo, September 17, 1912, DS 839.00/659D; Dana G. Munro, *Intervention and Dollar Diplomacy in the Caribbean, 1900-1921,* 262.
6. DS 839.00/659D.

boundary and that the receiver general of Dominican customs was being ordered to re-establish and operate the border patrol to make certain the line was respected.[7]

In dealing with the internal Dominican situation, the procedure suggested by Huntington-Wilson was somewhat altered. According to the new plan, two special commissioners were to confer with the United States minister, the receiver general of customs, and Dominican officials. They were then to decide whether or not to present Huntington-Wilson's draft note, now expanded to include the resignation of President Victoria. William T. S. Doyle, chief of the Latin-American Division, and Brigadier General Frank McIntyre, head of the War Department's Bureau of Insular Affairs, arrived in Santo Domingo aboard the *U.S.S. Prairie,* which carried a contingent of 750 marines.

After a week of consultations the two commissioners made three recommendations: announcement by the President that he would retire in 1914 (the end of the term for which Cáceres had been elected); elimination of the President's nephew from the government; and proclamation of a broad general amnesty. If the Dominicans carried out these reforms in good faith, the commissioners pledged their government's help in rehabilitating the economy, which was so chaotic that economic assistance seemed indispensable to re-establishing order. President Victoria at first refused to dismiss Alfredo but finally yielded after the commissioners presented a stiff note.[8] Also, he agreed to accept their two other recommendations.

When Victoria's compliance did not restore peace, the commissioners decided that he must resign the presidency immediately. To make certain that Victoria understood what was expected of him, they cut off his sources of income. Victoria did understand, and on November 18 he issued a call for a congress to name his successor. On November 26 he resigned the presidency and four days later the Dominican Congress chose Archbishop Adolfo Nouel as the new president, to serve for a two-year term. The commissioners approved the choice.[9]

Whatever experience the Archbishop had had in church politics, it was insufficient preparation for what he encountered in secular affairs. On December 10 he told Russell of his intention

7. DS 839.00/659; *FR, 1912,* 366-69; Munro, *Dollar Diplomacy,* 263.
8. DS 839.00/679, 775; Munro, *Dollar Diplomacy,* 263.
9. Munro, *Dollar Diplomacy,* 264.

to resign; he could not accept the humiliating conditions the rebels were exacting as the price for supporting his administration. Knox immediately consulted Taft and sent a cable in the President's name asking the Archbishop to complete his term and pledging the support of the United States. Nouel remained in office reluctantly; he informed the commissioners that his continuation in office would depend on the fluctuating circumstances.[10]

To solve the immediate financial problems of the country, the Dominican Congress on December 9 authorized President Nouel to contract a $1,500,000 loan, for which the government pledged $30,000 a month from its share of the customs receipts. On February 22, 1913, the Dominicans and the National City Bank of New York signed a contract calling for the immediate payment of $500,000, with the balance payable as required. The proceeds of the loan were to be used to pay salaries that were in arrears and expenses caused by the revolt. The funds could be disbursed only with the approval of the secretary of the American legation and the general receiver of customs.[11] The Taft Administration gave its formal consent to the arrangement on March 1.

Even with the additional funds and increased control by the United States over Dominican expenditures, the fundamental problems remained unsolved. Before the end of March the Archbishop quit his venture into civil politics and sailed for Europe. Nevertheless, the idea of the Dominican showcase persisted in the thinking of the State Department. The showcase had to be maintained, even if it meant, as it did under President Woodrow Wilson, taking over the government of the Dominican Republic as well as the management of its finances.

10. DS 839.00/750, 752A; *FR, 1912*, 378-79.
11. Munro, *Dollar Diplomacy*, 267-68; *FR, 1913*, 459-60.

3

Nicaragua

Of the nations in Central America, one of the most restless internally and most difficult internationally was Nicaragua. Although Nicaragua adhered to the Washington Conventions of 1907, her dictator José Santos Zelaya was plainly no more eager after their inception than he had been in the past to live in peace with his neighbors. When reports reached the State Department that Zelaya was about to go on the prowl again, Knox asked the Navy to keep warships in Central American waters.[1] After Adee mentioned to Huntington-Wilson that Root had talked about Central American affairs nearly every day with the Mexican ambassador, the Assistant Secretary took the hint and on March 12, 1909, gave the new ambassador, Francisco de la Barra, a full account of the Nicaraguan situation. Two days later De la Barra reported that his government was prepared to act jointly with the United States to compel observance of the conventions. To this end Mexico had ordered a gunboat to Central American waters with instructions to keep in touch with the American naval commander.[2]

The conference with De la Barra seemed to offer convincing evidence that Mexico took her moral commitment to the Washington Conventions seriously. At any rate the State Department so interpreted De la Barra's statements. At a Cabinet meeting on March 26 Knox read a paper that defined future policy toward Central America, a policy that assumed Mexico's cooperation. The Secretary's objective was to ensure the neutrality of Honduras and to re-establish its credit, which could be done if Honduras followed the Dominican pattern, and he suggested that the United States appoint a financial agent for Honduras. After en-

1. DS 18432/5, 8, 10, 18; *Foreign Relations, 1909,* 460-67; *New York Tribune,* March 18, 20, April 6, 1909.
2. DS 18432/12, 22, 24.

dorsing the steps Knox proposed, Taft declared that the United States was prepared to use a show of force in order to maintain peace among the Central American states.[3]

Later, when Knox talked to the Mexican Ambassador, he emphasized that moral suasion had usually failed in the past to maintain peace and stability in Central America. Now, however, a favorable combination of circumstances offered the United States and Mexico an opportunity to make real progress toward these goals by joint action. Specifically, Knox proposed a binding agreement among the Central American nations to regard as rebels any of their citizens who engaged in revolutionary activity against another country. Knox further proposed measures to maintain political and financial stability in Honduras and to guarantee her neutrality, for he believed—with some reason—that the presence of this weak, disorganized neighbor contributed to the Nicaraguans' everlasting political intrigues under Zelaya, which made that country the fountainhead of unrest in Central America. At the request of Honduras the United States and Mexico might appoint an adviser to help her straighten out her finances. The two nations might also consider inviting the Central American republics, except Nicaragua, to sign a new convention supplementing that of 1907. If Mexico received such proposals, what would her reaction be?[4]

Going far beyond the earlier convention, Knox was now asking Mexico, in effect, to acquiesce in American financial control of Honduras and to join the United States in guaranteeing Central American stability. If Mexico agreed, the two nations would assume the formal right to intervene in Central America. Knox's plan rested on three assumptions: Zelaya was the main cause of Central American turmoil; he could be controlled by neutralizing Honduras; and outside management of Honduran finances would stabilize that country's government and forestall intervention from another nation, either Central American or European.

During a conference with Knox and Huntington-Wilson on April 8, De la Barra raised so many questions it was apparent that his government was reluctant to follow the lead of the United States. In an effort to clarify the department's position, Knox again wrote him on April 12. In this note Knox stated that his suggestion was made in anticipation of an invitation from Hon-

3. George von Lengerke Meyer Papers.
4. DS 18920/1-2.

duras to nominate one or two financial advisers. If the request materialized, Knox hoped that the United States and Mexico would agree to name the consultants and that Honduras would retain them for an indefinite period. Their function would be to study the country's financial and economic position and, with approval by Mexico and the United States, to suggest necessary reforms. The results of such an undertaking would ultimately depend, in Knox's opinion, on the Honduran Government's cooperation and the advisers' skill.

To keep Honduras free from foreign entanglements, the supplementary convention would bind that country and Guatemala, El Salvador, Costa Rica, Mexico, and the United States to guarantee Honduran neutrality to each other. In this way Honduras would be encouraged to try sincerely to maintain her neutrality; Guatemala, El Salvador, and Costa Rica would all be pledged to refrain from violating that neutrality and to preserve it if it were threatened. The Mexican and United States promises to help keep Honduras neutral would give the convention added weight.

Knox reiterated to De la Barra his judgment that Nicaragua should not be invited to the conference. Indeed, he wanted to go further than mere exclusion. He suggested that Mexico and the United States issue a statement to the effect that, since Zelaya's behavior was subverting the Washington Conventions, it would be useless to send him an invitation. The joint announcement should express sympathy for the Nicaraguan people, the vast majority of whom undoubtedly wanted the conventions observed, and should indicate that Nicaragua would be welcome as a signatory to the new convention as soon as her government showed itself disposed to cooperate in keeping the peace.[5]

Hoping to get some encouraging action, the Secretary instructed Ambassador David Thompson in Mexico City to take up the question of a conference with President Díaz or the minister of foreign affairs, Ignacio Mariscal. When Thompson told the Foreign Minister that this was the psychological moment to call the Central American states together but that Nicaragua should be excluded, Mariscal's reaction was distinctly unsympathetic. Surprisingly, Mariscal took the attitude that Mexico had no interests south of Guatemala. Nor did she have any proof that Nicaragua was planning aggression on any of her neighbors. Mariscal also believed that the conference contemplated by the United States

5. Knox, April 12, 1909, to De la Barra. Philander C. Knox Papers.

would soon lead to armed intervention, an enterprise in which Mexico would refuse to join. As for excluding Nicaragua from the conference, Mexico could see no valid reason for such action.[6]

Mexico's unwillingness to back the United States against Nicaragua was due to the fact that Zelaya was a friend to whom Díaz was indebted. When relations between Mexico and Guatemala had been strained nearly to the point of war, Zelaya had offered Díaz 10,000 men if Mexico needed them. The informant who relayed this "extraordinary confession" to Thompson also told him that Díaz had already written to Zelaya, urging him to come to an understanding with the United States. Because of their friendship Díaz believed Zelaya would follow his advice.[7]

De la Barra's alternative proposal and Huntington-Wilson's comments on it revealed sharply the divergence of opinion between the two countries. The Mexican Ambassador suggested that the United States persuade the Central American countries to pledge to Mexico and the United States that they would observe the neutrality of Honduras. Huntington-Wilson objected. Although the United States wanted to meet Mexico's wishes as nearly as possible, there was a definite limit to allowable concessions. "That limit," as defined by Huntington-Wilson, "was this: we desired to accomplish something which would be a real and radical step forward, and failing this we thought it was useless to do anything." Huntington-Wilson argued that both governments were under a moral obligation to enforce the observance of the Washington Conventions and that converting this moral right and obligation into a conventional one would yield beneficial results. By underlining the possibility that force might be used to compel allegiance to the peace conventions, it would reduce the chances of such a contingency, to which the United States was as unwilling to resort as Mexico. Viewed in this light, De la Barra's alternative was no solution at all. As Huntington-Wilson noted, the American proposal would give Mexico and the United States the duty as well as the right to intervene, whereas the Mexican substitute would give the two nations the right without imposing an absolute obligation.[8] In other words, the United States was proposing a political agreement of which the Mexicans wanted no part.

Although Knox was ready to make some concessions to get Mex-

6. Knox Papers.
7. DS 18920/14. Moreover, Mexico considered President Manuel Estrada Cabrera of Guatemala much more serious a threat to its interests than Zelaya.
8. Huntington-Wilson-De la Barra conference, April 17. DS 18920/7-8.

ican cooperation, his conference with De la Barra on April 21 convinced him that no real meeting of minds could ensue. When the Ambassador told Knox that his government would consent to the appointment of financial experts but with the understanding that this action would entail no obligation on Mexico's part to carry out the plans the experts formulated, Knox agreed that responsibility would cease with the appointment. If the United States wanted a new conference of the Central American states, Mexico would participate but would insist that Nicaragua be invited; again Knox concurred. He added, however, that he thought a new convention would accomplish little or nothing if Mexico and the United States confined themselves to interposing their good offices as they had done in 1907. The Mexican Ambassador demurred; he thought good offices would be enough.[9]

Events in Nicaragua soon pointed up the differences in the United States and Mexican positions. For weeks the department had been receiving reports that Zelaya was readying an expedition against El Salvador, and on April 24 word came that his troops were on the move. Through the Navy the department ordered American warships to stop any expedition across Fonseca Bay. The Mexican Government, on the other hand, announced that it would station a gunboat there as a moral force but would not use it to intervene actively.[10]

Although Nicaraguan troop movements continued, no hostile action ensued. By the end of May United States naval observers on the scene concluded that, in view of so little danger of any outbreak of hostilities, the ships could be withdrawn. Not so certain of Zelaya's intentions, the department asked the Navy to keep one ship on duty in the area.[11] Apparently acting on advice from Díaz, Zelaya had considerably toned down his aggressive gestures. No factor positively indicates a cause-and-effect relationship, but it was an interesting coincidence that, after being without a minister in Managua for at least two years, Mexico filled the post in June.

Despite Zelaya's improved behavior, he still managed to annoy the United States. In mid-May the department received a copy of an editorial in the official *Diario de Nicaragua* that attacked the United States and suggested a Nicaraguan-Japanese alliance to

9. Knox Papers.
10. DS 18432/101A, 107.
11. DS 18432/110.

stop the United States' imperalistic advances. That same month Zelaya negotiated a large loan in London with the Ethelburga Syndicate to consolidate the Nicaraguan foreign debts and to build an east-west railroad. Although the United States tried to prevent the sale of the bonds in England and France, where both governments were sympathetic to Washington's aims, the British were powerless to act and French official intervention to prevent the sale was fruitless.[12]

By midsummer the Central American political pot began again to boil. Zelaya interfered in the Costa Rican presidential elections by throwing his support behind Ricardo Jiménez, and from Managua came word that the dictator was collecting arms and ammunition for the revolutionists in El Salvador. Since Mexico had stated that she had no interests south of Guatemala, Knox assumed that he was free to act without consulting De la Barra. He told Taft of his conviction that the United States and Mexico jointly, or the United States alone, should be in a position to apply an effective remedy at any time. There should be some conventional right to intervene promptly in Central American affairs without waiting for outbreaks and with a view to averting rather than quelling disturbances.[13] He had in mind, of course, the authority to intervene in Honduras specifically, but such jurisdiction would obviously extend to any other country as well.

Knox soon had an opportunity to show if he intended to use such authority, for in the fall of 1909 a revolt broke out against Zelaya. The United States did not regard this revolution as merely a domestic affair. Since Knox and the department considered Zelaya the primary source of restlessness in Central America, they always viewed Nicaraguan affairs within the framework of regional politics. If his compatriots should remove the dictator, the Administration would no longer face the problem of containing him.

Charles A. Beard has alleged that North American financial involvement and the Secretary's personal interests influenced the Taft Administration's policy toward Nicaragua. In *The Idea of National Interest,* Beard implies that, because Knox had once served as counsel for a North American company with interests in Nicaragua, he reflected this old connection in determining the United States' course toward that country. Basing his interpreta-

12. *New York Times,* May 18, 1909; DS 5691/19A, 20, 23A, 28-30.
13. Knox, September 28, 1909, to Taft. William Howard Taft Papers.

tion on evidence given at a congressional hearing by Thomas P. Moffat, the United States consul at Bluefields in Nicaragua, Beard also concludes that American investments in Nicaragua were large enough to affect departmental thinking. In short, citizens of the United States had trouble with Zelaya in their dealings in Nicaragua; therefore they wanted a change of government, and the State Department acted on behalf of privately owned businesses.[14] Beard's case seems to be on shaky ground, for a thorough search of State Department files and of personal papers indicates that Dana G. Munro's interpretation of the situation is the correct one. His book *Intervention and Dollar Diplomacy in the Caribbean* demonstrates that the department had no connection with the Nicaraguan revolution in its earlier stages and that Knox's former legal affiliation had no bearing on his official acts.[15] Yet, given the attitudes and experiences of the men in the department, it does seem that they would commit United States support for anyone who opposed Zelaya.

Led by General Juan J. Estrada, a member of Zelaya's Liberal party, the October 1909 revolt against the dictator centered in the port of Bluefields on Nicaragua's eastern coast. Although Estrada had once served as governor of Bluefields (a presidential appointment), he eventually broke with Zelaya. Estrada received some financial support from members of the Conservative party and from foreigners living in Bluefields who opposed Zelaya's discrimination against them and resented his monopolistic policies. But apparently the major contribution, around $90,000, came from the ruler of Guatemala, Manuel Estrada Cabrera.[16]

In July 1909 Moffat notified the department from Bluefields that if Estrada could get his hands on $50,000, he might consider leading a revolt. The department was cool to the idea and it remained so in October, when the revolt actually took place. Although Adee told Moffat to conduct his office in a strictly neutral manner and to do nothing that might indicate recognition of Estrada, the Consul did not obey instructions; he showed that he favored the revolution. Just when the department became aware of Moffat's exact position is not clear. The lack of reliable reports from the field makes the study of this period in United States-Nicaraguan rela-

14. Charles A. Beard, *The Idea of National Interest,* 171-76.
15. Dana G. Munro, *Intervention and Dollar Diplomacy in the Caribbean, 1900-1921,* 174. In Knox's personal papers there is an indication that he sold a number of his holdings before entering the Cabinet as Secretary of State.
16. DS 817.00/2957.

tions difficult. For some time the United States had maintained no minister in Managua, and immediately after taking office, Knox also recalled the *chargé*, John Gregory, because of the difficulties with Zelaya. When the revolt broke out, the legation in Managua was in the charge of a noncareer vice-consul, a Nicaraguan named Caldera, whose dispatches conveyed little information. The Navy sent the department copies of reports from its officers, which differed greatly from Moffat's. The only clear fact is that the department had to make decisions with too little hard information.

Although the department's position was formally neutral and impartial, it made little effort to hide its sympathy for Zelaya's enemies. The department's files indicate that, although the Administration meant to preserve the diplomatic niceties, it also intended ultimately to support any anti-Zelaya group. There is no evidence, however, that the Government of the United States was in any way involved in the origins of the Estrada revolt.

In a country torn by revolution, it is not at all unusual for some episode to occur that a foreigner can use as a pretext for a stern protest from his government. In view of the department's prejudice against Zelaya, its reaction to the execution of two American citizens was almost a foregone conclusion. On November 19 the newspapers carried the story that Leonard Groce and Leroy Cannon, commissioned officers in the revolutionary army, had been captured and shot by government forces. The following day representatives from State and Navy met at Knox's home and discussed the situation with him for nearly three hours. From the conference two points emerged clearly: Knox was convinced that Zelaya had acted unjustly and with unwarranted brutality; the United States would demand full reparation for the executions.[17]

Behind the scenes the department quietly (and, one gets the impression, almost gleefully) canvassed the kind of demand it should make on Nicaragua, besides that for indemnity. Believing that Zelaya's retirement was imminent, Knox thought the United States should remit a large part of the indemnity to the government that would succeed him and give the small remainder to the victims' relatives. Huntington-Wilson raced ahead with the thought that "what action we do take should be such that even if Zelaya, with the assistance of Mexico, were able to meet the demand, we should not put ourselves in the position not to be able

17. *New York Tribune,* November 21, 1909.

by the satisfaction of the demand to proceed further in the elimination of Zelaya." To hasten Zelaya's departure, Huntington-Wilson suggested the seizure and retention of Corinto and Managua,
pending the establishment of a responsible government, and the
severance of diplomatic relations.

Henry Hoyt, counselor of the department, thought the occupation of Corinto would be "a mighty good idea." Adee agreed and
recommended adopting "the British fiction . . . of a pacific demonstration in force": occupy the city and hold the customhouse as a
pledge for settlement of American demands. As for occupying the
capital, Adee wanted no part of it. Perhaps future events might
make an occupation necessary, but, as he pointed out, such action
would be a hostile demonstration or, to put it bluntly, "actual war"
and would probably involve some fighting. He was equally opposed to Huntington-Wilson's other proposal, severance of diplomatic relations. Instead, the department's Nestor suggested noti-
fying the Nicaraguan *chargé* of the plans to make a pacific
demonstration in Corinto and to demand reparations.[18]

The assistant secretary of the Latin-American Division was
apparently consulted only about occupying Corinto, to which he
reacted with little zeal. If the United States did take such drastic
action, W. T. S. Doyle advised justifying it by citing the cruelty and
oppression of the Zelaya regime, the dictator's interference in the
affairs of the other Central American states, and his violation of
the Washington Conventions. The executions should serve as the
occasion rather than the cause. Doyle confessed that his opinion
in the matter was strong, in view of the questionable ethical and
legal situation of Cannon and Groce; he doubted whether, when
the facts were investigated, the United States could make an un-
equivocal case for the two men.[19]

The department had another decision to make in connection
with the Nicaraguan affair: how should it answer the proposal
that Mexico now made for joint action? Seeming quite sure that
Zelaya's retirement could be arranged, Mexico suggested install-
ing a Liberal in the presidency, pending a constitutional election.
Huntington-Wilson considered this plan merely a scheme to replace Zelaya with one of his own creatures, which would nullify
the revolutionaries' actions. Knox's protracted efforts in the
spring to secure Mexican cooperation had been wasted, Hunting-

18. Huntington-Wilson Memo, November 26, 1909. DS 6369/334.
19. Doyle to Huntington-Wilson, November 29, 1909. DS 6369/342.

ton-Wilson concluded, for the Mexicans apparently had only been playing with the United States. Their belated offer of cooperation sprang from "the most contemptible motives": the Mexicans now wanted "to butt in" because they thought Zelaya would be overthrown; if they cooperated with the United States at this point, they would share the credit for eliminating him from Central American affairs.[20] The answer to Mexico was refusal to participate in joint action.

The department also ultimately abandoned the idea of unilateral intervention, because it believed that "if the action is likely to be prolonged or to result in a modification of political conditions that Congressional authorization should be requested."[21] Instead, on December 1 Knox broke off diplomatic relations with Nicaragua.

The note to the Nicaraguan *chargé* was an indictment that minced few words.[22] In it the United States charged Zelaya with keeping Central America almost continuously "in tension or turmoil" and with wholesale violations of the international conventions. His administration had imposed such a tyranny as to be "a blot upon the history of Nicaragua and a discouragement to a group of Republics whose aspirations need only the opportunity of free and honest government." The majority of the Central American states had often turned to the United States for help against this despotism. Now, through revolution, the Nicaraguan people themselves were doing the same. The United States had also suffered directly from Zelaya's tyranny: Two Americans had been killed "by direct order of President Zelaya"; a series of petty annoyances and indignities had driven the American minister from Managua, and the consulate there was now reported menaced. The "sinister culmination" of events made it difficult for the United States to delay active response "to the appeals so long made, to its duty to its citizens, to its dignity, to Central America, and to civilization."

The note not only stated that "the United States is convinced that the revolution represents the ideals and the will of a majority of the Nicaraguan people more faithfully than does the Government of President Zelaya"; it also offered a reward for a success-

20. DS 6369/334.
21. DS 6369/345.
22. *FR, 1909*, 455-57.

ful revolution. In taking up the indemnity question, Knox offered to make his demands considerably lighter if he were dealing with a government entirely dissociated from the present intolerable regime. Using its own standards of measurement, the department wanted, primarily, a new and stable government in Nicaragua. Reparation for the lives of two soldiers of fortune had become secondary.

The department's stand on Nicaragua won little support at home. The press buzzed over the note's bluntness, for it seemed to put the full blame for the Americans' executions on the president of a sovereign nation, holding him responsible like a common malefactor. Even further, it implied recognition of the Estrada faction. The note reminded the *New York Evening Mail* of a western sheriff's proclamation against an outlaw.[23]

At the British Foreign Office Charles Harding, permanent under-secretary, greeted Knox's action sympathetically and wrote Bryce that "it will be a very good thing if he [Knox] treats Nicaragua with a firm hand. It will be to the advantage of everybody concerned."[24] The Latin-American diplomats in Washington, on the other hand, were greatly agitated. The measure of their distress was revealed by the fact that Knox immediately discussed the situation with them in order to allay their misgivings, and he apparently succeeded in changing their attitude from apprehension to "stoical resignation."[25]

Although Mexico let it be known through the press that she would not be drawn into the affair, behind the scenes the Díaz administration was making ready to send Enrique Creel back to Washington on a confidential mission. The former ambassador, a good friend of Elihu Root, seemed an excellent choice in the situation, and the department notified Mexico that his mission would be "particularly welcome." Huntington-Wilson, however, still was not convinced that Mexico sincerely intended to cooperate for peace.[26] Unfortunately, Creel did not make a good impression at his first meeting with Knox, on December 14. Because Creel intimated that Mexico understood the Latin-American view better than did the United States, Knox thought him "officious."

23. *Literary Digest,* December 11, 1909.
24. Harding to Bryce, December 10, 1909. James Bryce Papers.
25. *New York Times,* December 8, 1909.
26. *New York Tribune,* December 3, 1909; Huntington-Wilson to Thompson, December 10, 1909. DS 6369/394A.

Moreover, in order to keep the Liberals in power, Creel seemed to be advocating a joint protectorate, with Mexico playing the principal role.

At the same conference Creel also told Knox that Díaz had advised Zelaya to submit his resignation to the Nicaraguan Congress, and two days later Zelaya stepped down. His successor was José Madriz, a Liberal and a former judge of the Central American Court at Cartago, who was unanimously elected President of Nicaragua by Congress on December 20. He pledged to uphold the rights of the citizens, grant free elections, and establish a policy of equal opportunity for all.[27]

Viewed from Washington, the change in head of state did not solve Nicaragua's problems. The department's representatives in Nicaragua, El Salvador, and Costa Rica unanimously opposed recognition of Madriz. Since the new regime was merely the old Zelaya group behind a new façade, it would perpetuate a situation the department considered diplomatically intolerable. Another count against Madriz was that he endorsed Mariscal's policy of antagonism to Estrada Cabrera. In spite of Creel's strong support for Madriz and his denial of the charge that the new president was Zelaya's creature, the department refused to recognize the Madriz government.[28]

Before Creel left Washington for Mexico at the end of December, he conferred with Taft on the matter of Zelaya's future. Mexico had offered Zelaya refuge but then, aware that the United States might disapprove, had instructed Creel to discuss the matter with Taft and to tell him that asylum would not be granted if the United States opposed it. After consulting Knox, Taft informed Creel that, although the United States would offer no objection, this should not be taken to imply approval of Mexico's action or acquiescence.[29]

At the same meeting Taft confessed to Creel that he would not be content until the United States secured some formal right to compel peace among the Central American governments or, in his own words, "to have the right to knock their heads together until they should maintain peace between them." Although Taft got the impression that he and Creel were of one mind on this point, he was wrong. Reconciling the divergent views of the two

27. *New York Tribune*, December 21, 1909; DS 6369/400.
28. DS 6369/411, 415, 481, 508.
29. DS 6369/400.

nations proved impossible. The Taft Administration would not accept Mexico's reliance on the old moral influence approach. The differences between the United States and Mexico reached full demonstration when Díaz furnished a gunboat for Zelaya's journey to Mexico and received the fallen dictator on December 30, the day after he arrived in the country. Mexico also recognized the Madriz government immediately. Clearly, Knox could expect no help from this quarter in dealing with the Nicaraguan problem.

The reports filed by State and Navy men in Nicaragua continued to be conflictory. Moffat at Bluefields maintained his support of Estrada, as did the new United States vice-consul at Managua, whereas Rear Admiral W. W. Kimball, commander of the naval squadron in Nicaraguan waters, regarded the rebels as untrustworthy. He reported that the vice-consul and the faction of the Conservative party supporting Estrada were cooperating in an effort to bring about intervention by the United States. The Admiral did not hide his preference for Madriz, which was so open that Knox objected to the Secretary of the Navy that Kimball was exerting pressure against Estrada—not at all in line with the department's policy of keeping "strictly neutral."[30] At one point hope flared briefly that the two sides might settle their differences. They agreed to talks aboard a ship the United States would provide as a neutral meeting place. Unfortunately, Estrada's representative drowned en route to the conference, and the project was never revived.[31]

The members of the department were cheered when the rebel forces began marching toward the interior in February 1910, with Managua their objective. On Huntington-Wilson's instructions, Thomas Dawson, chief of the Latin-American Division, prepared a proclamation recognizing the Estrada provisional government and two letters for S. Castillo, Estrada's agent in Washington, to hand to the department when the revolutionists entered the capital. Since no one knew precisely when this would be, none of the documents bore dates. One of the letters announced the occupation of the capital and requested immediate recognition of the new government; in the other, besides promising to punish the murderers of Cannon and Groce and to hold free elections, the Estrada government declared its intention to reorganize its finan-

30. DS 6369/652, 656A, 683, 687, 761.
31. Munro, *Dollar Diplomacy,* 179-80.

cial affairs and to negotiate a loan with North American bankers. The Nicaraguans, in addition, promised to treat commerce and business with North Americans fairly and equitably. Huntington-Wilson expected Castillo to present the first letter to the department the moment Estrada took Managua. The United States would immediately recognize the new government, whereupon Castillo would deliver his second missive.[32] The department's Latin-American experts doubted the wisdom of Huntington-Wilson's whole procedure, but it never came to a test because, when Estrada's campaign failed, the diplomatic maneuver became pointless.

The Madriz government now tried to end the civil war; as the month of March waned, Liberal troops were approaching Bluefields. Their capture of the city would quash the Estrada revolt. Even though the Liberals' campaign had not yet achieved this objective, Admiral Kimball now wrote *finis* to the revolution and recommended recognition of Madriz as head of state. By the first week in April of 1910, several governments had already taken that step, including Mexico, Cuba, Venezuela, Panama, Germany, and Denmark. England considered recognition, but after consulting the State Department in Washington, deferred action. State still saw Madriz as an agent of Zelaya.[33]

May was the critical month for Estrada, for the new Nicaraguan government was planning to attack Bluefields by land and by sea. Since the story of the United States' intervention that saved Estrada has been told many times, only a very brief sketch will be given here.[34] The commanders of U. S. Navy vessels informed the combatants that they would not permit any fighting in the port city. To enforce this interdiction, one hundred marines moved into Bluefields. Nor would the United States permit a gunboat, whose Nicaraguan ownership was suspect, to bombard the city. Unable to engage the enemy, the Madriz army withdrew into the interior. Moffat reported: " . . . the Estrada Revolution exists today only because a strong hand saves it from annihilation."[35]

32. Huntington-Wilson Memo to Dawson, February 24, 1910; DS 817.00/1373.
33. Creel, now the Mexican Minister of Foreign Affairs, thought that Knox's position was wrong. He believed that Madriz had been a fearless critic of Zelaya and had an independent mind. FO 420/252/77.
34. Munro, *Dollar Diplomacy,* 183-84.
35. DS 6369/1185. The British commander, Thesinger, informed the Admiralty that large sums of money had been advanced to the revolutionists. Estrada and his staff remained in Bluefields, and the town's provisions contained reserves of food, money, and ammunition. If the United States had not acted, Bluefields would have been captured by the Madriz forces. FO 420/252/70.

Withdrawal of the government forces did not, however, mean immediate victory for Estrada, and Madriz retained the presidency well into August.

In mid-June Sir Edward Grey again inquired about the United States' recognition of the Nicaraguan government. After consulting Knox, Huntington-Wilson sent Reid, in London, a forceful restatement of the position Knox had outlined in his note of December 1, 1909, which had broken off relations with that government. "Zelaya, as you know," wrote Huntington-Wilson, "was an unspeakable carrion who mulcted his people of a huge fortune . . . and strangled all commerce and development during his sixteen years of outrageous despotism, which he rounded off with the brutal murder of two American citizens." In the department's view, the situation in Nicaragua was unchanged; Madriz was surrounded by the same old gang, and he was supported by Zelaya's money. Although American citizens living in Nicaragua had registered few complaints against Estrada, those against the Madriz regime were numerous. Indeed, the Americans in eastern Nicaragua seemed to approve unanimously the present policy of the United States Government.[36]

Fortunately for Estrada and probably for the United States as well, some of the areas under government control began to rebel against Madriz. These uprisings, along with Estrada's penetration of the interior and the continued hostility of the United States Government, finally drove Madriz from office on August 20. The next day Managua fell to the insurgents without a fight and on August 28, 1910, Estrada entered the capital. Three days later he was inaugurated as provisional president of Nicaragua.[37]

The department, now given the opportunity to practice its healing arts, was prepared. On the day Estrada entered Managua, the department cabled him the text of a message he was expected to send to Washington. The department demanded a number of pledges from Estrada in return for recognition of his government, the most important being that he would ask for a loan, to be secured by United States control of the customs. Washington used the "Dominican approach," not because of any threat of foreign intervention, but because it hoped in this way to stabilize Nicaragua and subsequently all of Central America. In addition, Estrada must promise to hold an election within six months, prosecute the murderers of Cannon and Groce and pay a reasonable indemnity,

36. Huntington-Wilson to Reid, July 1, 1910; DS 6369/1147.
37. *FR, 1910,* 758-59; DS 817.00/1352.

and ask the United States to send a commission to Nicaragua if any formal agreements were needed.[38]

The new president hesitated to comply with these demands, for there was money—one estimate was $5,000,000—in the treasury. But support from the north was essential, and on September 10 he dutifully sent the prescribed note. Upon its receipt the department informed the press that, in response to Estrada's suggestion, it was detailing an officer from the diplomatic service to Nicaragua to work with the new government.[39]

As its special agent the department selected the ubiquitous Thomas C. Dawson, who had previously helped establish United States control in the Dominican Republic and might be called the American specialist in the establishment of protectorates. On his arrival in Managua on October 18, Dawson immediately grasped that the reality of Nicaraguan politics differed markedly from Washington's optimistic theories. The Zelaya Liberals were the majority party (some estimates put it at five to one), and they were actively seeking return to power. On the other hand, divisive internal disagreements were weakening Estrada's party. Dawson realized that a popular election was not only impracticable—it was dangerous. Ever resourceful, he resorted to the device of forming a constituent assembly, which would choose the president and vice president and give legal effect to the measures the United States wished to see adopted. He persuaded the Nicaraguan leaders to agree in writing that Estrada should serve a two-year term as president, with Adolfo Díaz, a virtually unknown Conservative, as vice president.[40]

Having smoothed the way for "democracy" in Nicaragua, Dawson now turned his attention to the basic issue. As a result of his efforts, on October 27 the Nicaraguans agreed to a series of documents known as the "Dawson Agreements." They promised to ask United States financiers for a customs-guaranteed loan, to adopt a new constitution abolishing monopolies, to cooperate with the United States in setting up a commission to adjudicate all unsettled claims against the Nicaraguan Government, and to punish the murderers of Cannon and Groce.[41] Consider what one specialist can accomplish in ten days!

38. Munro, *Dollar Diplomacy,* 187.
39. *FR, 1910,* 762; *New York Tribune,* September 13, 1910.
40. DS 817.00/1473, 1687; 817.51/168; Munro, *Dollar Diplomacy,* 187-88.
41. *FR, 1910,* 765; *FR, 1911,* 652-53, for the texts of the agreements. Dawson's summary of his work in a ten-page report dated November 17, is in DS 817.00/1473.

The constituent assembly met in mid-December and "elected" Estrada and Díaz; according to Moffat, the Nicaraguans greeted the result of the election with "intense enthusiasm."[42] And since the new administration was the result of an election and not a revolution, the United States recognized it on January 1, 1911. Elliot Northcott became the new minister to Nicaragua and Franklin M. Gunther secretary to the legation. Accompanying Northcott to Managua was Ernest M. Wands, the financial expert who was to devise a plan for the complete rehabilitation of Nicaraguan finances.

The triumvirate faced the task of transforming the pledges in the Dawson Agreements into accomplished facts. Their attempts to implement the agreements led ultimately to the landing of a force of marines and the establishment of a United States protectorate over Nicaragua. There is no evidence that the Taft Administration deliberately pursued a policy with these ends in view. It bears repeating, also, that Taft and Knox were not puppets in the hands of their country's financial interests. Although control of customs collection meant supervision by United States officials, armed intervention was quite another matter that was, from all existing records, unintended.

Soon after arriving in Nicaragua, Northcott discovered how difficult his assignment was. The majority of the Nicaraguans were hostile to the United States, and control of customs by another country's officials was especially obnoxious to them. Popular resentment might not have proved insuperable if this control by foreigners had been backed by a solid native government, but the election had not quieted the domestic unrest. Nicaraguan politicians still disagreed as to who should be *the* leader, and conditions remained fluid and unstable. [43] Since D. G. Munro has, in his thoughtful analysis of the situation, detailed the political intricacies, there is no need to retrace this familiar ground. It is sufficient to record here that Estrada, who proved to be a weak president, was replaced by Vice President Díaz in May 1911. The new president's major adversary was the powerful Minister of War, Luis Mena, who controlled the army and the assembly and expected to sit in the presidential chair, whether by semilegal or illegal methods.

42. *FR, 1910,* 767.
43. *FR, 1911,* 654-58; DS 817.00/1608, 1687; 817.51/168; Munro, *Dollar Diplomacy,* 189-91.

Although the political maneuvering continued unabated, the department kept its eye on the major objective: the reorganization of Nicaraguan finances. After a month-long study of economic conditions at first hand, Wands recommended a loan, to be secured by United States control of the customhouses. When Díaz became president, the negotiations proceeded rapidly. Under the treaty signed in Washington on June 6, 1911, Nicaragua agreed to negotiate a loan to refund her debts and to provide capital for developing her resources. The security met the department's requirements. From a list of names presented by the underwriting bank's representative and approved by the President of the United States, Nicaragua would appoint a collector general to administer the customs duties.[44] The new arrangement practically duplicated the United States-Honduras treaty, signed months earlier, which in turn was modeled on the agreement with the Dominican Republic.

The Nicaraguan assembly immediately approved the treaty, but the United States Senate refused to accept either the Nicaraguan or the Honduran conventions, which it was considering simultaneously. Although Taft got his Reciprocity Treaty through Congress, 1911 was a poor year in which to drum up support for banking interests. Not only had the Republicans lost control of the House in the mid-term elections, but revelations about the "money trust" among key banking firms surfaced and troubled the legislators.

Taft's special message to Congress urging ratification indicated the importance the Administration attached to both treaties. On June 17 Knox sent a personal letter to Senator Shelby M. Cullom, chairman of the Senate Foreign Relations Committee, forcefully advocating acceptance. The Secretary argued that, by using diplomacy and capital to help neighboring republics, the treaties were practical instruments for bringing and maintaining peace. They would serve to reduce the need for interference in Central America and prevent the constant and intolerable turbulence in the neighborhood of the Panama Canal. Besides these benefits, the treaties would bring great commercial advantages, especially to the southern states.[45] But the Senate, ignoring all pressure from the Administration, postponed consideration of the treaties.

44. DS 817.00/1687; *FR, 1912*, 1074-75; Munro, *Dollar Diplomacy*, 193.
45. DS 817.51/154A.

In the meantime Wands discussed the loan with Brown Brothers and Company, Speyer and Company, and J. and W. Seligman and Company—all of them North American investment houses. All were so interested that they were willing to make offers even without a treaty, on the condition that Nicaragua agree to appoint a North American customs collector in case of default. But the department did not want Nicaragua to sign a loan contract until after the Senate had approved the convention. The department knew that, with the treaty, Nicaragua could get money at a lower rate of interest; without the treaty, the department would not get the collectorship that meant peace and sound financial administration. Huntington-Wilson looked to the Caribbean as a sphere of influence for the United States; the exclusion of European financiers from the fiscal life of Central America would help achieve this goal.[46]

Despite the negative considerations, Brown Brothers and Seligman signed several contracts with Nicaragua in September 1911, one of which provided for a $15,000,000 loan contingent upon the Senate's ratifying the convention. But since Díaz needed money immediately, the New Yorkers agreed to make a short-term loan secured by a customs collectorship under a collector general nominated by the banks and approved by the Secretary of State. Although Knox sanctioned the choice of Clifford D. Ham for the collectorship, he made it clear that the department would give this investment no support or protection beyond that accorded to all other legitimate enterprises of United States citizens abroad. By buying $1,500,000 Nicaraguan treasury bills at par, the bankers made it possible to set up a national bank and to start work on currency reform.[47]

With their economy showing signs of revival, the Nicaraguans again turned their full attention to politics. Deputies in the assembly who supported Mena for the presidency refused to approve the loan contract unless they were permitted to elect their man for the term beginning in 1913. Minister Northcott having resigned, Gunther, twenty-six years old and filling his first diplomatic assignment, was in charge of the Managua legation. Neither he nor the department raised any effective protest against the deputies' action, and on October 7 Mena's supporters voted

46. DS 817.51/118.
47. *FR, 1911,* 1079-80; Memo by Clark and Doyle, November 10, 1911, DS 817.51/263.

him into office as the next president. A few days later the assembly approved the loan contract.[48]

George T. Weitzel, the new United States minister to Nicaragua and former assistant chief of the Latin-American Division, arrived at his post in January 1912 and immediately began devoting most of his attention to the country's financial affairs. Although the Dawson Agreements had provided that all claims must be submitted to a mixed claims commision, the new government had paid out large sums to favored claimants who alleged that they had suffered losses under Zelaya. Prominent families, including those of Mena and Díaz, received large payments.[49] Not only were the funds in the treasury being dissipated, but current revenues did not meet government expenses. Ham, the banks' appointee, had begun supervising the customs collections in December 1911, but since much of this income was pledged to discharge certain claims, the Nicaraguan Government could not use this major source of revenue. The Díaz administration therefore appealed to the bankers for additional funds. Because the loan was so risky, the bankers agreed "much against their will" to advance credit, not to exceed $750,000, on certain conditions. Nicaragua pledged that she would pay no further claims such as had benefited the Mena and Díaz families, without the approval of the mixed claims commission. In addition, the government transferred the ownership of the Nicaraguan railroad to a new company, giving the bankers a lien on all the stock, with an option to buy 51 per cent of it. The banks also took over the management of the railroad, an arrangement that was to continue until all of their loans were repaid.[50]

The bankers had made large commitments, but so had the Nicaraguans. They were dismayed to find United States citizens collecting their customs, serving on the mixed claims commision, and controlling their national bank and railroad—all in the name of good government. But the dismay of the Nicaraguans was nothing compared to the tension in Washington as the department watched the economic and political events unfold in 1912. Try as they might, Taft and Knox were unable to get the Senate to agree to the Nicaraguan and Honduran treaties. The United States therefore remained in what might be termed an uncommitted-committed position.

48. Munro, *Dollar Diplomacy,* 200.
49. DS 817.00/1691; 417.00/120.
50. *FR, 1912,* 1099; DS 817.51/376, 477.

In July 1912, however, the Nicaraguans themselves acted to force a decision. For some time Díaz and Mena had been quarreling. Although Mena had a firm grip on the police and much of the army, he could not be certain that the United States would permit him to assume the presidency in 1913. Either unwilling or unable to wait until the appointed date, Mena began his revolt on July 29. In response to demands from United States citizens and other foreigners for protection, Minister Weitzel asked Díaz for assurances that he would protect foreign-owned property. Díaz' answer revealed the weakness of his government; because of the revolt, he was unable to comply with the legation's request. Instead, he countered with the request that "the Government of the United States guarantee with its forces ˇsecurity for the property of American citizens in Nicaragua and that it extend its protection to all the inhabitants of the Republic." Weitzel immediately turned to the North American talisman in Central America— armed force. On August 4 a detachment of 100 sailors arrived in Managua to serve as a legation guard. A short time later Taft ordered 350 marines to the capital, but by the time they arrived —in mid-August—Weitzel was estimating that 2,000 men would be necessary to suppress the rebellion.[51] As a result of his recommendation more marines were landed.

Even the additional troops did not prevent the revolutionists from continuing extensive operations, and by late August the department recommended that Taft should issue a statement on the Nicaraguan situation. Since it was summer and (naturally) neither the President nor the Secretary of State was in Washington, on August 30 Acting Secretary Huntington-Wilson sent his recommendations to Taft at Beverly.[52] He wrote Taft:

> We feel in this Department that the United States ought to exert its influence very strongly for the elimination of such elements [the Zelaya-Mena groups]. Not to do so and to sit by and see them triumph would, we fear, be a blow to our prestige in all the neighboring republics. . . . We are having so much trouble in Mexico, in Cuba and in Panama, and we have had for so long frequently to express "grave concern" and to lodge protests that what with the attitude of Senator Bacon's group in the Senate, which gives the impression that we are a house divided against itself, the authority of our words seems lessened. We think that if the United States did its duty promptly, thoroughly and impressively in Nicaragua, it would strengthen our hand and

51. *FR, 1912,* 1032-40; DS 817.00/1864.
52. *FR, 1912,* 1043-44; DS 817.00/1940A.

lighten our task, not only in Nicaragua itself in the future, but throughout Central America and the Caribbean and would even have some moral effect in Mexico.

Enclosed with Huntington-Wilson's letter was a draft declaration of United States policy, to be delivered to the Nicaraguan Government. With Taft's approval, it was sent to Managua on September 4, and Weitzel made it public on September 13. The United States reiterated its opposition to Zelayism and reaffirmed its support of the legally constituted government. Not only would the United States Government use its influence to restore lawful and orderly government; it would protect the lives and property of its citizens and maintain sufficient troops to guard the legation and keep communications open. Claiming that vicious elements among the rebels wanted to restore Zelaya's methods, the department drew a very long bow and characterized the origins of the revolt as "the most inexcusable in the annals of Central America." The United States justified its policy by pointing to its moral mandate under the Washington Conventions, Nicaragua's confession of her inability to protect Americans, and her request for American troops.

The declaration—reinforced by the presence of approximately 2,000 marines—and Mena's illness cooled the revolutionary fever. On September 24 Mena surrendered to the United States forces and by early October the revolt had ended. The United States withdrew its troops except for the hundred men left in Managua to guard the legation. At the time no one realized that these marines, the symbol of United States power in Nicaragua, would not be withdrawn until 1925. During all those years the United States was responsible for keeping a minority party in power. Nicaragua was indeed stable and the *status quo* prevailed, but all of the country's basic economic, social, and political problems remained unsolved.

By the fall of 1912, the United States had driven the three "bad guys"—Zelaya, Madriz, and Mena—out of the country and by its interference in the election had assured Díaz the presidency for the next four years. Díaz, whose term began on January 1, 1913, brought about no solutions to the State Department's problems, neither during the Taft nor during subsequent administrations. Even so, faith has continued among United States diplomats that a stable government can be established in the Central American country through loans and the control of a major source of revenue—the customs. If the need should develop, the marines can always land, and the situation be shortly in hand. But the American policy has never provided a workable, lasting answer to Nicaraguan problems. It could not, for there is no one answer to the multiple problems that beset such an inchoate nation. About the best that can be hoped for is to allow Nicaraguans to work on their own problems with no intervention from the north.

4

Honduras

Honduras, in the first decade of the twentieth century, was no nation; it was national incoherence. In this section of Central America, which had been the scene of seven revolutions within a fifteen-year period, public improvements consisted of fifty-seven miles of railroad and some inadequate docks. The unreal-ness (to the Anglo-Saxon mind) of its financial position was the reality of a total foreign indebtedness of $124,000,000 based on an annual income of $1,600,000. Here, certainly, was a country that needed help.

The Department of State's failure to secure Mexico's coopera-tion in neutralizing Honduras and stabilizing its financial situa-tion is part of this book's discussion of the crises in Nicaragua. Although perforce abandoning the idea of a new Central Ameri-can convention that would assure tranquillity in that area, the department determined to continue its own efforts to improve Honduras' economic situation. In January 1909 Washington Val-entine, a North American businessman holding railroad and wharf concessions at Puerto Cortés, had proposed a general re-funding of Honduran debts through a new loan secured by an agreement similar to that with the Dominican Republic. As early as March 9 Adee commented on the beneficial results of Ameri-can collection of Dominican customs and expressed the opinion that in the near future the United States might have to assume a corresponding function in Honduras. "Things are fast drifting that way."[1]

Since British nationals held most of Honduras' indebtedness, the British Government was interested in Honduras too. In March, Sir Lionel Carden proposed to President Miguel Dávila

1. DS 17624/3-4; Dana G. Munro, *Intervention and Dollar Diplomacy in the Caribbean, 1900-1921,* 218.

that Honduras pay off British bondholders in forty annual installments by using revenues from the railway and wharf at Puerto
Cortés and from a 15 per cent surcharge on import duties.[2] Dávila
agreed, and the Government of Honduras undertook to pay Valentine for his interests in the railway and wharf.

Unhappy with this arrangement, Philip M. Brown, the United
States minister, protested to the Honduran Government, and the
State Department upheld him. Adee believed that the British
wanted a preferential lien on Honduran revenues to the prejudice
of the country's obligations toward North Americans and that the
rate of interest asked by the British was exorbitant. He concluded,
"the only practical outlet for Honduras from her financial
predicament is an arrangement like that made for Santo
Domingo. I believe Honduras is ripe for it."[3]

Dávila retreated from his agreement with the British, and in
late April he told Brown that he now thought the proposed arrangement would be highly disadvantageous to Honduras. His
government would be most grateful if, through the friendly
offices of the United States legation, a satisfactory plan could be
made with a North American syndicate for the general refunding
of the entire debt of Honduras.[4] Huntington-Wilson put his mind
to the problem, for he believed that an important decision faced
the department.

> As things now are, apparently we shall continue to be fre-
> quently involved in Central American troubles and to find our-
> selves each time in a somewhat impotent position. I believe we
> should either strengthen and regularize our means of working
> for peace, or else let the Central Americans fight it out, holding
> them responsible for the safety of our material interests and let
> them see how they like being left severely alone.[5]

For his part, Huntington-Wilson favored sending the legation a
draft convention, which Honduras could then return to the United
States as its own proposal.

Once again the "Dominican solution" provided a formula. Honduras was hopelessly in debt, and England was exerting diplomatic pressure for a financial settlement. The tumultuous political conditions that had prevailed in the past gave no evidence of
abating in the future. In the department's view, the only way

2. Munro, *Dollar Diplomacy*, 218-19.
3. DS 17624/8.
4. DS 17624/20-25.
5. DS 17624/79.

Honduras could become politically and financially stable was through a loan secured by American control of her customhouses. The success of Huntington-Wilson's scheme depended upon an American loan, but would responsible financiers be interested, in view of the financial chaos in Honduras? Both J. P. Morgan and Company and James Speyer indicated their willingness to proceed, on condition that the United States would control the collection of customs.[6]

Since J. P. Morgan and Company had excellent connections in England, that house could more easily arrange a settlement with the British Council of Foreign Bondholders than could Speyer. With this consideration in mind, the department asked J. P. Morgan to arrange the refunding loan. After Morgan had reached an agreement with the British bondholders, State saw to it that Carden notified the Honduras Government of its release from its agreement with the English.[7]

In the meantime, Minister Brown's doubts about the Dávila government were deepening. Since corrupt and powerful influences within the country were working to prevent any negotiations with the North American financiers, Brown did not believe that the government was powerful enough to carry negotiations to conclusion. He suggested to his superior officers that it might be desirable to postpone definite talks until "in the course of events" a responsible government came to power. Washington rejected the idea of delay. Believing that it was "now or never," the department informed Brown that "the weakness of the present government would be a favorable factor in facilitating the negotiations." Indeed, the very difficulties of the political situation made the time auspicious for energetic efforts to consummate the loan, which would be "of vast importance and benefit to Honduras and of excellent political effect, and will thus contribute greatly to our national, commercial and other interests in Central America."[8]

Although Dávila sent agents to the United States for the loan negotiations, Brown continued to discourage the project. The President was losing control of the country, Brown reported, and was showing symptoms of mental illness. Furthermore, even if Dávila's agents reached an agreement with J. P. Morgan and

6. DS 17624/26-26B; 815.51/93; *Foreign Relations, 1912,* 545-54.
7. DS 17624/34, 36, 38; Munro, *Dollar Diplomacy,* 220.
8. DS 17624/37, 52.

Company, there was no guarantee that the executive or the assembly would approve it. Although the department planned to forward this gloomy report to the bankers, Huntington-Wilson vetoed the idea. It would be unwise, he felt, to throw cold water on their efforts, now that negotiations were actually in progress. Since Brown tended to exaggerate conditions, Huntington-Wilson was not prepared to rely on his judgment.[9] As a matter of fact, the department was so dissatisfied with Brown that, in December 1909, it replaced him with Fenton McCreery, who had had previous experience in the Dominican Republic. McCreery did not reach his post until April 1910.

In December 1909 the bankers and the Honduran agents signed a contract providing for the flotation of a $10,000,000 loan of 5 per cent bonds, $7,500,000 to be issued immediately. From the latter amount $6,000,000 would be set aside for the external debt; the balance would be used to pay internal claims and to rebuild and extend the railroad, which the bankers would operate during the life of the loan. The unsold bonds would be held in reserve for whatever future internal improvements the bankers deemed advisable. Consummation of the contract depended upon the execution of a treaty between the United States and Honduras granting control of customs revenues to the North Americans.[10]

The State Department needed to exert a great deal of pressure before Dávila would send his agents full powers to sign the treaty with the United States Government that the bankers demanded as a prerequisite for the loan.[11] In the convention of January 1911 Honduras agreed to negotiate a refunding loan secured by the customs duties. As long as the bonds were outstanding, the customs would be administered by a customs general appointed by the Honduran Government from a list of names presented by the bankers' representative and approved by the President of the United States.[12]

On February 15 the Honduran minister signed the loan contract with J. P. Morgan and Company and three other New York banks. The contract authorized a 5 per cent loan of $10,000,000, of which $7,500,000 would be issued immediately. The bankers agreed to purchase $6,354,000 of the bonds at 88, paying for them with $2,-100,000 in cash and over $19,000,000 in old British bonds. The bal-

9. DS 17624/18; 7357/672.
10. Munro, *Dollar Diplomacy,* 221; DS 17624/86, 91-92.
11. Munro, *Dollar Diplomacy,* 222-23; DS 815.51/112B.
12. Munro, *Dollar Diplomacy,* 223; *FR, 1912,* 568 ff.

ance of the $7,500,000 would be held in reserve to redeem any other outstanding bonds whose holders might subsequently accept the arrangement. Of the cash Honduras received, about $700,000 was to be applied to the internal debt and a like amount paid to Valentine for his concession and claims. The remainder could be used to extend and improve the National Railroad.[13]

But neither country was ready for the treaty. The Senate of the United States refused to ratify either the Honduran or the Nicaraguan conventions. Hondurans disliked both the treaty and the loan contract: the treaty, because it meant control of their customs by a United States citizen; the loan, because it gave the Hondurans very little cash. Shortly after signature of the treaty, the Hondurans resumed their national pastime, revolution. Manuel Bonilla and Lee Christmas, apparently supported by the United Fruit Company, headed the revolt. In the hope of getting support from the United States, Dávila made a desperate effort on January 31 to procure the assembly's approval of the convention, but it was rejected by a 33 to 5 vote.[14]

Since revolution (unless used to oust its opponents) drew down the State Department's anathema, Washington urged an immediate armistice and offered to mediate. When both sides agreed to armistice and arbitration, the department again chose Thomas Dawson as its emissary. On February 21 this perennial troubleshooter presided at a conference at which the two factions agreed to let him select the provisional president. After receiving nominations from both camps, Dawson chose Francisco Bertrand, one of the revolutionists' candidates. Dávila resigned, and in the election held during October, Bonilla won the presidency.[15]

Because of the unsettled conditions in Honduras, the New York bankers were no longer interested in the loan. The department began working with the Whitney Central Trust and Savings Bank of New Orleans, which was cooperating with Samuel Zemurray of the United Fruit Company. But even this shift did not bring about a loan contract, for the department kept insisting upon control of customs and Bonilla would sign no agreement to grant what State wanted.[16] As it turned out, Bonilla was quite ill, and his popularity waned shortly after he took office. Although the new

13. Munro, *Dollar Diplomacy,* 224-25.
14. Munro, *Dollar Diplomacy,* 228.
15. Munro, *Dollar Diplomacy,* 226-30.
16. Munro, *Dollar Diplomacy,* 231-35.

banking firm pushed its project, it had no real chance of success, and this chance faded entirely with Bonilla's death.

Four years of valiant effort toward change had been expended; the *status quo* continued. One could hardly claim that dollar diplomacy was a success in Honduras.

5

Guatemala

Conditions in Guatemala differed somewhat from those in other Central American countries in that the dictator, Estrada Cabrera, maintained a politically stable government. Its economic and financial aspects, however, were not so sturdy, for Guatemalan revenues were declining and the nation was heavily in debt to English bondholders. The last sizeable financial negotiation had taken place in 1895 when the debt, both internal and external, had again been refunded by a bond issue of £ 1,600,000 at 4 per cent, secured by a special tax on each bag of coffee exported. But Estrada Cabrera managed to circumvent the contract by reducing the tax or by diverting the receipts to other uses, so Guatemala seldom paid interest on her bonded indebtedness.[1] Although the State Department was concerned about this situation, no feeling of urgency underlay its relations with that country.

In spite of Guatemala's financial position, J. & W. Seligman and Company, James Speyer, and the Windsor Trust Company were all interested in floating a loan for her. Despite the receptiveness of these investment houses, the most comprehensive plan for Guatemala's financial rehabilitation came from Minor Keith of the United Fruit Company and his counsel, Bradley W. Palmer of Boston.

When Palmer presented Keith's plan to the department in October 1909, he showed a remarkable insight into the department's thinking. Possibly his friendship with Attorney General George Wickersham and a conference with Taft and Knox had helped to

1. Coffee was Guatemala's chief export, the value in 1913 being estimated at $12,000,000, with bananas next at approximately $800,000. Dana G. Munro, *The Five Republics of Central America*, 266, 289; *Foreign Relations, 1913*, 566-67; DS 814.51/112.

fill in his background of information. Keith wanted Guatemala to authorize a government bond issue of $30,000,000, carrying 5 per cent interest and payable in fifty years. Within ten years the bankers would establish a sinking fund to retire all the bonds at or before maturity. The initial issue would be approximately $17,-500,000, since Guatemala's present income did not justify a larger amount. The proceeds would be used to settle and adjust the national debt, internal and external, and to construct a modern city with adequate port facilities and sanitary works at Puerto Barrios, Guatemala's port on the Atlantic side. The government would receive whatever cash was left after the expenses of issue had been paid.

The remaining bonds ($12,500,000) would be used to subsidize the extension of the Guatemalan railroad to the border of El Salvador, to reform the banking system and establish a national bank of issue, and to reform the currency and set a fixed gold standard. As security for the loan Guatemala would pledge the customs, which would be collected by the agent of the bankers who purchased the bonds. When the national bank was established, it would become the collecting agency.

In addition to the loan, Keith and Palmer also proposed that the United States Government guarantee their projected railroad to El Salvador's border. They would obtain for the United States Government such contractual interests in the line as to ensure not only the passage of United States Government mail and property, but also mail and cargo whose origin or destination was the United States. The United States would thereby have a direct interest in Guatemala and El Salvador that would be of such scope as to justify its intervention if either country were threatened by invasion. Keith and Palmer were confident that United States interest in the railroad would ensure permanent peace in the region. Both men blamed the United States for Guatemala's irresponsible attitude toward her foreign debts. Because the Monroe Doctrine protected Guatemala from intervention by a European Power, she totally disregarded her obligations, and, in fact, a spirit of repudiation existed throughout the nation's business and governmental circles.

Keith's plans were so far-reaching that Guatemala hesitated to accept them. The government needed some friendly advice and help from their neighbors to the north—or perhaps "the quiet insistence" from the United States—to encourage the authorities to reach a decision as to what must be done. Primarily, Guatemala needed to learn the importance of honoring her obligations. In the unlikely event that the government would not accept the State Department's recommendations to begin active negotiations for a loan, the department then should insist that Guatemala make every reasonable effort to repay her existing debts.[2]

Huntington-Wilson had Doyle check Keith's proposal. He reported back that Keith's was the most comprehensive and accurate résumé of present conditions in Guatemala that he had ever seen. His plan was feasible, and if the department wanted to take action, it ought to move promptly, since the situation was worsening daily.[3]

At this stage Palmer called to the department's attention the activities of Adolfo Stahl and the group known as "the American syndicate." Palmer informed the department that the syndicate's loans to Guatemala carried exorbitant rates on interest, ranging from 20 per cent to 30 per cent, even though the security was excellent. Moreover, "these contracts," said Palmer, "are filed with the representative of the United States in Guatemala and the Syndicate doubtless understand that they enjoy the protection of our government."[4] He suggested that the department look into the syndicate's operations.

The department followed Palmer's advice with an inquiry about the syndicate's practices to Sands, the minister in Guatemala. After reviewing the correspondence, Sands concluded that the legation and the syndicate understood that the routine depositing of loan contracts had no legal value. Sands, completely naïve in financial maneuverings, could not fathom why the contracts had been deposited, since the loans were considered in Guatemala to have been questionable transactions. His casual attitude was all the more remarkable, in view of his opinion that the syndicate's operations were pernicious and that Stahl was "a man than whom no one in Central America has a worse reputation."[5]

Sands's report made no impression on the department; it was necessary for Palmer to write another letter, this one dated Janu-

2. Palmer Memorandum and letter to Knox, October 8, 1909, DS 10859/25-26; Frazier Memorandum, October 8, 1909, DS 10859/32-33.
3. DS 10859/25-26.
4. DS 10859/39; D. H. Dinwoodie has a good summary in his article, "Dollar Diplomacy in the Light of the Guatemalan Loan Project, 1909-1913," *Americas,* January, 1970.
5. DS 10859/45; 814.51/106.

ary 22, 1910, in order to get action. Palmer quoted from one of Stahl's contracts deposited at the legation: "The holders of the bonds shall have the right to ask the protection of the United States . . . from any violation from what has been stipulated." Picking up this piece of information, Huntington-Wilson notified his chief, "I do not suppose that you would wish to have the United States bound . . . to intervene on behalf of bondholders." Knox now took the matter in hand and sent identical letters to Speyer, Palmer, Seligman, and the Windsor Trust Company.

> It is only fair to state, categorically and once for all, that the Department of State will not entertain any complaint or diplomatically intervene on behalf of an American syndicate in reference to such a loan [to Guatemala] unless after a thorough examination of the terms thereof the Department shall have become convinced that the arrangement is an equitable and beneficial one and one duly regardful of American equities and vested interests in Guatemala which may be entitled to be safeguarded in any such arrangement.[6]

Knox's statement put the banking community on notice that they must first clear their loans through the department. Once Washington had approved a transaction, the United States Government would give full diplomatic support to the company behind it. The department's instructions to Sands on February 25 confirm this interpretation. The department disapproved of the legation's filing contracts that specifically either stated or implied the United States Government's notice or approval of their contents. From now on, the language of each loan contract should be carefully examined for references to the Government that would imply that the lender might ask for diplomatic support in the future. After telling Sands to return Stahl's contracts to him, the department warned the Minister to be more cautious in such matters in the future.[7]

During 1910 and 1911 the department kept urging Estrada Cabrera to accept a North American loan, but Estrada Cabrera successfully put off a decision. By January 1912 the English were tired of waiting for the Guatemalan President to act. Sir Lionel Carden, the British minister, demanded that the revenues from the coffee tax, which amounted to approximately $800,000 and were pledged to English bondholders, be restored within thirty

6. DS 10859/45, 54; 814.51/55A.
7. DS 10859/48, 65; 814.51/150, 155.

days. If Guatemala did not comply, Great Britain threatened to
take the dispute to The Hague. When Michael Innes, the British
chargé in Washington, told Huntington-Wilson about Carden's
demand, he added that he did not expect action from Estrada
Cabrera. "Nothing except a pistol held at Cabrera's head would
move such a rascal, and I doubt whether he will sleep less peace-
fully for all our paper thunderbolts, particularly when he is
threatened with nothing more formidable than arbitration."[8]
Innes was right. Estrada Cabrera stalemated the ultimatum by
claiming that he was seriously negotiating with American bankers. It soon became apparent, however, that the President was
simply maneuvering to circumvent the British.

Knox planned to visit Guatemala in March, so the British suggested that he confer with Carden before his departure. "It seems
rather cheeky," Huntington-Wilson wrote Knox, "for them to
want you to discuss things with a Minister whom we tried to get
them to recall owing to his obstruction of our interests." Nevertheless, the Assistant Secretary thought Knox should receive
Carden—but not too cordially—for news of such a meeting might
have a favorable effect on Estrada Cabrera. It would show him
that Great Britain and the United States were in accord and that
he therefore could not play one government off against the other.
As Huntington-Wilson saw the situation, the department's main
objective was to force Guatemala to come to an agreement with
the bankers.[9]

When Carden met with the Secretary on March 16, he tried to
convince Knox that Britain did not oppose the United States' interests or policy in Central America. She did, however, expect a
legitimate return from her own and her citizens' interests there;
obviously, they were not getting it. Carden suggested that an Anglo-American arrangement on matters affecting British interests
in Central America would do much to create a greater spirit of
harmony between the two countries. Such an agreement, by
removing all possible grounds for future misunderstandings—
which the Central American governments might use to play
Great Britain off against the United States—would greatly facilitate the pacification and development of those countries, which
the United States had so much at heart. From what Knox said at
their meeting, Carden understood that the Secretary welcomed

8. DS 033.1100K77/149.
9. DS 713.51/4; 713.41.

his suggestions; at any rate Knox agreed to further talks when Carden visited Washington in early summer en route to England.[10]

Toward the middle of June Carden returned for his scheduled discussion at the State Department.[11] In the course of their conversation he told Knox that he would like to be assured of the United States' refusal to countenance any loan to Guatemala that did not provide for payment of the debt owed in England. The Secretary remarked that it was his understanding that, in the cases of both Guatemala and Honduras, it had always been the intention of the North American bankers to provide for legitimate British claims but that the department did not ordinarily review such loan arrangements until the bankers had reduced them to fairly concrete terms. Carden's second suggestion was a corollary to his first point; he developed the idea that the United States should support legitimate British contentions, making it unnecessary for Britain to bring independent pressure, which, in some cases, gave the appearance of conflict of interest between the two governments. Knox was receptive to this idea, but not to Carden's third proposal: that the United States not sign any reciprocal agreements with Central American countries that would be detrimental to British commerce. Knox thought this proposal a "preposterous suggestion."

Later that day Carden sent Knox the draft of an Anglo-American agreement. Knox's reply of June 15 made it clear that the United States would not sign any agreement with Great Britain on Central America; nothing was to be added to what he had already told Carden in their conference.

In spite of their failure to reach a formal agreement, the British continued to cooperate with the United States, hoping that somehow the State Department could make Estrada Cabrera pay his debts to English bondholders. The department tried to secure Guatemala's assent to refunding the loans, but the wily Estrada Cabrera could never be brought to signing an agreement. By December 1912 the English had lost interest in the financial scheme developed in the United States, and they rejected the entire refunding plan.

The English rejection strained Huntington-Wilson's diplomatic

10. Carden came away from the interview feeling that Knox's knowledge of Central America was most superficial. FO 420/256/62.
11. For a summary of the talk, see Scholes, "Sir Lionel Carden's Proposed Agreement on Central America, 1912," *Americas,* January, 1959.

surface. On January 3, 1913, he expressed his resentment to Innes.[12] Bluntly comparing the attitude of Great Britain to that of Shylock demanding his pound of flesh, Huntington-Wilson said that it was time for the British to realize that Central America "lay especially in our sphere of influence, and that we could not consider it very friendly on their part to demand one and only one solution of a question in that sphere, especially when it was known that by so doing they would be blocking a well-recognized policy of the United States." He was quite sure, Huntington-Wilson added, that if the United States attempted such tactics in a country recognized to be in the British sphere, the English would be displeased.

Huntington-Wilson's little sermon on international sin did no good. The English refused to reconsider the refunding plan, which left them free to act alone, and the State Department was helpless to intervene because it could not get Estrada Cabrera's signature on a loan contract. Shortly after Knox left office, the English "pointed the pistol" at Estrada Cabrera's head, telling him that if the coffee revenues were not restored to the bondholders by mid-May of 1913, the British would send a warship, break off diplomatic relations, and take direct measures to collect the coffee tax. Estrada Cabrera capitulated. Oddly enough, he seemed pleased with the British arrangement, once he had signed.[13]

12. DS 814.51/202.
13. *FR, 1913,* 568 ff.

6

Mexico

For a generation the firm hand of President Porfirio Díaz had kept once-turbulent Mexico relatively quiet and peaceful. But during the Taft Administration—and much to Taft's dismay—the great Revolution of 1910 swept through the country, igniting the smouldering discontent into fires that were to burn for years to come. The increasing opposition to the government stemmed from a number of reasons, among them the concentration of ownership of land and other wealth into fewer and fewer hands; a growing middle-class interest in public affairs and an accompanying resentment against the political monopoly by the small ruling group; inequitable taxation that penalized the commercial, middle, and poorer classes; an incompetent and corrupt judiciary; and a deep hatred of the United States. Mexicans of all classes resented American commercial aggressiveness and shared the feeling that their own government gave the Yankees advantages in every area of enterprise. Generally speaking, Díaz was not personally the focus of this discontent. The Mexicans directed their hatred at the *camarilla porfiriana,* the clique around Díaz, and particularly against Vice President Ramón Corral.

The popular opposition to the regime remained muted, unorganized, and submerged until 1908, when an article by an American journalist altered Mexico's history by bringing the discontent to the surface. Indeed, one Mexican author called the article the "Revolution's Book of Genesis."[1] In an interview with James Creelman, Díaz—almost eighty at the time—announced his determination to retire at the end of his term in November 1910. He told Creelman that the day he had been waiting for had arrived: The Mexican people were now capable of choosing their govern-

1. D. Arenas Guzmán, *La consumación del crimen.* Interview in the March, 1908, issue of *Pearson's Magazine.*

ment without danger of revolution. If an opposition party were organized, he declared, he would welcome it. Although the people took Díaz at his word, no immediate movement to oust him from the presidency resulted from his pronouncement. Mexicans were willing to let him live out his days in office, but they were intensely interested in the incumbent of the vice-presidential position.

After publication of the Díaz-Creelman interview several new parties appeared and, although two were official machines to support the Díaz regime, several others took the old man literally and offered at least partial opposition. The Democratic party opposed renaming Corral vice president and gradually marshaled its support behind General Bernardo Reyes, another *porfirista,* for this office. Far more significant was the Anti-Reelection party under Francisco I. Madero, member of a wealthy northern family of landowners and a well-educated man in his mid-thirties who had studied in France and at the University of California. He adopted as slogans "Free Suffrage" and "No Re-election," although he conceded that Díaz should be allowed to die in harness and that "No Re-election" applied to offices other than the presidency.

In March 1909, to the surprise of few, Díaz announced that he had decided after all to run for office again, and that Corral would be second on the ticket. Elections were scheduled for June and July 1910. Five months after the announcement Taft set out on a long trip through the West, and on October 16 he met Díaz at El Paso and crossed with him to Mexican soil amid a great show of border neighborliness. Díaz had requested the meeting to strengthen himself among his own people through a colorful demonstration of international friendship, and Taft was happy to aid his cause, for he knew that a billion dollars or more of North American investments in Mexico would be greatly endangered if Díaz died and his government went to pieces. As Taft remarked candidly, "I can only hope and pray that his demise does not come until I am out of office." Although no more than empty ceremony, he felt that the meeting accomplished its real purposes.[2] Events were soon to prove him wrong.

At the time Díaz and Taft were shaking hands for the photographers, Madero was well launched on a speaking campaign that was to take him into many parts of Mexico, preaching his doctrine of effective suffrage and no re-election. Although Madero did not

2. Taft to Mrs. Taft, October 15, 1909, William Howard Taft Papers.

completely ignore the urgent social and economic problems facing the country, he offered no more than a vague, sketchy program for dealing with them. Only for political ills did he offer specific prescriptions. In November 1909 his prospects improved when General Reyes, never more than a reluctant candidate, accepted an assignment from Díaz that amounted to ceremonial exile in Europe. By April 1910, when Madero's party convened to nominate a candidate, he had decided that "No Re-election" must apply to Díaz as well as to subordinate officials; on April 17 he accepted his party's nomination for the presidency.

For the rest of the spring Madero traveled around the country, attracting large and sympathetic crowds despite some government harassment, and official observers began to fear that he might win a genuinely free election. Rather than take this risk, the Díaz regime arrested Madero on June 15, had him convicted of sedition on trumped-up charges, and imprisoned him at San Luis Potosí. Many of Madero's followers in other parts of Mexico were similarly silenced. With his opposition behind bars and his cohorts counting the ballots, Díaz won an overwhelming victory, but the travesty of the election convinced the opposition that democratic practices were worthless and that revolution was the only means to power.

The election won, the government staged a lavish celebration of the centennial of Mexican independence in September. Champagne flowed, bands played, soldiers marched, and orators expounded, yet the gala was not an unqualified success, because these reminders of the heroes who had fought for Mexico's freedom stiffened the opposition and sharpened the desire to renew the current generation's political life. By reawakening national pride the centennial celebration undoubtedly contributed to the outbreak of the Madero revolution.[3]

On October 6, 1910, Madero escaped to San Antonio, Texas, where the revolutionary junta maintained its general headquarters. After being proclaimed president of the junta and leader of the revolution, Madero issued the Plan of San Luis Potosí, calling on his countrymen to revolt against their government. On November 20, the date designated by Madero, anti-Government demonstrations took place throughout Mexico. United States Ambassador Henry Lane Wilson reported that, although the move-

3. Jesús Romero Flores, *Del porfirismo a la revolución constitucionalista,* 115-16, 121.

ment was apparently unorganized and without responsible leadership, it had spread over the entire country. The uprising, he reported, was remarkable for its intensity and bitterness, indicating a deep-seated antipathy to the Government. In Mexico City people of every rank openly and aggressively expressed their hatred of Corral and the *camarilla* and their approval of the revolutionary movement. Wilson alerted the State Department to expect real trouble if a popular leader took control of the rebellion.[4]

Shortly after the revolt broke, the Mexican Government tried to persuade the United States authorities to arrest Madero and also some of his agents in the States or at least to keep them under strict surveillance. The Mexicans claimed that the activities of Mexican revolutionaries in the United States violated both international and American neutrality laws. Although the department rejected the charges, it pledged stringent enforcement of legislation related to international and domestic neutrality. Even though key officials of the department watched Mexican developments, they obviously were not deeply troubled. Knox went to Palm Springs, California, on March 4 and Huntington-Wilson left Washington for a stay in South Carolina.

When Ambassador Wilson, who had returned to Washington for personal reasons, called on the President on March 6, he described the Mexican situation in the most pessimistic terms and expressed the opinion that the Díaz government was on the verge of collapse. On paper the Mexican army numbered 34,000 strong; in reality it consisted of only 14,000 men. Since 90 per cent of the people sympathized with the revolution, Wilson did not believe that Díaz could suppress what was in fact a popular uprising, and he warned that the coming upheaval would endanger North American lives and property.[5]

The Ambassador's foreboding prognosis led Taft to summon immediately Secretary of War Jacob M. Dickinson, General Leonard Wood, Secretary of the Navy George von L. Meyer, and Admiral Richard Wainwright to the White House. At this meeting the President ordered Wood to mobilize 20,000 men north of the border and to keep them there for several months on patrol duty and maneuvers. The Army should station the troops where they would be readily available if the United States had to intervene in Mexico.[6] The military authorities spent most of that night and almost

4. *Foreign Relations, 1911,* 367-68.
5. Taft to Roosevelt, March 22, 1911, Taft Papers.

all of the next day working out their plans to man the border with Mexico in Texas and California and to concentrate ships of the Atlantic Fleet in the Gulf of Mexico and the armored cruiser command of the Pacific Fleet in southern waters.[7]

Taft's quick decision to mobilize the troops (he did not even consult the State Department) was a direct result of the interview with Wilson. The Ambassador's report crystallized Taft's own growing uneasiness over the Mexican situation, for the violent anti-American feeling revealed during the November riots in Guadalajara and Mexico City had already aroused his fears. Although he wanted to believe that such prejudices were only local, Wilson offered no comfort; dislike of the Yankee, he reported, prevailed throughout the country among all classes.[8]

Taft explained to the Mexican ambassador that the transfer of troops to Texas and California was not intended as a hostile act, and he assured De la Barra that the increased patrols were intended for more effective policing of the border. Taft also sent a message to Díaz on March 7, expressing the hope that unfounded and sensational newspaper speculation about the maneuvers would cause no misapprehension in Mexico. The Mexicans were not reassured. "The newspapers here boil with conjecture," Dearing noted, "the Mexicans are in a ferment." To the department Dearing pointed out the obvious: Mexicans thought the mobilization foreshadowed some unfriendly action. While Dearing believed that Díaz would take the assurances at face value, he was convinced that Mexicans, Americans in Mexico, and most of the diplomatic corps unanimously agreed that the troops' mission was not confined to military drill maneuvers.[9]

Realizing that Wilson's views, if publicized, would make him *persona non grata* to the Mexican Government, Taft could not use the Ambassador's report to justify mobilization. Indeed, he could not, in the circumstances, even admit that movement of troops and ships was a mobilization. Therefore, he issued a state-

---

6. Taft to Roosevelt, March 22, 1911, Taft Papers; Leonard Wood Diary, March 6, 1911.
7. *New York Tribune,* March 8, 1911.
8. Both Knox and Huntington-Wilson, as has been noted, were out of town. Fred Dearing, the *chargé* in Mexico City, was taken very much unawares by the decisions made in Washington: "Our army's spring manoeuvres, God Bless my Soul, are announced to take place along the border! All as mild as a May morning. But it's all very sudden." Fred Dearing Papers.
9. Taft to Roosevelt, March 22, 1911, Taft Papers; DS 812.00/922; Dearing Papers; *FR, 1911,* 415-16, 420.

ment that was intended to give the impression that the Army's decision to order 20,000 men to the Mexican border for spring maneuvers was merely coincidental in its occurrence at a time of unrest within Mexico.

But the press, refusing to accept this explanation, discussed the possibility of American intervention in Mexico. When newspapers began printing facts and figures about the troops moved into the border area and their equipment, it became difficult for the Administration to maintain its fiction. In addition, Washington increasingly believed that intervention would become necessary to protect foreign lives and property in Mexico. As a result, Taft announced that the troops' real purpose was to eliminate filibustering and the smuggling of men and arms across the border. The United States Government was determined that the revolution in Mexico must end.[10]

Mexican sensibilities were more deeply wounded when the Navy ordered warships on Caribbean duty to call at Mexican ports. Taft and the department first learned of these instructions when the Mexican ambassador asked the department to issue an explanatory statement to calm public opinion in Mexico. Taft acted immediately, ordering the ships to stop only for coal and to leave immediately. In addition, he informed De la Barra of his orders.[11]

This done, Taft turned back to the Navy. To Secretary Meyer he made known his annoyance at not having been told of the Navy's additional orders, which exceeded the plans for mobilization. On March 6, he reminded the Secretary, the men in conference at the White House had decided to mobilize Army and Navy units in Texas and at San Diego; no one had mentioned sending ships to Mexican ports. He hoped that Meyer would prevent these "small fry" from appearing again in Mexican ports and that he would restrict all maneuvers to areas north of the border.[12] To Roosevelt, Taft frankly reported that the Navy, eager for combat, had to be held in leash.[13]

10. *New York Tribune,* March 8, 1911; Taft to Roosevelt, March 22, 1911, Taft Papers.
11. DS 812.00/921-22; *FR, 1911,* 422.
12. DS 812.00/955.
13. Taft to Roosevelt, March 22, 1911. Taft Papers. Dearing wondered if Washington realized how many Americans there were, and Mexicans too, who were praying for some incident that would resurrect the old American imperialism, the resurrection to be followed by intervention, annexation, and finally absorption of Mexico. It was not surprising that the Mexicans were touchy. Dearing Papers.

The Mexican crisis disturbed not only the Mexicans. Members of the Cabinet were upset because they had not been consulted, and rumors around Washington described Knox as angry to the point of resignation.[14] To mollify his Secretary of State, Taft wrote him a long letter of explanation, to which the Secretary replied petulantly by reciting the litany of his burdens: De la Barra, howling for stricter enforcement of the neutrality laws; Wilson, predicting the regime's explosive collapse; Americans with interest in Mexico, demanding protection against real and fancied dangers; Americans with no interests in Mexico (but with large newspaper investments at home), hoping for the worst; the Monroe Doctrine, constantly requiring a measure of benevolent supervision over Latin-American countries; the delicate entente with the Latins, needing the kind of nourishment and mainte-nance to be found in champagne and other alcoholic preserva-tives. Although Knox foresaw a "shindig" in Congress over the Mexican situation, he concluded that the person on whom respon-sibility rested must do his duty as he saw it, on the basis of the facts presented to him.[15] This recital was less than all-out support graciously conveyed, but despite its excess of complaint and its reserve of approval, it satisfied the President.

On March 13 the Administration decided to make an unofficial but authoritative statement on Mexican policy through the *New York Tribune*.[16] The story declared that the primary purpose for stationing troops along the border was to stop violations of the neutrality laws, which had assumed appalling proportions. This statement was a complete turnabout in public information, for no government department had previously been willing to concede that any serious infractions of border agreements had occurred. Although tighter control of the border would eliminate filibuster-ing and cut off the flow of arms to the insurgents, the Mexican Government needed several additional months to curb the guer-rillas. Although the Administration denied contemplating an in-vasion of Mexico at the present time, it did intend to offer help in pacifying the country if the Mexicans proved unable to cope with the revolution within a reasonable period. If the United States ultimately had to intervene, it would do so only to restore order and on condition that a general election be held immediately.

14. A. Butt, *Taft and Roosevelt*, II, 602-3.
15. Knox to Taft, March 14, 1911. Taft Papers.
16. *New York Tribune*, March 14, 1911.

When a new executive took over, the troops would leave. The presence of United States troops on the border served to assure all foreign nations that their interests in Mexico would be protected; it also served to warn them that whatever happened, they were not to intervene.

Sincerely wishing to avoid intervention, Taft gave the Army strict instructions not to cross the border, and he firmly resisted all pressures to change these orders. In March Governor O. B. Colquitt of Texas asked Taft to send troops into Mexico to apprehend certain revolutionary leaders, but the President forcefully declined. In April, when two Americans were killed and several wounded in Douglas, Arizona, as the result of fighting in Agua Prieta across the border, Taft issued a calming statement. He described the international situation as one that demanded extreme moderation on the part of all American citizens, and he added that he had taken steps to prevent a repetition of the tragedy.[17] After more trouble in Ciudad Juárez early in May, Mrs. Taft asked her husband if there would be war. He replied that he did not know, but that he was going to do everything in his power to prevent one.[18]

His ambassador in Mexico did not share this restraint. Wilson wanted to "fire a hot telegram" to the department, reporting that the Mexican Government had not replied to his note on the Douglas incident, and, since the party in power was unmistakably courting trouble with the United States in order to divert attention from its own failures on the domestic scene, its silence was a towering and intolerable affront. Dearing was able to dissuade him from dispatching the telegram. Wilson's trouble, Dearing concluded, was that he thought of himself, not as subordinate but as a coordinate, not as the executor of policy but as a participant in its formulation.[19]

Díaz had tried in every way to restore domestic order. Civil repression, military force, and conciliation had all failed. When the extreme measure of suspension of constitutional guarantees brought no results, Díaz changed his cabinet and promised broad reforms that included no re-election, electoral reform, correction of local abuses, the independence of the judiciary, and the division of large estates. He even packed Corral out of the country. In

17. On March 16 and 24, Taft Papers; *New York Tribune,* April 15, 1911.
18. Butt, *Taft and Roosevelt,* II, 645.
19. Dearing Papers.

Taft's view, the presence of the troops on the border had forced the Mexican Government to face reality, but Dearing did not agree. Rather, he believed that the government had retreated because, realizing its authority was crumbling, it feared the consequences.[20]

Whatever the reason, the government's promises did little to check unrest. The revolution continued to gain strength and by May Díaz had reached the end of his resources. Madero, who had returned to Mexico in February, now consented to negotiate a settlement, but he balked at Díaz' remaining in office. Finally, the government representatives agreed that Díaz and Corral would resign, but for the rest Madero was content to leave the *porfirista* structure intact. On May 25 Díaz resigned and on the following day he departed for that haven of exiles from the Western Hemisphere, Europe. De la Barra, the former ambassador to the United States, became provisional president, and in the months he held office, he won the respect of both the State Department and the embassy in Mexico City.

With the Mexican elections scheduled for mid-October, Knox on the seventeenth recommended to Henry L. Stimson, the new Secretary of War, that all troops deployed in the maneuvers along the border be recalled and only those needed for patrol duty and for the enforcement of the neutrality laws be kept in the border area.[21] Stimson followed Knox's advice, and all "maneuvers" terminated at the end of the month.

On November 6, 1911, Madero was inaugurated as President of Mexico, but in spite of the Administration's fervent hopes for his success in bringing peaceable conditions, the internal disorders continued. Madero in fact soon found himself adopting Díaz' insistence that the United States strictly enforce the neutrality laws. Wilson's reports were pessimistic; by the end of January 1912 he had already lost faith in the new regime. Madero seemed incapable of establishing effective control of the country, and Wilson had evidence of new illegal confiscations of American property and the imprisonment of Americans on false or whimsical charges. Although Mexico's new president was honest, sincere, and a devoted patriot, in Wilson's opinion he lacked stability of character and the capacity for hard work, and he had no definite administrative program. Madero at the moment seemed to

20. Dearing Papers.
21. DS 812.00/2416/2295.

want to deal justly with all matters that the embassy brought to his attention, but the Ambassador doubted whether this attitude would continue as pressures increased.[22]

Concluding from Wilson's reports that the internal and international situations probably would deteriorate still further, Knox anticipated that Americans would suffer much more in the future than during Madero's revolution, when neither side was willing to incur the displeasure of the United States Government. Knox therefore recommended that Taft increase the border guard—unobtrusively—to spare the Mexicans' national pride. Wasting no time, Taft instructed Stimson to station enough men on the border to protect American citizens' lives and property in Mexico.[23] Apparently, the War Department did not actually order the troops to move; all mobile forces were merely to hold themselves ready for action. The department also considered advising Americans to leave the country.[24]

The news that troops had been alerted on both sides of the border led to rumors of American intervention. Advice poured in to the department and the President. One Texas interventionist suggested that Taft hurl the "hirelings of the war department into the land of tamales" and take forcible possession of the haciendas of the "half breeds in the land of Montezuma." Advocates of restraint, such as Edward L. Doheny, who had interests in Mexican oil, declared that there was no real danger to foreigners and foreign-held property.[25] Those who demanded protection were fewer than others who believed that intervention would arouse such hostility that no United States citizen would be safe in Mexico. To calm at least the Mexicans, Knox instructed all consular offices to deny the reports of intervention. Although agreeing that this would be helpful, Huntington-Wilson thought an even better device for scotching the rumors would be to make the military hold their tongues. He cited as one inflammatory source a newspaper interview with an Army colonel who spoke casually of a possible campaign on Mexican territory.[26]

On February 26 a critical situation developed in Ciudad Juárez when the rebels informed the United States consul that they were

---

22. DS 812.00/2710. On the margin of this dispatch Dearing pencilled comments reinforcing a number of Wilson's opinions, including those on Madero.
23. *FR, 1912*, 716; Taft Papers.
24. Wood Diary; DS 812.00/2797A.
25. Doheny to Taft, March 5, 1912. Taft Papers.
26. DS 812.00/2797A; *FR, 1912*, 720.

about to attack the city and advised him to move all foreigners to safety. After discussing the available alternatives, Dearing (now back in Washington) and Clark drafted a telegram instructing the consul to warn the rebel leader that in no circumstances must his troops fire into American territory; any violation would lead to serious consequences. Dearing and Clark believed that Wilson should convey the same warning to the Mexican Government with regard to its forces and should suggest that the federal troops make any contemplated resistance outside of Ciudad Juárez or perhaps even withdraw without making a defense. Clark and Dearing then proceeded to the White House for Taft's approval of their action, which he gave at once. "You know I am not going to cross the line," he remarked. "That is something for which Congress will have to take the responsibility." Then the President added, "But I suppose it will do no harm to threaten them a little." For whatever reason, the federal troops surrendered Ciudad Juárez to the anti-Madero forces without a shot.[27]

Yet the tempo of affairs was quickening; on February 24 Wilson had suggested that the department consider whether it might not be wise to err on the side of safety and advise United States citizens to leave Mexico. The incident at Ciudad Juárez was the climax that forced a decision, and on March 2, after the Cabinet in special meeting had discussed and approved the measure, Taft finally issued a statement suggested a year earlier by Huntington-Wilson. After reminding United States citizens living in Mexico that it was illegal for them to work against a government with which the United States was at peace, Taft warned that anyone who ignored these laws did so at his own peril. The department emphasized that the proclamation was not a declaration of neutrality nor a recognition of a state of belligerency in Mexico; it was simply a warning to all United States citizens. On the same day, the department instructed Wilson, at his discretion, to advise North Americans to leave any area where lawlessness endangered their personal safety.[28]

Under two different presidents Mexico had complained of the relaxed American attitude toward enforcing neutrality legislation, domestic and international. The Taft Administration insisted that it was enforcing the laws in accordance with established policy. It argued that the United States was not obliged to prevent

27. DS 812.00/2912/3031; *FR, 1912*, 880-81.
28. *FR, 1912*, 731-33.

commercial trading in arms and ammunition even in a condition of recognized warfare, much less in time of peace. Nor did this country's commitment relieve Mexico of the duty of policing its own border with its own forces to prevent violations of Mexican statutes. Under normal conditions, the Secretary of State maintained, the United States had no other international duty than to be neutral and impartial. If, on the other hand, the United States agreed to Mexico's demands, it would in effect be cooperating with a foreign government to help it suppress a revolution and restore internal peace.[29]

On March 8 Huntington-Wilson repeated to the Mexican ambassador that, since neither international law nor domestic legislation made the commercial export of arms and ammunition a crime, the United States executive was powerless to stop such traffic. The ambassador was ungracious enough to repeat the dictum of an earlier Secretary of State: "No sovereign power can rightfully plead the defects of its own domestic penal statutes as justification or extenuation of an international wrong to another sovereign state."[30] Whether or not the barb spurred the action, in any event a change in policy occurred when Taft decided to ask Congress for legislation to stop the shipment of war matériel into Mexico. Congress was sympathetic, and on March 14 both houses passed a joint resolution making it unlawful to export, without the President's approval, arms and ammunition to any American country experiencing armed rebellion. Taft issued his proclamation on the same day, because Root felt that exporters would take advantage of a delay to ship huge quantities of equipment.[31] Regulating the export of arms to Mexico now rested with the executive branch, which in general approved all requests made by the Mexican Government and by United States citizens or companies in Mexico.

During March and April the service departments conferred and drew up their plans in case intervention became necessary. On March 26 Wood talked with Stimson about a possible invasion of Mexico, and on April 15 Stimson convened the Joint Board to consider Army-Navy cooperation in such an event. Apparently the board agreed that if intervention should be necessary, the Navy would seize Veracruz and then either establish a naval

29. *FR, 1912,* 708-9; DS 812.00/2445.
30. *FR, 1912,* 740-44. Fish to British Minister.
31. *FR, 1912,* 745; *New York Times,* March 14-15, 1912; Taft Papers.

blockade on both coasts or take the as yet unoccupied ports on the Pacific and on the Gulf. For its part, elements of the Army would go into Veracruz and on up to Xalapa or Orizaba, while others defended the border.[32] The State Department did not expect the services to be called upon to execute their plans. Knox felt that conditions were not yet so bad as to compel intervention; in fact, he regarded intervention as a remote contingency.[33]

During this tense period that old bugaboo—Japan's designs in Mexico—popped up again. Senator Henry Cabot Lodge learned that a Japanese syndicate was negotiating to purchase from the American owners a vast tract of land—4,000,000 acres in Lower California—running for 350 miles along Magdalena Bay. Since the land had no commercial value and could serve only as a naval coaling station, Lodge wanted the government to inform the owners that the United States could not permit its sale except to other Americans or to Mexicans. On April 2 he introduced a resolution calling on the President for information.[34]

The Senator's facts were essentially correct. Frederick H. Allen, counsel for the owners, had been discussing the matter with the department since the summer of 1911 in an effort to learn the government's reaction to the proposed sale. Although Knox did not answer directly, he left no doubt of his disapproval.[35] Allen then offered to withhold for the United States Government such land in the neighborhood of Magdalena Bay as it might like to buy at some future time, but Huntington-Wilson explained that, since the considerations were strategic, this decision lay with the Navy Department. The American owners informed the department in December that they intended to sell only a minority interest to the Japanese, but the department refused to elaborate on Knox's original statement.[36]

Lodge's speech in the Senate on February 29, 1912, and his subsequent resolutions created a flurry of diplomatic activity. The department received assurances from Madero that no Mexican-Japanese understanding existed, and the Japanese Government categorically denied any interest in the project, which it had, as a matter of fact, discouraged. After Ambassador Charles Page Bryan reported from Tokyo that he could learn nothing of such a

32. DS 812.00/3031; Joint Board Minutes, Record Group 225; Wood Diary.
33. *FR, 1912*, 893-94.
34. DS 894.20212/31, 45.
35. DS 894.20212/12.
36. DS 894.2012/18-19.

scheme, Taft instructed the department to inform Japan that Lodge had introduced his resolution without the Administration's knowledge or approval.[37]

The reassuring information furnished by the executive was not sufficient to deter Lodge. In July he introduced another resolution declaring that the United States would view with great concern the occupation by a foreign company of any strategically important area in the Western Hemisphere.[38] The Senate approved it by a 51–4 vote.

Taft and Knox never believed that Japan was making an effort to get a foothold in Mexico, and most of the press agreed. Nothing in the department's files indicates that Japan and Mexico at any time considered disposition of the land near Magdalena Bay. Writing privately to Root on August 8, Mexican Ambassador Manuel Calero described Lodge's fears as quite unfounded, since Mexico would never consent to foreign occupation of Magdalena Bay or any other portion of her territory.[39] Lodge himself, in reporting his resolution, stated that the Senate Committee on Foreign Relations had found no evidence that the Japanese or any other government was involved in the syndicate's attempt to buy land in Lower California. Taft thought that Lodge had a "bee in his bonnet" and had been fooled by a lawyer hunting a fee from a defunct client.[40] Certainly Taft never took the Lodge resolution seriously.

Yet the Lodge resolution, as Perkins indicates, was nothing less than "a veto on the transfer of private property from private individuals to private individuals." Although Taft never gave much weight to Lodge's proposal, subsequent administrations invoked its authority to prevent the transfer to foreign interests (not governments) of Mexican property owned by Americans.[41]

Although the arms embargo proclaimed in March enabled the Mexican government forces to recapture some important areas in the north, Madero was not able during the following months to consolidate his political position. On August 28 Wilson sent a long report to Knox that painted a disheartening picture of the Mexican scene. Everyone, Mexicans and foreigners alike, suffered from the activities of the guerrilla bands and the brigands. Nominally the Madero administration was pro-United States, but Wil-

37. DS 894.2012/30, 32.
38. D. Perkins, *Hands Off: A History of the Monroe Doctrine*, 273.
39. Elihu Root Papers.
40. Taft to David Starr Jordan, August 5, 1912. Taft Papers.
41. Perkins, *Hands Off*, 274.

son emphasized that it was in reality conducting a campaign against North American interests in Mexico, the object apparently being to enrich the Madero family and its entourage. He foresaw the harassment and confiscation of many important American interests unless the Mexican Government was taught that United States nationals and property must receive the same protection that Mexican nationals and their interests enjoyed in the United States.[42]

Because of this report, Taft himself acted. In a conference with Calero on September 4, Taft pointed out how patient and helpful to Mexico the United States Government had been, noting that the amendment of the neutrality law was vital to the Madero government's very existence. In return the United States expected more consideration for its interests than Mexico had thus far shown. He could not tolerate Mexican indifference much longer, Taft told the Ambassador. Many Americans had been killed, and in each case the Mexican Government had done nothing but make a superficial investigation. Taft frankly warned the Ambassador that if conditions continued to worsen, he would have no recourse but to call a special session of Congress to consider official action. Calero promised that he would do his best to stir his government to greater activity. The same day, Taft discussed the Mexican situation with Wood, who told him that the Army had perfected its plans.[43]

During their interview Taft had told Calero that the United States was sending the Mexican Government a long note listing the specific cases that showed negligence on its part. Although Wilson presented the note on September 15, it was mid-November before Calero indicated to Taft the general outline of his government's reply. The President had assumed that the response to his note would be unsatisfactory, and Calero's outline confirmed his assessment.[44] Taft's patience was fraying. "I am getting to a point," he wrote Knox on December 14, "where I think we ought to put a little dynamite in for the purpose of stirring up that dreamer who seems unfitted to meet the crisis in the country of which he is President."[45]

Early in January of 1913 Ambassador Wilson returned to Mexico after an extended leave, during which Mortimer Schuyler had

42. *FR, 1912,* 828-32.
43. *FR, 1912,* 834; DS 812.00/5392; Wood Diary; Taft Papers.
44. *FR, 1912,* 842-46; DS 812.00/5697.
45. DS 812.00/5697.

served as *chargé* of the embassy. Soon Wilson was reporting that both economically and politically the situation was "gloomy if not hopeless." This dispatch and others like it, "so uniformly and particularly discouraging" and so conflictory with Schuyler's, confused the department. Was the greater pessimism due to a difference in point of view between Wilson and Schuyler? Knox urged Wilson to give some concrete reasons for the tone of his reports.[46] Wilson denied that he and Schuyler interpreted events differently and that his dispatches were pessimistic; they were, he declared, factual.

On January 27 Knox, still greatly disturbed by Wilson's reports, wrote Taft about them. In this long letter Knox enclosed three sets of dispatches and instructions, each illustrating differences of opinion between the department and Wilson. The first set related to Wilson's increasing pessimism, "which appears to the Department to be unjustified, if not, indeed, misleading." The second showed that Wilson had taken a stand of his own with regard to claims. On this point, in the Secretary's opinion, his expressions amounted almost to criticism of the department and betrayed a desire to force the department to change its policy. The most recent document might be interpreted, the Secretary told Taft, almost as indicating "an intention on the part of the Ambassador to force this Government's hand in its dealing with the Mexican situation as a whole, the apparent disagreement between the Ambassador and the Department being so fundamental and so serious that the Department feels it would err if it did not bring the matter pointedly to your attention." Included in this latest set was Wilson's dispatch of January 18, which advocated vigorous and drastic action to secure redress for damages and, perhaps incidentally, the downfall of a government hateful to the vast majority of Mexicans. That government was obviously antipathetic to the United States, to which it had given innumerable evidences of its bad faith, inefficiency, hostility, and insincerity.[47] Although Knox refused to believe Wilson, the Ambassador had good grounds for his pessimism, which Consul William W. Canada echoed from Veracruz. The pervasive undercurrent of discontent and the widespread expectation of new conflict led Canada to predict an imminent eruption, worse that the earlier one.[48]

46. DS 812.00/5913A; *FR, 1913,* 692-93.
47. DS 812.00/7229A; *FR, 1913,* 886-87.
48. DS 812.00/5907.

But Madero was optimistic, although unjustifiably so; from no quarter could he depend on unqualified support.[49] The opposition press and leadership kept up a constant harassment of his government. The moneyed interests—landowners and Mexican and foreign businessmen—made no move to use their influence in his favor. Most ominous, the army's support, on which the government depended completely, was dubious. And Madero clearly refused to believe their gloomy forebodings. He simply ignored reports of impending revolution.

The storm, which broke on February 10, lasted for "Ten Tragic Days," as the Mexicans call this period in their history. Félix Díaz, General Reyes, and other leaders whom Madero had imprisoned for plotting against his government were freed by their followers, and under Díaz' leadership attempted to capture the National Palace. Although the attack failed and Reyes was killed, the rebels were not subdued. As the two opposing factions faced each other in Mexico City, Wilson, in concert with his diplomatic colleagues, demanded that both Madero and Díaz give effective protection to the foreign colony. Wilson also telegraphed the department advising "prompt and effective action."[50]

Knox immediately instructed Wilson to outline precisely just what action the United States should take. When the Ambassador recommended sending warships and marines to Mexico's Atlantic and Pacific ports, Knox requested the Navy to order ships to Veracruz and Tampico, to detain the vessel already at Acapulco, and to send another to Mazatlán. The department's press release announcing the movement of ships emphasized that these orders represented no change in American policy; they were not designed to favor either of the parties involved in Mexican politics; the vessels' sole purpose was to observe and report. As a further precaution, the Administration also cut off all arms shipments to Mexico, even those Taft had already approved.[51]

On February 11 serious fighting between government and rebel forces again broke out in the heart of the capital. That evening Wilson telegraphed the department:

> I am convinced that the Government of the United States, in the interest of humanity and in the discharge of its political obliga-

49. S. Ross, *Francisco I. Madero,* 276-77.
50. Ross, *Madero,* 278-81; *FR, 1913,* 700. Wilson estimated that there were about 5,000 Americans in the capital and a total of about 25,000 foreigners.
51. DS 812.00/7229A; *FR, 1913,* 701-2.

tions, should send firm, drastic instructions, perhaps of a menacing character, to be transmitted personally to the Government of President Madero and to the leaders of the revolutionary movement. If I were in possession of instructions of this character or clothed with general powers in the name of the President, I might possibly be able to induce a cessation of hostilities and the initiation of negotiations having for their object definite pacific arrangements.[52]

William Doyle and his Division of Latin-American Affairs were opposed to sending the instructions requested by Wilson. Doyle ticked off the reasons for this stand, the first being Wilson's admission that the greatest force such an instruction would bear would be perhaps to put the United States Ambassador in a position to bring about a cessation of hostilities. Such an instruction would be wholly undesirable unless the United States were prepared to make good its threats. Also, before the President could act, Congress must authorize him to use the Army and Navy to force Mexico to comply. Such action by Congress would probably be construed, no matter how mistakenly, as the first step in armed intervention. Should the Administration decide to follow the course recommended by Wilson, Doyle warned, it must be with the knowledge that its action might plunge the country into a war that would necessarily be waged by a new administration. He concluded that the United States had gone as far as it should in the circumstances; all it need do for the moment was maintain a state of alert preparedness. The department notified Wilson that the President opposed sending him the instructions he had requested.[53]

During this time, while the fighting swirled through the capital and opposing forces gave little thought to the security of noncombatants, United States citizens converged on the embassy by the hundreds. Chaos within and without meant that the Ambassador worked in the most trying circumstances, which might explain at least in part his reasons for sending so drastic a telegram. As the man on the spot he had to be prepared to act promptly and decisively on his own responsibility if he thought the situation called for it. Yet Wilson was not an unbiased observer. Although professing faith in Madero's sincerity and honesty, from the beginning of the Madero regime Wilson had voiced serious doubts about the President's ability as an administrator, and the Ambassador's

52. *FR, 1913,* 704.
53. *FR, 1913,* 706.

long letter to Knox on February 4, 1913, indicated nothing but contempt for the government. After its fall he termed it "a wicked despotism" and charged that during its entire existence it had been anti-United States.[54]

Knox's earlier misgivings about the decorum of Wilson's conduct were reinforced when he learned through an Associated Press report that Wilson had refused to evacuate the embassy even though warned that it would be in the line of fire. On February 14 Knox instructed Wilson to leave the embassy if a protest proved ineffective:

> Almost intolerable as is the situation, it should be remembered that fighting within cities is by no means without precedent and that the convenience of foreigners and the dignity of diplomatic establishments can not in all cases be interposed in a manner to affect the issue of such fighting where the danger to foreigners and diplomatic representatives is incidental and where they may escape such danger by removal.[55]

Madero's position was becoming increasingly precarious. On the morning of February 14 Wilson discussed the situation with Mexico's Minister of Foreign Affairs Pedro Lascuráin, who expressed the opinion that Madero ought to resign. In the afternoon Wilson learned that the Cabinet had already urged the President to do so, but that he had refused. In view of this situation, Wilson invited the representatives of Great Britain, Germany, Spain, and France to the United States embassy to determine a common line of action. After a discussion that lasted from one o'clock in the morning until almost three, the conferees agreed unanimously that, although they were without instructions from their governments, they should ask Madero to resign and to turn the executive power over to Congress. Madero firmly rejected this unofficial message of friendly advice, which was conveyed to him through the Spanish minister. The Mexican President refused the right of diplomats to interfere in a domestic question. He would not resign; he was the constitutional President of Mexico.[56]

During Wilson's meeting in the morning with Lascuráin, the Foreign Minister had asked him whether the United States had any intention of landing troops in Mexico. Wilson replied that he had no instructions or authority in the matter, but since the con-

---

54. *FR, 1913,* 696-99, 713-15, 724-25, 741-42.
55. *FR, 1913,* 708-10.
56. *FR, 1913,* 708-12.

versation was entirely personal and unofficial, he added that if the situation grew intolerable the United States would need to consider providing the protection that the Mexican Government seemed unable to give. Whether because of a misunderstanding arising from this conversation or for some other reason, Madero assumed that the United States had ordered marines to Mexico City. He immediately wired Taft, asking him to prevent disembarkation, since landing troops would only worsen the present bad situation.[57]

Momentarily apprehensive over Wilson's conduct, the department asked him for an explanation. Before Wilson's answer reached Washington, however, a rereading of several dispatches apparently dispelled the fear that the Ambassador had not acted circumspectly, so Taft's response to Madero went over the wires. Although denying the accuracy of the report that "orders have already been given" to land troops, Taft made no promises that such orders would not be issued in the future. Indeed, the message closed with the intimidating statement that events of the past two years, coupled with the present disturbances, had aroused the feeling in the United States that Mexico's future was bleak and that the paramount duty of the United States Government was to relieve the situation promptly.[58]

Knox explained to Wilson the balance between intimidation and conciliation for which the department had striven in composing the telegram. Taft was afraid that stories of intervention would arouse the people to attack Americans, whereas Knox feared that too emphatic a denial might destroy the sobering effect of the idea that in certain contingencies the United States would be compelled to intervene. Keeping in mind both Taft's policy and the local situation, Wilson's job was to see that Mexican opinion, both official and unofficial, achieved a happy medium between exaggerated apprehension and wholesome fear.[59]

Madero's ouster became inevitable when General Victoriano Huerta, the commander of the government troops and the man responsible for protecting the President, joined the opposition. On the afternoon of February 17 Huerta informed Wilson that at any moment he and Díaz would put into operation their plan to

57. *FR, 1913,* 713-16.
58. *FR, 1913,* 715.
59. *FR, 1913,* 717.

remove Madero from power. Huerta was not boasting; within the next twenty-four hours he communicated to Wilson the news that he had arrested the President, Vice President Piño Suárez, and the Cabinet. The problem now was what to do with Madero. Would it be better, Huerta asked the Ambassador, to send him into exile or to an asylum? Wilson replied that he "ought to do that which was best for the peace of the country."[60]

Once Wilson learned of Madero's fall, he began worrying about its aftermath. To forestall trouble he invited both Huerta and Díaz to the embassy to plan for maintaining order in the city. After much disagreement the two generals finally came to these terms: Huerta would be the provisional president and Díaz would name the Cabinet; later, in the regular election for the presidency, Huerta would support Díaz.[61] These details settled, the Ambassador congratulated the department on the "happy outcome" of events. The next day, after receiving pledges of immunity for his followers and safe-conduct into exile for himself and Piño Suárez and their families, Madero agreed to resign.

As soon as Huerta was installed as provisional president on February 20, Wilson telegraphed the department, ostensibly asking for instructions but in fact urging the United States to recognize Huerta immediately. Then, without waiting for a reply, that same evening he assembled the diplomatic corps. All the diplomats having agreed that recognition was imperative for the new government's survival, they decided that they would recognize Huerta the following day. Again acting on his own initiative, Wilson informed all consular officers in Mexico to publish the fact that the Senate, the Chamber of Deputies, and the people of Mexico City supported the Huerta government and to urge Mexicans to back the new regime, which would be recognized by all foreign governments.[62]

The department, however, did not feel the need to act so quickly. While it accepted Wilson's assurances that the Huerta government had acquired power legally and intended to re-establish peace and order, the new regime still had to prove that it could and would do its duty by foreigners and their governments. Before recognition would be forthcoming, Mexico had to pledge that she would satisfactorily resolve the many questions that

60. *FR, 1913,* 718-21; DS 812.00/6271.
61. *FR, 1913,* 720-23.
62. *FR, 1913,* 725-27, 732.

were unsettled with the United States. To make sure that its language would not be misinterpreted, the department included a list of the specific items, mostly involving claims.[63] But Wilson believed that he could get the desired results from the new government without refusing full recognition; indeed, he seemed to think that the government would settle the claims as a personal favor to him. As he informed the department, the Mexicans understood that he expected immediate action and they gave every indication of being grateful for his good offices in ending the conflict. At any rate, Wilson wanted to put off carrying out the instructions until after his interview with government officials on February 24, to which delay the department agreed.

Although the news from Mexico did not indicate any imminent crisis, Taft decided to reinforce the border patrol once more, and 5,000 men were subsequently ordered from Fort Omaha to Galveston. Once more Taft had acted, not only without consulting his Department of State, but without even informing it of his action; Huntington-Wilson picked up the weighty news in a casual conversation. Wood and Stimson being out of Washington, Huntington-Wilson suggested that the President authorize the State Department to issue a statement. Taft agreed, but he issued the statement himself in New York.[64] No new crisis had developed to cause the movement of troops, the public was assured. The troops were the second and last precautionary measure, the first having been the dispatch of warships to Mexican ports.

The "Ten Tragic Days" now began moving swiftly to their savage climax. On February 19 Wilson reported the rumor that Gustavo Madero, the former President's brother, had been killed, a rumor confirmed by Huerta later that day. Blaming the soldiers for the crime—they had killed Gustavo on their own initiative—Huerta assured Wilson that the government was taking every precaution to protect Francisco Madero and Piño Suárez. Earlier, the department had reminded Wilson that he had a certain responsibility for Madero's safety, since Huerta had consulted him regarding treatment of the men in the displaced government. Now Knox informed Wilson that, although Gustavo's assassina-

63. *FR, 1913,* 728-31.
64. *FR, 1913,* 730. Stimson told Wood that if there were trouble with Mexico, he would like to get in it even if he had to go in a subordinate capacity. Wood characterized these remarks as simply an indication of Stimson's desire to be of service, for the Secretary of War knew that the chance of any real action was remote. Wood Diary.

tion had created a very unfavorable impression in the United States, Taft was pleased with Huerta's assurances that no injury would come to the former President and Vice President.[65] Knox wrote out the draft of this telegram in his own hand.

In spite of Huerta's soothing words, the families and partisans of the two men as well as many members of the diplomatic corps were gravely concerned for their safety. A number of people pleaded with Wilson to intercede with Huerta to make certain that Madero and Piño Suárez would be sent out of the country unharmed. Wilson did indeed talk to the General on the prisoners' behalf, but by all accounts his efforts were half-hearted. After three tense days came the denouement: Just before midnight on February 22, when Madero and Piño Suárez were being transferred from the National Palace to the penitentiary, their party was "attacked" and both men were killed. According to the official version of the affair, they died when their supporters tried to rescue them.[66]

Wilson could not observe any reaction among the people to Madero's tragic death; the capital was quiet, and so, apparently, was the rest of the country. In fact, he thought the Mexicans were undisturbed by the political murders and quite satisfied with the Huerta regime. He predicted that Mexico was on the eve of peace, except perhaps in the districts immediately south of the capital. Wilson deplored the possibility that Britain might withhold recognition because of Madero's murder, since that would endanger the Huerta government, on which the safety of all foreigners depended. He was disposed, he informed Knox, to accept the government's version of the affair and consider it a "closed incident," and he urged the department to do the same.[67]

Knox refused to be hurried in his decisions. He warned the Ambassador to be "carefully guided by the President's direction that, for the present, no formal recognition is to be accorded those *de facto* in control, except upon specific instructions from the Department." Not satisfied with this cautionary message, Wilson sent another emphatic telegram for the consideration of the President and the Secretary. In his reply Knox made it plain that he did not take murder so lightly. The press in the States, he told the Ambassador, was practically unanimous in suspecting that

65. DS 812.00/6271.
66. *FR, 1913*, 723-24, 732.
67. *FR, 1913*, 736.

the Huerta government might be involved in the deaths of Madero and Piño Suárez and was expressing horror at the fact. At the least, "that horrible occurrence" had been possible because those responsible for the victims' safety had not taken adequate precautions. To make sure that Wilson could not misunderstand what the department expected of him, Knox repeated the instruction to avoid any action that would confer recognition on the provisional government. In the meantime the department would consider the question on the basis of the usual tests: the Mexican people's readiness to support the new government; Huerta's disposition and ability to protect foreigners and their interests and to carry through his government's international obligations.[68]

Despite Wilson's efforts, he could not persuade the Taft Administration to grant recognition to the Huerta regime. The whole problem, along with so many others, was left to President Woodrow Wilson.

68. *FR, 1913,* 738, 741, 747-48.

7

Summary

Dollar diplomacy has always had sinister connotations, yet, as conceived by Taft and Knox, its objectives were high-minded. Indeed, in essence it anticipated United States foreign policy after World War II: to help underdeveloped countries establish viable governments and to integrate them into the twentieth century. Taft and Knox had perforce to choose private capital as their instrument, whereas President Truman was able to use the nation's capital. In either circumstance, the most important consideration was the preservation of vital American interests abroad. But from the point of view of the policy's broader implications—the improvement of social and economic conditions in Latin America with the concomitant burgeoning forth of American trade and investment—the results were meager. More recent ventures have demonstrated how difficult it is to force-feed an economically backward area into a moderate state.

The lack of tangible results from dollar diplomacy was accompanied by an intensification in the Latins' hostility toward the United States, which arose not so much from the policy itself as from the North Americans' motivation and approach. Taft and Knox shared the prevailing view of Anglo-Saxon superiority and betrayed their convictions by the tactless way in which they treated the Latin Americans. One gets the impression that Knox went about implementing American policy in the same impersonal way that he would have revived a defunct or ailing corporation. If one sent in technicians and pumped in money, the chances for success were good. Diplomatic support of private capital meant that the Latin Americans had to conform to the idea that what was good for the United States was good for Latin America. The Latin Americans resented and rejected these efforts to make them over in the North American image. The history of the twentieth century indicates that such remodeling is impossible. Also, Taft and Knox designed their policy toward Latin America on the basic miscalculation that revolutions in that part of the world were motivated merely by money. They forgot that love of power, prestige, and the desire for domestic changes toward economic justice and personal dignity could be equally compelling reasons for revolt.

Far East

8

Background for Taft's Far Eastern Policies

Count Johann von Bernstorff, the German ambassador in Washington, characterized the Far East as President Taft's *"Lieblingsfrage,"* a description confirmed often enough by Taft himself. His preoccupation with the Orient arose from his long tenure in the Philippines and his diplomatic missions to Japan as Roosevelt's emissary. His personal inclination to make the area a focal point of his foreign policy was reinforced by the determination of several State Department officials—Willard Straight, William Phillips, and the influential Francis Huntington-Wilson—to make the United States' policies count in the Far East.

No previous administration had ever become intimately involved in internal Chinese affairs. Rather, the United States Government had maintained the role of a disinterested friend to China and more than once had openly dissociated itself from the methods adopted by the other Powers to enforce their treaty rights. During the Taft Administration, however, this attitude of detachment changed: The State Department promoted concessions for American banks and corporations, intervened actively in support of American interests, and both cooperated and competed with the European Powers and Japan.

Since the days of the clipper ships, Americans had entertained a romantic and sentimental interest in China. This attitude and the expansion of missionary activity with its consequent need for increased funding gave many Americans a sense of involvement in the well-being of the growing number of their coreligionists among the Chinese. Knox appealed to these feelings in justifying his activist Far Eastern policy, declaring, "When we support the 'open door' in China, that is not the so-called 'dollar diplomacy,'

but the recognition of a high moral duty."[1] The Administration's
real motivation, nevertheless, lay in the conviction that expansion of United States trade in the Far East was imperative. The
Chinese situation—both internal and international—was so complicated, however, that ordinary economic and diplomatic tech-
niques were ineffective. Here economics and politics were inex-
tricably entangled, and Knox grasped, as the European diplomats
had before him, that the undertakings of foreign capitalists conferred on the Powers the means and grounds for asserting political control when and as any issues affecting the political destiny
of China arose. In addition, each of the Powers was convinced
that, without political support, economic and financial opportunity would be denied to it by its competitors. The United States
Department of State at last began to use economic levers in its efforts to become politically influential in China and
thus keep the door open to American trade and investment. But
Knox knew that the United States was neither diplomatically
nor politically strong enough to prop open the financial door.
Great Britain was to fight his diplomatic battle, and the British, French, and Germans were to furnish his financial ammunition.

The shift in American policy came about, almost as an after-
thought, over the issue of the Hukuang loan, but although this
loan for railroad construction in the Yangtze Valley first engaged
the Americans' attention, they did not regard it as affecting the
principle of the Open Door. It was Manchuria, for some years the
center of American trade and diplomatic involvement, which the
department regarded as vital to its political and economic program; and when, in the fall of 1909, the Taft Administration belatedly focused its attention on the north, the avowed objective of its
diplomacy was the preservation of the Open Door policy against
a clear and present danger. Now the stakes were much higher and
the competitors unyielding; ultimately, the United States, unwilling and unable to support its claims, was forced to withdraw from
this game of *Weltpolitik*.

The Western Powers had already been competing for years for
trade and influence in China when the peace terms of the Sino-
Japanese War of 1895 added another competitor to their ranks and
another dimension to foreign rivalry for advantages. Japan's defeat of China revealed not only Japan's strength but China's
weakness, yet it was the Western Powers who exploited that vic-

1. Speech given at Cincinnati, Ohio, November 5, 1910; Philander C. Knox Papers.

tory after preventing Japan from doing so. Now came what the Chinese called "the cutting up of the melon," by which they meant the scramble on the part of foreign nations for territorial concessions and spheres of influence.[2] Germany led off by seizing Kiaochow Bay in March of 1898; during the same month Russia demanded a lease on Port Arthur and the Liaotung Peninsula; England got a naval station at Weihaiwei and additional territory around Hongkong; and France took a lease to Kwangchow Bay in South China, both countries acting in April. Each country also claimed a sphere of influence in the interior: France in the south, Britain in the Yangtze Valley, Russia in the north, Germany in Shantung, and Japan in Fukien.

The Powers coupled their efforts to secure territorial concessions with efforts to gain contracts for railroads, since the Chinese court, indifferent to the whole subject of modern technology, showed no interest in pushing such construction.[3] Not until after the Boxer Rebellion did the government grasp the necessity for a network of railroads throughout the country. In most cases, domestic capital being unavailable, the railroads were built with the proceeds of foreign loans for the account of the Chinese Government. To protect their investment the Europeans demanded certain types of control: supervision of expenditures, management of the railroad for the life of the loan, and either the right to first mortgage on the property or the pledge of Chinese internal revenue as security.

The so-called "concessioned" lines carried far wider privileges, which bore great political as well as economic potential. In addition to giving the concessionaire outright control over the construction and subsequent operation of the railroad, the typical contract also included jurisdictional rights over certain areas along the track and, in a strip ten miles wide on either side of the right-of-way, the right to set up telegraph lines and to exploit the area's natural resources. Such a concession was therefore, by its very nature, exclusive and could only be matched by other concessions elsewhere. The German railroad in Shantung and the

2. In spheres of influence, each of the Powers sought to establish the following privileges: a guarantee by China that she would not alienate the area to any other foreign Powers; an understanding that the Power's nationals should have preferential or in some cases practically exclusive rights to make loans, construct railroads, operate mines, and so forth.
3. In 1894 China had about 200 miles of track; in 1913, about 6,000 miles. Foreign corporations owned a little over 2,000 miles, in which they had invested $383,-000,000. Ownership of the remaining mileage rested largely with the Chinese Government. C. F. Remer, *Foreign Investments in China*, 139-40.

French in Yunnan were "concessioned" lines, but the best-known was the Russian railroad in Manchuria. In 1896 China had granted Russia the concession for the Chinese Eastern Railway (the C.E.R.), thus providing a shorter route to Russia's Pacific provinces. Two years later, when Russia got the lease to the Liaotung Peninsula, she forced China to include in the agreement another "concessioned" road connecting Harbin and Port Arthur. The section from Changchun to Port Arthur—later transferred to Japan under the Treaty of Portsmouth—became the South Manchuria Railway (the S.M.R.).[4]

The burst of European activity in China did not place any restrictions on American trade—which was in fact of no great importance.[5] Nor was any nation's, relatively. Although in 1908 Britain ranked first among the exporters to China with 18.4 per cent of the trade, followed by Japan with 13.3 per cent and the United States with 10.4 per cent (which dropped to 7.5 per cent in 1913), Britain's primacy did not represent a large volume of goods. In any list showing per capita trade of the countries of the world, China was close to the bottom, and this ranking remained unchanged in 1913, even though her trade had doubled since the turn of the century.

The impediments standing in the path of increased trade were great: Foreigners could live only in certain ports, the rivers by and large were the transportation system, the Chinese were in general xenophobic and poverty-stricken. Americans suffered additional handicaps in competing for this restricted market. Their government made little effort to promote their interests, and they themselves did not display the imagination and industry of their rivals. On the last point the American minister, William J. Calhoun, observed in March 1912 that United States businessmen had been losing rather than gaining a share of the market. "[I]f the Americans expect to do any business in this country worthy of consideration," he commented, "they must organize and push it as other nationals are doing." Nor was the American public willing to invest its money in China. The lack of railroad concessions, for example, meant that American factories got no orders for rails and rolling stock.[6]

4. E-tu Sun, *Chinese Railways and British Interests, 1898-1911,* 10; A. E. Campbell, *Great Britain and the United States, 1895-1903,* 160.
5. U. S. Bureau of the Census, *Historical Statistics of the United States, Colonial Times to 1957,* 550, 552.
6. P. A. Varg, "The Myth of the China Market, 1890-1914," *American Historical*

The illusion persisted in certain sections of the American business community, however, that the potential for trade with China was enormous.[7] In addition to profits, the Chinese market also offered an escape from the ills of American overproduction, which many regarded as inevitable. Disturbed by events in China that threatened at some future date to bar American traders from a great market, merchants began to pressure the McKinley Administration to "do something."

That "something" turned out to be Secretary of State John Hay's first Open Door notes of September 1899. Hay's advisers, recognizing that the United States must accept spheres of influence as existing facts, felt that the most the United States could obtain in the Far East was equality of commercial opportunity. The notes therefore made no mention of railroad and mining concessions or of capital investment in general. Hay obviously accepted the impairment of China's territorial integrity as a *fait accompli,* for by requesting the most-favored-nation status for American commerce in all future as well as present spheres and leased territories, he revealed the American assumption that the existing foreign spheres of influence and territorial concessions would continue and even, in the future, expand.[8]

In view of the Boxer Rebellion and the subsequent Russian occupation of Manchuria, Hay had second thoughts about the Open Door. He now came to believe that its preservation would not be possible unless China had complete control over her own territory. Therefore, the circular note of July 3, 1900, announced the intention of the United States Government "to seek a solution which may bring about permanent safety and peace to China, preserve Chinese territorial and administrative entity, protect all rights guaranteed to friendly powers by treaty and international law, and safeguard for the world the principle of equal and impartial trade with all parts of the Chinese Empire." Griswold remarks of Hay, "He had committed the United States to the policy of striving to deter its competitors for the Chinese market from violating the territorial and administrative integrity of the Chinese nation." Events in China soon disillusioned Hay of any ex-

Review, February, 1968; DS 893.77/1217.

7. In Great Britain the same notion prevailed. C. J. Lowe, *The Reluctant Imperialists: British Foreign Policy, 1878-1902,* 227.

8. A. W. Griswold, *The Far Eastern Policy of the United States,* 66-75, 80; see T. J. McCormick, *China Market: America's Quest for Informal Empire, 1893-1901,* for the commercial aspects of the Open Door.

pectations that his policy would prevent the break-up of the empire. He gradually resumed the position of the first Open Door notes, recognizing that it was now Russia and not China who controlled Manchuria. The Chinese Empire survived the Boxer Rebellion and its consequences, not because Hay had tried to harmonize the Powers' policies, but because the Powers persisted in their competition.[9]

In October 1900, at London's instigation Germany and England concluded an agreement also designed to maintain China's integrity and the Open Door. If a third Power sought any territorial advantages, the two countries would discuss common action. Early in 1901 Britain learned that Russia planned new encroachments in Manchuria and inquired what Germany would do if the threat materialized. The Germans replied that they would do nothing; the agreement did not cover Manchuria.

Britain and the United States were not the only Powers who feared Russian aggression. Japan's special concern was to prevent Russia from acquiring Korea, an area the Japanese regarded as of immense strategic importance for their security. Opinion in Japan was divided—the great statesman Marquis Ito favored a direct understanding with Russia, whereas Foreign Minister Jutaro Komura and Tadasu Hayashi, the ambassador in London, wanted a defensive arrangement with England. Komura's and Hayashi's arguments persuaded their government, and the Anglo-Japanese accord was signed in January 1902; with President Roosevelt's approval, Britain recognized Japan's special interests in Korea. The impending war between Russia and Japan began in April 1904, but an Anglo-French entente, reached in May 1904, reduced the possibility that England might become involved with Russia and France in the Far Eastern hostilities.

Roosevelt had not been happy with Russian predominance in Manchuria, and when war erupted, his sympathies were with Japan because she was "playing our game." Shortly before hostilities ended, Roosevelt, using Taft as his emissary, again assured Tokyo that he approved of Japanese suzerainty over Korea. Yet Roosevelt was convinced that a system of balanced antagonisms in the Far East would best serve America's national interests, and when Japan's decisive victories threatened this goal, he brought pressure on both combatants to end the war.[10] Japan did very well

9. Griswold, *Far Eastern Policy,* 81-84.
10. R. A. Esthus, *Theodore Roosevelt and Japan,* 106.

in the final settlement: Russia paid for her defeat with the abandonment of her ambitious designs in southern Manchuria and Korea. Under the Treaty of Portsmouth, signed in 1905, Russia recognized Japan's paramount interests in Korea; she also transferred to Japan, subject to China's approval, the lease of the Liaotung Peninsula and the railroad concession between Changchun and Port Arthur, now renamed the South Manchuria Railway.

China approved the transfer of the lease and the concession in the Komura Treaty, also known as the Treaty of Peking, signed on December 22, 1905. In an additional agreement China granted Japan a concession to rebuild and exploit for fifteen years the temporary railroad that the Japanese had laid between Antung and Mukden during the war.

Another document that came out of the negotiations was the secret protocol of 1905, the conference minutes dealing with agreements to be executed in the future. Early in 1906 the Japanese communicated to the United States and England a summary of the protocol's contents.[11] In Article 3 China promised not to construct any trunk line near or parallel to the S.M.R. or any branch prejudicial to its interests. The British ambassador in Tokyo, Sir Claude MacDonald, commented that the importance of the article depended on its interpretation, but that the Japanese might possibly construe it so as to block all railway construction in Manchuria. And Japan took precisely this point of view. The Chinese, on the other hand, never officially denied either that the Japanese claim was valid or that they themselves were bound by the protocol; they quarreled only with Japan's interpretation of the document. The Chinese Foreign Office reminded the Japanese in May 1908 that "at the time this engagement was concluded ... the [Chinese plenipotentiaries] considered that the meaning of the word 'parallel' was too wide."[12]

In spite of Russia's losses under the Treaty of Portsmouth, she continued as the dominant Power in northern Manchuria, and through the treaty provisions and special arrangements with China, Japan held a very strong position in Korea and southern Manchuria. Neither Russia nor Japan was ready to relinquish her rights and influence in the areas each dominated. Each valued her strategic advantages and also was aware that the United

11. Esthus, *Roosevelt*, 116-17.
12. *Documents on British Foreign Policy, 1919-1939*, R. Butler, *et al.*, eds., 2d series, IX, 17-18, 118-20, henceforth cited as *BF*; J. V. A. MacMurray, ed., *Treaties and Agreements with and Concerning China, 1894-1919*, I, 554-55.

States wanted China to regain control over these territories in order to grant Americans free access.

In the years immediately following the Russo-Japanese War, two men who would be instrumental in shaping and carrying out the Taft Administration's Far Eastern policy were serving as diplomats in that theater. As Japan moved into her new spheres on the mainland, both Huntington-Wilson and Straight were deeply suspicious of her motives. Each had developed suggestions for keeping her encroachments in check. Huntington-Wilson, then stationed at the American embassy in Tokyo, was convinced that the only way to keep the door open in Manchuria was to use "strong pressure."[13] The United States and England could exercise this pressure effectively because Japanese statesmen, realizing that money and support from those quarters were essential to their nation's development, were afraid to give offense.[14] After his recall to Washington in the spring of 1908, Huntington-Wilson tried to impress upon Secretary of State Elihu Root the importance of "keeping . . . alive" the policies of the Open Door and Chinese territorial and political integrity. Despite this prodding, the Secretary made no move.[15]

Straight also regarded Manchuria as a crucial area, but his plans for its salvation depended more on economics than on politics. He saw little future for American trade under existing conditions.[16] As long as Americans supplied merely those few manufactured articles the Chinese market could absorb, the profits would remain insignificant. To make the traffic lucrative, American financiers must lend China the money to build railroads and develop natural resources, for only by investing large amounts of capital could Americans create a demand for their manufactured goods.[17] Although both Russia and Japan were

13. Huntington-Wilson to Root, February 5, 1906, March 15, 1906, and April 12, 1906, Tokyo Post Records.
14. Huntington-Wilson, Memorandum, July, 1906, quoted in A. Vagts, *Deutschland und die Vereinigten Staaten in der Weltpolitik,* II, 1247-48. American and British financiers had floated the Japanese war loans, and in November 1905 Japan secured another loan in the British market to take over the S.M.R.
15. DS 551/92, 99, 102; Esthus, *Roosevelt,* 240-42.
16. Soon after the Japanese assumed control of the South Manchurian concession in August 1906, foreign merchants began to grumble that their trade was subject to restrictions and restraints not enforced against Japanese nationals. A thorough investigation at this time, and again in 1911, by the China Association (a British group) failed to uncover any satisfactory proof of deliberate discrimination. Sir H. Parlett, *A Brief Account of Diplomatic Events in Manchuria,* 19-20.
17. Straight Memorandum, December, 1907, DS 2413/97-99; H. Croly, *Willard Straight,* 237-38.

firmly established in northern China and would resist a new competitor, Straight regarded Japan as the chief threat to American trade. She seemed to be repeating the policy of absorption she had pursued so successfully in Korea. But in Manchuria Japan had not yet won commercial dominance, and Straight believed that the United States still had a chance to preserve the Open Door and what remained of China's authority.[18]

Straight was more fortunate than Huntington-Wilson, for Edward H. Harriman listened sympathetically to his ideas. Already in control of a transcontinental railroad in the United States and a line of trans-Pacific steamers, Harriman dreamed of developing this network into a global system of transportation. His original plan had hinged on the acquisition of the S.M.R., but when Komura talked his government out of the sale, Harriman then decided that a line farther west would serve equally well as a connection with the Trans-Siberian Railroad. In 1906 Straight was appointed to head the Mukden consulate, and before leaving the United States, he discussed with Harriman the chances for American investment in Manchuria. At this time Harriman apparently gave Straight a somewhat vague commission to submit plans for the development of railroads in Manchuria with American capital.[19]

Straight arrived in Mukden in October and at a most opportune moment. Worried by Japan's presence in Manchuria—and also by Russia's, to a lesser degree—the Chinese were determined to strengthen their control over the Three Provinces. Peking intended, furthermore, to follow its usual pattern of playing the barbarians off against each other so that the power equilibrium thus created would eliminate the domination of either Russia or Japan and permit China to carry through her plans.[20] As Straight put it, Peking wanted funds from the United States or England, or even from an Anglo-French-American combine, in order to shield herself behind the political support such capital would bring.[21]

In the month of Straight's arrival the Dowager Empress appointed two commissioners to study conditions in Manchuria and to recommend measures for its reconstruction. On the basis of the

18. Croly, *Straight,* 207-8, 212.
19. Croly, *Straight,* 199, 238, 241; G. Kennan, *E. H. Harriman: A Biography,* II, 2-3, 7-22, 24-25.
20. Sun, *Chinese Railways,* 142-43.
21. DS 2413/97-99.

ensuing report, the Court in April 1907 issued a reform edict for the economic and administrative revitalization of Manchuria. The Three Provinces became a single administrative unit under a viceroy, to whom the three governors were subordinate. Hsü Shih-ch'ang was appointed viceroy and Tang Shao-yi governor of Fengtien Province. Mukden thus became both a viceregal and provincial capital.[22]

The proposals of the Hsü administration for the development of the Three Provinces included the construction of a rail network linking the most important cities. Priority was given to the extension of the Chinese Imperial Railways from their terminus at Hsinmintun to Fakumen, the first 55 miles of a projected 400-mile line to connect with the Chinese Eastern in Tsitsihar.[23] Although Hsü and Tang discussed with Straight plans for railroad construction with American money, Tang eventually suggested a broader scheme of economic development. He wanted to establish a bank and to float two loans, the first American and the second international. Straight passed Tang's proposal on to "one of our Railway Kings," but Harriman rejected it—this was in the fall of 1907—on account of the uncertain state of the market.[24]

Straight had by this time concluded that his original idea of saving China through unilateral investment would not work. Even with the best will in the world and unlimited resources (which were not available), the burden was too heavy for Americans to carry alone. He therefore accepted the necessity of sharing concessions and profits; competition for concessions should be replaced by some measure (the operative phrase, in Straight's thinking) of financial cooperation among the more politically disinterested Powers in lending money to China. Working together would also give them a common interest in preserving her integrity. If these countries refused to lend money, they would be surrendering a clear field to Japan and Russia.[25]

In late November of 1907 Straight talked at length with Taft, then Secretary of War and an influential member of the Roosevelt Administration, in China on a mission for the President in the Far East. Taft expressed the belief that China was turning to the United States as her one disinterested friend, and when Straight

22. Sun, *Chinese Railways,* 142.
23. Sun, *Chinese Railways,* 143-44.
24. DS 2413/97-99; Croly, *Straight,* 242; Straight to Fletcher, March 17, 1908, Henry Fletcher Papers.
25. Croly, *Straight,* 244-46.

asserted that the Americans' moment had come, the Secretary agreed. Straight outlined Tang's loan project, which appealed to Taft, as did the idea of applying the Boxer indemnity to the loan.[26] To one suggestion Taft gave little encouragement: that of American participation in an international loan. Straight was certain, however, that when Taft got home he would advise the Administration "to regard Manchuria as a fair field and not as one which must be approached with special regard for the susceptibilities of the Japanese." While Taft in fact told Straight that he would try to "do something" with the loan idea if China made the first move, he never pushed the subject.[27] He may have been reluctant to do so because he was aware of Root's position on the matter of Chinese loans.

When Harriman, the principal source of American funds, declined to invest in Manchuria, the Chinese turned to the British. On November 8, 1907, they signed a contract with Lord ffrench, representative of Pauling and Company, a British construction company, for building the Hsinmintun-Fakumen railroad and with J. O. P. Bland of the British and Chinese Corporation for its financing. No public mention was made at this time of the plans for the road's eventual extension to Tsitsihar. Hsü and Tang suggested that the whole line be treated as a branch of the Chinese Imperial Railways. Since the road would thus be part of the national system, it would technically not be a Manchurian project, and other nations—by implication Japan and Russia—would have no excuse for objecting to its construction.[28] To the British minister in Peking, Sir John Jordan, the Tang-ffrench arrangement appeared to be a statesmanlike way of attacking the Manchurian problem and one to which Japan could not reasonably object.[29]

But the Japanese had indicated as early as August 1907 that they would indeed object if China tried to carry through such a scheme. Ito told the British ambassador that his government considered the Fakumen project parallel and competitive with the S.M.R., since the Japanese were certain that, once the line reached Fakumen, China would not halt construction but would go on to Tsitsihar. Instead of rejecting the protest, however, the

---

26. The Americans asked $25,000,000 to indemnify its nationals for damages suffered during the Boxer Rebellion.
27. Croly, *Straight*, 250-51; Straight to Fletcher, March 11, 1908, Fletcher Papers; Esthus, *Roosevelt*, 236-37.
28. Sun, *Chinese Railways*, 144; Croly, *Straight*, 242-43.
29. Jordan to Campbell, October 1, 1908, FO 350/5.

Chinese merely argued that the road was neither parallel nor potentially competitive, thus tactitly acknowledging the protocol's validity.[30]

China appealed to England for support, but the British made no effort to come to the rescue. Quite the contrary; in a statement in the House of Commons on March 24, 1908, British Foreign Minister Sir Edward Grey said in effect that there could be no doubt as to the validity of the protocol. "The statement was of course made," one British diplomat noted many years later, "for the purpose of the particular argument in pursuance of a policy of discouraging British enterprise in a direction unpalatable to the Japanese."[31] Certainly Grey had no desire to offend the Japanese, whom he regarded as most satisfactory allies. In his estimate they had never attempted to strain the alliance or in any way to stretch its terms in their favor.[32] The truth of the matter was that the projected line would compete with the S.M.R., as the Foreign Office claimed and even Straight never denied.

In spite of the failure of the Fakumen project, the Manchurian administration continued its efforts to secure British and American capital, and in August 1908 Tang signed with Straight a memorandum embodying more specifically the plan submitted to Harriman the previous year. The so-called "Tang memorandum" provided for a loan of $20,000,000 to establish a bank for financing railroad construction and developing mining, lumbering, agricultural, and other industries in the Three Provinces. The remitted Boxer indemnity and a Chinese imperial guarantee would secure the loan. The memorandum contained several tentative projects, among them the purchase of the C.E.R. from Russia and the construction of a railroad from Tsitsihar to Aigun on the Amur River.[33]

Just before signing the agreement with Tang, Straight had been recalled by the department. He had been involved in an altercation with a Japanese national, and he feared that Washington was

30. *British Documents on the Origins of the World War, 1898-1914,* G. P. Gooch and H. Temperley, eds., VIII, No. 365, 467, henceforth cited as *BD;* Sun, *Chinese Railways,* 144-45. Contrary to C. Vevier, *The United States and China, 1906-1913,* 51, the Chinese did not deny that the protocol was binding. Rather, as Sun notes, by arguing that the road was neither parallel nor competing, they implicitly recognized Japan's alleged right to protest against Chinese railroad plans. Sun, *Chinese Railways,* 145.
31. Wellesley to Lindley, December 17, 1931, *BF,* 2d series, IX, Nos. 8, 16.
32. Grey to Bryce, March 30, 1908, James Bryce Papers.
33. DS 2112/98.

displeased over the incident. Such was not the case; he was being called home, Third Assistant Secretary William Phillips wrote, because "certain powers that be" in Wall Street were beginning to think of Manchuria as a field for investment. Straight's assignment in the States would probably be to discuss the available opportunities with the interested financiers.[34] Straight found Harriman and his bankers, Kuhn, Loeb and Company, ready to do business with the Chinese, and they authorized Straight to open negotiations with Tang, who was due to visit in the United States in November. Ostensibly, the purpose of Tang's mission was to thank the Americans for remitting the Boxer indemnity; actually, it was to contract a loan for Manchurian development.[35]

Tang arrived in Washington on November 30, but immediately his hopes for American support were dashed by the news that within a few hours the United States would conclude an agreement with Japan. The notes exchanged by Root and Ambassador Kogoro Takahira in effect tacitly recognized Japan's sphere of influence in southern Manchuria in return for Japanese cooperation in limiting the immigration of her laborers to the United States. This recognition of Japanese dominance in the area meant that Roosevelt, although not abandoning the idea of equal commercial opportunity, would take no active measures to protect the Open Door.[36] Roosevelt revealed how he assessed the situation in a letter to Taft two years later:

> Our vital interest is to keep the Japanese out of our country, and at the same time to preserve the good will of Japan. The vital interest of the Japanese, on the other hand, is in Manchuria and Korea. It is therefore peculiarly our interest not to take any steps as regards Manchuria which will give the Japanese cause to feel . . . that we are hostile to them, or a menace . . . to their interests. . . . The "open-door" policy in China was an excellent thing, and will I hope be a good thing in the future, so far as it can be maintained by general diplomatic agreement; but as has been proved by the whole history of Manchuria, alike under Russia and under Japan, the "open-door" policy, as a matter of fact, completely disappears as soon as a powerful nation determines to disregard it, and is willing to run the risk of war rather than forego its intention. . . .
> Now on the other hand, whereas our interests in Manchuria

34. Willard Straight Papers.
35. Croly, *Straight,* 255, 269-72.
36. C. E. Neu, "Theodore Roosevelt and American Involvement in the Far East, 1901-1909," *Pacific Historical Review,* November, 1966.

are really unimportant, and not such that the American people would be content to run the slightest risk of collision about them, our interest in keeping the Japanese out of our own country is vital. . . .[37]

In spite of the American-Japanese notes Tang continued to negotiate with the bankers through Straight. Tang also informed Root that, besides the Manchurian loan, China wanted another, much larger sum to abolish likin (an additional tax levied on imports that were in transit between provinces or between districts within provinces), raise the tariff, and establish a uniform currency. As Root observed to Straight, these objectives were all in conformity with American policy and with the Sino-American Treaty of 1903. But he also set out for Straight the basis on which the loan must be negotiated.

As for the negotiation of a loan, whether in the United States or Europe, which has been mentioned as a necessary condition precedent to the carrying out of the treaty provisions above referred to, the State Department has no wish or authority to involve the United States in any obligation either legal or moral with reference to such a loan.[38]

Actually, internal events in China had doomed Tang's mission even before he reached the United States. In mid-November, while Tang was en route, both the Empress Dowager, to whom the mission largely owed its initiative, and the Emperor died. The Regent subsequently dismissed Tang's patron, Yuan Shih-kai, the president of the Foreign Office and an influential member of the government, and recalled Tang, who soon left the United States for London.[39]

The failure of Tang's mission meant that Harriman had lost a chance to acquire a financial interest in Manchuria. Almost simultaneously Harriman's plans for a world-wide transportation system received another blow, this time from Japan. The Russians had decided that the C.E.R. was a financial liability that they wanted to write off. In the summer of 1908, while Tang and Straight were laying their plans in Mukden, the Washington

37. Roosevelt to Taft, December 22, 1910, *The Letters of Theodore Roosevelt,* E. E. Morison, ed., VII, 189-90. To Lord Grey, governor-general of Canada, Roosevelt expressed himself even more bluntly. He told Grey that Japan should not only be allowed but encouraged to go into Manchuria. Any interference with her natural expansion would bring trouble on the American-Canadian Pacific coast. Grey to Bryce, January 20, 1911, Bryce Papers.
38. P. C. Jessup, *Elihu Root,* II, 53-54.
39. Croly, *Straight,* 272-78.

agent of the Russian Ministry of Finance, Gregory Wilenkin, was in St. Petersburg discussing the disposition of the railroad with his chief, Minister V. N. Kokovtzov. They decided to seek an agreement with Japan for the sale of both the C.E.R. and the S.M.R. to an international syndicate. When Wilenkin returned to the United States that autumn, he proposed to Jacob Schiff of Kuhn, Loeb and Company that Schiff take the initiative in carrying out the project.

Since the success of the project depended on Japanese cooperation, Schiff informally sounded out Baron Eiichi Shibusawa, a Japanese banker, who consulted the Japanese Foreign Office. Foreign Minister Komura instructed Shibusawa to tell Schiff that Japan would not under any conditions consider selling the railroads and to advise the banker not to get involved in the scheme in any way because Japanese policy on the question of Manchurian railroads was fixed. There was no possibility of any change in the policy.[40] And, in view of Japanese objectives in Manchuria, no other answer was possible. It was true that the railroad company was empowered only to carry on the business of railroad traffic and certain accessory enterprises such as mining, and it had no diplomatic, judicial, or governmental functions. Nevertheless, its interests formed the real backbone of Japanese power and expansion in Manchuria.[41]

In December 1908 the South Manchuria Railway Company succeeded in floating the last installment of its bonds, part of the proceeds being intended for work on the Antung-Mukden line.[42] On January 11, 1909, China and Japan began formal negotiations on a number of points at issue between them, all involving Manchuria. The agreements, which were signed in August and September and which met most of the Japanese demands, greatly increased the Taft Administration's concern over the future of Manchuria.

40. Croly, *Straight,* 278-79; E. H. Zabriskie, *American-Russian Rivalry in the Far East . . . 1895-1914,* 149; Komura to Takahira, January 22, 1909, JFO, MT Series, Reel 14.
41. O'Brien to Root, December 15, 1908, DS 19272/——.
42. DS 5767/49.

9

China and the Powers: The Hukuang Loan

Before becoming deeply involved in Far Eastern affairs, the Taft Administration had a chance to rehearse the new role, active intervention in Chinese affairs. The opportunity came with negotiations for the so-called Hukuang loan. This loan was to finance railroad construction in the Yangtze Valley.[1] The United States Government used every available form of diplomatic pressure to compel China and Britain, France, and Germany to allow American nationals an equal share of the investment. The direct involvement of the Department of State in securing contracts for American business broke the traditional pattern of American-Chinese diplomacy, which had been official detachment, dating from Bayard through Olney to Root. Although he believed that the United States Government ought to do what it could to promote trade in China, Root thought it a great mistake for it to intervene directly to help individual bankers and traders. Shortly after becoming Secretary of State, he cautioned Minister William W. Rockhill to avoid scrupulously any appearance of soliciting favors for individual Americans or for American corporations. Rockhill might forward to the Chinese Foreign Office American applications for privileges and concessions, but he should do so without comment.[2]

Root's restatement of what he considered the traditional American policy might well have been a response to the activities of E. H. Conger, Rockhill's predecessor in Peking, who had openly sought concessions for Americans. In 1903 Conger learned that British capitalists had asked for preference if China needed

1. Szechuan and the three other provinces known collectively as the Hukuang: Hunan, Hupeh, and Kwangtung. Actually, Szechuan and Kwangtung were never involved in the contracts.
2. P. C. Jessup, *Elihu Root,* II, 53-55.

money to build a railroad through Hunan and Hupeh provinces to Cheng-tu in Szechuan. He reminded the Chinese Government that Americans had long ago applied for a similar concession and that only a few months earlier he himself had called the attention of Prince Ch'ing, president of the Foreign Office, to this fact. At that time he had asked that if foreign funds were needed, China give preference to Americans either to lend the money or build the road, since they had been the first to suggest such a route. Conger therefore formally protested against any arrangement depriving Americans of what he termed their just claim to consideration.[3]

The Foreign Office replied that it had informed the British the Chinese proposed to build the Hankow-Szechuan road themselves. If local capital were not sufficient, however, the provinces could then ask the Throne's permission to borrow in England and the United States, since companies from both countries had applied for the concessions. In repeating this promise the following year, Prince Ch'ing added that it was China's prerogative to decide the matter of concessions and that mere application could not be considered equivalent to an option.[4]

The British group seeking the concession was in reality an Anglo-French coalition. In October 1904 a group of British financial houses headed by the British and Chinese Corporation joined a French group led by the Banque de l'Indo-Chine to form the Chinese Central Railways Company. The company earmarked a small interest in the concession for Belgian financiers and another for any American group that might indicate within the year that it wished to participate.[5] In July 1905 H. M. Durand, the British ambassador in Washington, wrote to the Department of State that his government would soon approach the Chinese about financing the Hankow-Szechuan line. Were any Americans prepared to share the loan? Second Assistant Secretary A. A. Adee replied that, although the department was publicizing the opportunity, no one had so far shown any interest.[6] In September the British embassy repeated its inquiry, and again the answer was negative.[7]

At this time the Chinese Government was not seeking foreign

3. *Foreign Relations, 1909,* 175.
4. *FR, 1909,* 146, 155-56.
5. *FR, 1909,* 147; E-tu Sun, *Chinese Railways and British Interests, 1898-1911,* 9.
6. *FR, 1909,* 147.
7. *FR. 1909,* 148.

capital for railroad construction in the Hukuang, because the provincial gentry were determined to finance their own roads. This
powerful class constituted the only group in the Chinese economic structure with sufficient wealth and responsiveness to
world influences to become actively interested in the new industrial developments. Property holders, officials, and *literati,* the
gentry were bound together by ties of family, wealth, and participation in the power structure at the local level. They were also the
keystone of Manchu political control in China, and although they
had not yet abandoned their support for Peking, they were dissatisfied and restless. The granting of railroad concessions to foreigners ranked high among their grievances. In contrast to the
Boxer period, however, the focus of their discontent was now less
the foreigner than the dynasty. The Manchus, themselves bitterly
resented as aliens by the Chinese, were judged guilty of yielding
to the barbarians.[8]

The activities of the American China Development Company
had done much to aggravate the provincials' resentment against
foreign concessionaires. In 1898 the company had received a
concession to build a railroad from Hankow to Canton, and although specifically bound by the agreement to retain control of
the undertaking, the Americans had breached their contract by
selling a majority of the shares abroad. Extravagance and mis-
management further discredited not only the company itself but
the United States as well. Supported by the gentry, Chang Chih-
tung, the powerful governor-general of the Hukuang provinces,
persuaded the Throne to revoke the concession in December 1904.
China agreed to pay an inflated indemnity: $6,750,000 for the loan
bonds and shares and for the existing property, which included
the twenty-eight miles of completed track.[9] Chang borrowed the
indemnity money from the government of Hongkong, using E. H.
Fraser, the British consul general at Hankow, as his intermediary.
In return for the loan Chang promised Fraser to give preference
to British nationals in the Hankow-Canton concession if domestic
capital was not available and if the British could meet other foreign bids.[10]

Despite the gentry's determination to build the railroad themselves, they could not raise the funds. In the summer of 1908 the

8. Sun, *Chinese Railways,* 21-22, 91.
9. Sun, *Chinese Railways,* 73-75.
10. Sun, *Chinese Railways,* 82-83.

central government announced that it would take over all rail-roads whose construction was unduly delayed. Although this im-plied raising foreign loans, the Chinese press did not seriously contest the government's action.[11] In July Peking moved another step toward control by appointing Chang director-general of the Hankow-Canton railroad.[12] Chang had never believed that the provinces could put up the money and had always favored secur-ing foreign capital. The last step toward foreign financing of the railroad came soon after Chang's appointment, when the Em-peror gave his permission to borrow abroad.[13] In mid-October Jor-dan reported that the prejudice against foreign financing seemed to be dying out. Chang was intensely eager to borrow money for the southern line but wanted it on impractical terms.[14]

Mindful of his pledge to Fraser, Chang approached the British and Chinese Corporation for a loan,[15] expecting conditions simi-lar to those of the Tientsin-Pukow contract signed with the Ger-mans in January 1908. The Germans had made a number of concessions in China's favor because growing Chinese national-ism made such a policy expedient and because China exploited the competition between the British and the Germans for the contract.[16] But J. O. P. Bland, the corporation's representative, insisted on the more onerous terms of earlier loans, which Chang refused to accept. Although Chang blamed Bland personally for the stiff conditions, the bank representative in fact was voicing convictions that he shared with his principals, the British Foreign Office, and the British minister.[17]

Chang had optimistically expected to close the deal for the Han-kow-Canton loan quickly, but the negotiations with Bland made little progress. Presently, with Chang's encouragement, Germans, Belgians, and Japanese all entered the competition.[18] It was the Germans, however, with whom Chang really wanted to do busi-ness. A few years earlier he and Heinrich Cordes, Peking repre-sentative of the Deutsch-Asiatische Bank, had discussed a loan

11. Jordan to Campbell, August 6, 1908, John Jordan Papers.
12. Sun, *Chinese Railways,* 99.
13. Sun, *Chinese Railways,* 84; Rex to Bülow, March 12, 1909, *Die grosse Politik der europäischen Kabinette, 1871-1914,* Vol. 32, No. 11603, 3-5, henceforth cited as *GP.*
14. John Jordan Papers.
15. Sun, *Chinese Railways,* 99-100.
16. Sun, *Chinese Railways,* 99, 134-36.
17. Jordan to Campbell, October 29 and November 12, 1908, Jordan Papers.
18. Jordan to Campbell, January 21, 1909, Jordan Papers; Sun, *Chinese Railways,* 101-2.

for construction of the Hankow-Szechuan line.[19] Chang, recently appointed director-general of this western trunk line, now told Cordes that, although he intended to give the Hankow-Canton concession to the British, for political reasons he wanted German capital for the road west to Szechuan.[20]

Foreign Minister Grey realized that Chang's letter to Fraser did not guarantee the loan to British capital and that China was still free to accept the most favorable offer. Therefore, when the Deutsche-Asiatische Bank told the Hongkong and Shanghai Bank of Chang's approach and suggested that German and Anglo-French interests should cooperate in the loan, Grey approved. He regarded German participation in the Hukuang financing as preferable to ruinous competition. Also, Britain could later rely on Chang's pledge to safeguard her rights with regard to engineers and materials.[21] Charles Addis, London manager of the Hongkong and Shanghai Bank, began negotiating in January for a tripartite agreement that would eliminate the rivalry for Chinese loans, thus forcing China to borrow on the bankers' terms. As a result of Addis' efforts and despite the French Government's resistance to inclusion of the Germans, on March 1, 1908, the three banking groups signed a provisional arrangement.[22]

The competitive eagerness of foreign financiers to lend money to China stemmed from the fact that until 1911 she was a good credit risk, always prompt in meeting her obligations, and loans to the Chinese Government were therefore a profitable business.[23] On March 3, Chang, faced with the prospect of a hostile European combination, offered the loan to the British on the terms of the Tientsin-Pukow contract with the Germans, signed in January. These terms he presented as an ultimatum. The British and Chinese Corporation, the Banque de l'Indo-Chine, and the British Foreign Office all considered Chang's offer unacceptable, and, feeling secure in their arrangement with the Germans, the

19. At the German Government's instigation, the strongest private German houses had combined with two government banks to form the Deutsch-Asiatische Bank. The objective was to facilitate the financing of concessions abroad.

20. Sun, *Chinese Railways*, 99, 103; Rex to Bülow, March 12, 1909, *GP*, 32, No. 11603, 3-5.

21. FO 405/197/7, 21.

22. FO 405/197/18; Jordan did not learn of these negotiations until after the agreement was signed. Jordan Papers. Even after the outbreak of the revolution, the amortization and interest charges on the Chinese Government's foreign railroad loans were, on the whole, paid up until 1920. C. Hou, *Foreign Investment and Economic Development in China, 1840-1937*, 37.

23. *BD*, 2d series, VIII, No. 95, 156.

British declined the loan on March 4. The Germans immediately announced that, since the bankers' agreement was not final, they would accept the loan if Chang offered it to them on the same terms, which he did. Cordes signed the preliminary agreement with Chang on March 7.[24]

But Chang still wanted British capital in order to keep a balance of power in the Yangtze Valley, and the Germans themselves expected ultimate British participation. As a matter of fact, Chang and Cordes had earlier agreed that if British objections were strenuous, Chang would allot the Hankow-Canton line to them and the Germans would shift their interest to the Hankow-Szechuan railroad.[25] Jordan admitted that his government had little grounds for complaint. Chang had made the first offer to the British bank, which rejected it "in the belief," Jordan wrote, "that we had formed a combination which would force him to accept more onerous terms." Nevertheless, Jordan carried out his instructions to protest against the Sino-German contract.[26] Having made his point, Chang agreed to reopen negotiations with the British interests, now under the leadership of the Hongkong and Shanghai Bank represented by E. G. Hillier, at whose suggestion Chang agreed to include the French.[27] Negotiations also continued in Europe among the three banking groups in an effort to reach a final settlement.[28]

Beyond calling the attention of J. P. Morgan and Company to the preliminary agreement for the Hankow-Canton railroad, the United States Department of State showed no interest in the loan.[29] Instead, at this time it was pursuing another phase of the China problem. The treaty system developed between China and the Powers in the nineteenth century fixed the Chinese import tariff at about 5 per cent, a figure that soon became nominal because of the continued rise in prices; the effective rate was never more than 4 per cent.[30] In order to increase its revenue during the Taiping rebellion, China had imposed the likin, the internal tax on goods in transit. The amount collected on goods moving within a province usually did not exceed 10 per cent, but when goods crossed several provinces the tax could run as high as

24. Jordan, Annual Report, China, 1909, FO 405/195.
25. Sun, *Chinese Railways*, 105, 134-35; *GP,* 32, No. 11603, 3-5.
26. Bertie, Annual Report, France, 1909, FO 425/335; FO 405/195.
27. Sun, *Chinese Railways,* 105, 134-35.
28. FO 405/195.
29. DS 5315/187.
30. Hou, *Foreign Investment,* 107.

15–20 per cent. By treaty foreign goods were exempt from this inconvenient and onerous tax and paid in lieu of it a flat 2.5 per cent transit charge.[31] Peking wanted to abolish likin but could not afford to do so without raising the tariff, for which she needed the Powers' approval.

The United States, Great Britain, and Japan having all promised to support China's efforts at tariff reform, in December 1908 the Chinese Government asked the Powers to send delegates to a conference on tariff revision, abolition of likin, and financial reform. Believing that foreign commerce would benefit from such changes, Knox instructed the American representatives in the major capitals to find out if those governments intended to act on the Chinese proposal. The Germans were uninterested, since their new loan was secured partly on likin revenues; Russia and France were noncommittal; England and Japan did not reply.[32]

In Phillips' judgment, the Germans had killed the scheme. Straight, however, was not inclined to quit the fight for financial remedies, since he believed that China could not save herself without American help. Arguing that a strong China was the best assurance for permanent peace in the Pacific, he urged the department to act alone, if necessary, in supporting Peking's efforts to reform. Straight considered the various objections that his colleagues might raise against unilateral action—among them that likin was a guarantee not only for the recent German transaction but for earlier loans as well. He suggested finding some other security as a substitute.[33] Consequently, on April 26 the department made another effort to interest London and Tokyo.[34]

Stories in American newspapers early in May indicated that the tripartite bank negotiations were under way in Berlin. The press also reported that the final agreement would probably increase the amount of the loan to China and include the railroad from Hankow west to Chengtu.[35] This intelligence did not suggest any new line of thought to Huntington-Wilson. On May 11 he asked Phillips to prepare a draft memorandum for presentation in London and Berlin, recording American disapproval of likin as security for the loan. The department argued that such a hypothe-

31. Hou, *Foreign Investment*, 108, 147.
32. DS 788/199-200, 213, 224.
33. DS 788/214, 224.
34. DS 788/224.
35. *New York Tribune*, May 9, 1909.

cation would hinder the promised abolition of the transit tax and therefore violated the spirit of the 1903 treaties.[36]

Phillips, however, was reluctant to continue along this path. On May 15 he recommended to Knox that the department do nothing on the liken matter until England had replied to the note of April 26.[37] Three days later, after studying the details of the interbank agreement signed in Berlin on May 14—the so-called Berlin compromise—Phillips told the Secretary that, since likin was the first guarantee for the loan, China could not now abolish the tax.[38] On May 19 he informed Huntington-Wilson that, as long as there was hope for a reply from Britain, he hesitated to lodge a formal protest on the likin guarantee.[39]

The British eventually informed the United States Department of State that they could not discuss the subject at this time;[40] Phillips was not really interested in receiving the British answer, for he had a more important and foresighted reason to oppose a protest. In the future, he believed, American banking interests would jump at the opportunity to participate in a Chinese loan secured by likin. In that case, if the United States now protested to the Powers, it might find itself in the embarrassing position of being unable to stop its own nationals from accepting that same guarantee.[41] Still not getting Phillips' point, Huntington-Wilson argued that the department *might* be able to deter American capitalists from loans with likin as a guarantee by refusing to endorse such transactions, but he nonetheless agreed that the protest should be delayed.[42]

But Phillips' objective was not to "deter" American capitalists; on the contrary, it was to secure a share of the loan for them. Having noted the inclusion of the Hankow-Szechuan railroad in the interbank agreement, Phillips on May 21 suggested to Knox the basis for an American claim to participation: the assurances made to Conger in 1904. After reviewing the correspondence with the British in 1905 on financing the western line, Phillips concluded: "I do not, therefore, consider that we have relinquished our rights . . . ," but before making a protest to protect those rights, Phillips favored a more thorough investigation of the whole sub-

36. DS 788/266.
37. DS 788/239-41.
38. DS 5315/207.
39. DS 788/267.
40. Reid to Knox, May 29, 1909, DS 788/262.
41. Phillips to Huntington-Wilson, May 19, 1909, DS 788/267.
42. DS 788/267.

ject.[43] To get more information on the financial side of the picture, on the same day he wrote to J. Selwin Tait of the International Banking Corporation to ask whether his bank and its associates would be willing to undertake approved Chinese government railroad loans.

Straight and Huntington-Wilson did not even bother to wait for Tait's reply to Phillips' inquiry. Once Phillips had shown the way, his admonition to proceed cautiously along that way was disregarded. On May 24 Straight recorded in his diary, "Telegram sent to Peking which started the row about the Chinese loan. Bill [Phillips] tried to ask a question merely, but with H. W. approving, my telegram went, telling Rockhill, if press reports were true, to take immediate action."[44] Straight's account leaves the impression that the Secretary took no part in the decision to move on the Hukuang loan. Yet, in discussing the subject with Mitchell Innes of the British embassy, Knox excused the last-minute intervention on the ground that he had only just realized that likin dues were involved. This statement led Innes to think that the action resulted from Knox's direct initiative.[45] Bernstorff, however, reported that Taft had told him that the intervention was his own idea, because of his great interest in the Far East.[46]

Rockhill tried on three occasions to convince the president of the Foreign Office, Prince Ch'ing, that China should not sign the preliminary agreement until the Americans received a share of the loan.[47] His representations did not advance the American cause; rather, they had the opposite effect. Liang Tun-yen, an influential member of the Foreign Office, impressed upon Jordan the need for immediate action, giving as reasons not only the increasing agitation among the provincial gentry but especially the American efforts to renew their claims to a share in the Hankow-Szechuan line.[48]

If the United States Department of State wanted American capital to share in the loan, it needed to interest some financiers. Tait, apparently assuming the subject to be dead, answered Phillips' inquiry of May 21 by stating that his bank would have been glad to handle the Hankow-Szechuan concession.[49] On June 3

43. DS 5315/208-9.
44. DS 5315/238; H. Croly, *Willard Straight,* 282.
45. Innes to Bryce, June 17, 1909, James Bryce Papers.
46. *GP,* 32, No. 11619, 17.
47. *FR, 1909,* 145.
48. Jordan to Grey, June 4, 1909, FO 405/197/230.
49. DS 5315/238.

Phillips suggested that Tait get together a group of bankers interested in China, but as it turned out—and as Phillips learned from Tait—a syndicate had already been organized under the leadership of J. P. Morgan and Company.[50] On June 3 Huntington-Wilson wired Rockhill that a representative of a powerful American financial group would reach Peking within six weeks. In the meantime Rockhill was to do what he could to keep open all opportunities.[51]

In view of the fact that American financial and commercial interests are often accused of using the American government to further their own interests, it is only fair to say that in this case one can accept as genuine the bankers' statement that they engaged in the China business largely from patriotic motives. Although, as Vevier points out, four of the five banking houses in the American group had already been involved in some sort of economic activity in China, the financiers did not respond with great enthusiasm to the invitation to become the United States Government's "wedge" in promoting American influence in China.[52] On the contrary, the bankers moved reluctantly. At first they told the Administration that they did not care to press a claim for a share in the Chinese railroad investment because it would pay only 5 per cent, and their money could earn as much or more at home. But Taft, seconded by Knox, insisted that the banks should proceed. By underwriting a part of this loan, the bankers would establish the principle of American participation in developments in China and would provide the United States with a better foundation for any action the Government might care to take.[53]

On June 10 the American Group came formally into being. In addition to J. P. Morgan and Company, the members were the National City Bank, the First National Bank, and Kuhn, Loeb and Company. They agreed to supply capital for American participation in the Hukuang loan and to send an agent to Peking.[54] Despite the desire of the International Banking Corporation and the China Investment and Construction Company to participate, they were frozen out by the State Department—over their bitter pro-

50. DS 5315/242-43.
51. DS 5315/212.
52. C. Vevier, *The United States and China, 1906-1913,* 107.
53. Bryce to Grey, August 31, 1909, reporting a conversation with his old friend Charles R. Crane, the newly appointed American minister to China. FO 405/191/53.
54. *New York Tribune,* June 10, 1909.

tests—on grounds that in all fairness must be regarded as mere technicalities.[55] Knox, however, defended the department's decision, stating that it was using Wall Street "for the purpose of getting somewhere." When the department decided to use the Hukuang loan as a wedge for American opportunity in China, it selected the sturdiest instrument available. It would have been culpable had it done otherwise, the Secretary asserted.[56]

On June 2 Knox instructed Reid to remind the British that China had promised Conger that if she could not find domestic capital for construction of the Hankow-Chungking railroad, British and American capital would be given first chance to offer the money. The Secretary referred to the correspondence with Britain's Ambassador Durand and denied that the United States had ever relinquished its rights.[57] But Grey gave no satisfactory answer; he merely disavowed any knowledge of China's commitment to the United States. He did promise, however, to inquire into the matter and to talk further with Reid about it.[58] Knox interpreted Grey's reply to mean that Grey was disclaiming his government's interest in the matter and referring the United States to the English bank in China.[59] His feelings hurt, his suspicions aroused, and his temper ruffled, Knox fired off an immediate protest to Peking in an effort to prevent the signature of the final loan contract.[60]

Fletcher, the American *chargé* in Peking, carried out his instructions and protested to the Foreign Office on June 5, but Chang, the responsible official, simply ignored the Americans and their claims.[61] The following day he signed the preliminary agreement for a loan of £ 5,500,000 sterling at 5 per cent, with the issuing price of 95. Of this amount £ 2,500,000 would be used to construct the Canton-Hankow line, about 600 miles long; an equal sum would be spent for the road for Hankow to Ichang, about 480 miles; the remainder would be used to redeem the American China Development Company bonds. The Chinese Government, which guaranteed the loan, pledged as security provincial likin, salt, and rice taxes.[62]

55. See DS file 5315 for June through August; also Vevier, *China*, 108-9.
56. Knox, Memorandum, n.d., Philander C. Knox Papers.
57. *FR, 1909*, 145-46.
58. Reid to Knox, June 3, 1909, Whitelaw Reid Papers.
59. Bryce to Grey, June 22, 1909, FO 405/197/269.
60. *FR, 1909*, 148; FO 800/278.
61. *FR, 1909*, 155.
62. *FR, 1909*, 152-54.

With one notable exception the loan terms closely followed those of the Berlin compromise signed by the three European banks in May. The bankers had agreed that the British would appoint the engineers for the Hankow-Canton railroad, the Germans to have the same right for the Hupeh section (Hankow to Ichang) of the Hankow-Szechuan line. The engineering rights of the remaining two thirds of the western road, from Ichang to Chengtu, went to the Chinese Central Railway, representing the British and French groups.[63] The agreement signed in Peking, however, provided for construction only as far as Ichang. For the so-called Chengtu extension the government intended to use Chinese funds because the people of Szechuan, through which the extension ran, vehemently objected to the intrusion of foreign capital into their province.[64]

Apart from returns on the actual loan itself, the advantage of lending money to a weak government was that the creditor could sell materials to the debtor under compulsory preference clauses. The financiers making the loan more often than not indirectly derived large profits from these commercial contracts.[65] In this particular loan, the right to appoint engineers, equivalent to the right of construction, meant that the holder of that right, the bank itself or its designate, acquired some degree of monopoly in supplying materials. In addition to the profits on supplies, agencies often charged a 2½–5 per cent commission for acting as purchasing and construction agents.[66]

Jordan, who only three days earlier had said "*nunc dimittis* to the railway loan and all its worries," was now indignant about "our American friends [who] have put their oar in . . ."; he was especially annoyed because, although he and Rockhill saw each other almost daily, Rockhill had not so much as hinted that the Americans were interested. Jordan was ready to believe that Henry Fletcher, due to take charge of the embassy after Rockhill's departure late in June, would be reasonable. But the news that Straight was to represent the American Group filled Jordan with gloom—"a very pushing sort of fellow who will want to make a *coup.*" The Minister sympathized with the Chinese. He realized that they wanted to sign the final loan contract but that they could not flout the Americans, who had returned the Boxer indemnity

63. *FR, 1909,* 207-9.
64. *FR, 1909,* 152-54.
65. Memorandum, December 7, 1916, DS 893.75/10.
66. Hou, *Foreign Investments,* 35.

and had done them other favors "of a less altruistic sort."[67] Count von Rex, the German minister in Peking, was equally unhappy with Rockhill, whom he reproached for having quietly—and happily—observed the Germans struggle for months to breach the English monopoly in the Yangtze Valley. Now that the work had been done for them, the Americans came in to demand their share of the business. Rockhill, embarrassed, made no answer.[68]

On June 8 Whitelaw Reid cabled to Washington a summary of his conversation with Foreign Minister Grey on the loan. Because the Americans had not responded in 1905 to the invitation to participate, Grey stated, "that offer must be regarded as having lapsed." Complicated and expensive negotiations, which were common knowledge, had continued since that time, and never once had American financiers indicated a desire to take part in them. The Foreign Secretary concluded that at this stage the British Government would scarcely feel justified in interfering with the British banking group's arrangements.[69]

When *Chargé* Fletcher discussed the matter with the Chinese Foreign Office, with Chang, and with the bank representatives, he heard the same story everywhere: It was inexpedient to delay signing the final contract. Chang said that he would not have objected to admitting the Americans if they had approached him earlier and that he would welcome their participation in future loans. The bank representatives also seemed inclined to look favorably on the prospect of cooperating with American interests in the future.[70] Although he did not confide his opinion to the department, Fletcher himself realized the danger of reopening contract discussions with the Chinese and thought the Americans ought to do their negotiating with the bankers in Europe.[71]

On June 9, in a circular instruction to London, Paris, and Berlin, Secretary of State Knox urged those governments to permit American financiers' entry into the Hukuang loan. After stressing "the menace to foreign trade likely to ensue from the lack of proper sympathy between the powers most vitally interested in the preservation of the principle of equality of commercial opportunity . . . ," the Secretary added, "the United States regards full and frank cooperation as best calculated to maintain the open

67. Jordan to Campbell, June 7 and June 22, 1909, Jordan Papers.
68. *GP,* 32, No. 11629, 28-29.
69. Reid Papers; *FR, 1909,* 149-50.
70. Fletcher to Knox, June 10, 1909, *FR, 1909,* 157-58.
71. Jordan to Grey, June 10, 1909, FO 405/197/241.

door and the integrity of China." The United States Government considered that the creation of a strong four-Power financial combination would promote these goals. Although Knox reasserted the American right, along with the British, to construct the Hankow-Szechuan railway, he intimated his willingness to surrender that right for a greater good, the creation of "a highly desirable community of interests."[72]

Knox thus appealed to the Powers to use this occasion to strengthen the policy of the Open Door; nowhere did he imply that he had caught them out in a violation of that policy. The Americans did not insist on a share in the Hukuang project in immediate pursuit of the traditional Open Door policy. What Knox did argue was that financial cooperation among the four Powers would do much in the long run to reaffirm and strengthen the Open Door concept. He did not maintain that European refusal to give Americans a part of the Hukuang loan was a breach of that concept—obviously because none of the Powers involved had any intention of excluding Americans from the Yangtze Valley. Britain, Germany, and France objected to American entry into this specific loan on pragmatic grounds; Knox based his protest on what he claimed was a breach of contract by the Chinese.

Germany and France denied that they had any power to persuade the Chinese to admit the Americans to the Hukuang project, suggesting that the solution might lie in an arrangement between the American Group and the European bankers.[73] But of course the British held the key that secured the door against American entry. When Grey reiterated his argument that the Americans had not responded to the original invitation, Reid on his own initiative struck a telling counterblow. No court of law, said the Ambassador, would sustain the British contention that one holder of a joint concession had the power to declare its partner's share invalid because the latter had not put up any money for three years. Grey agreed to submit a memorandum on Reid's views to the financiers but added that, as far as he was concerned, they were the final authority.[74] Reid's rebuttal was convincing. As Addis of the Hongkong and Shanghai Bank noted, the American contention that "neither [Britain nor France] can claim to place

72. *FR, 1909,* 152.
73. *FR, 1909,* 150-51, 156-57.
74. Reid to Knox, June 10, 1909, Reid Papers.

a term upon the undertaking given by China to America . . . is, I am afraid, indisputable."[75]

Although Grey had not yet explicitly consented to American participation, Knox interpreted the replies to his note as meaning that the three European governments would not oppose American participation if the bank representatives in Peking agreed to it. He therefore asked the Far Eastern Division to draft new instructions for Fletcher. In view of the extensive considerations involved in the loan, Knox wanted to put the American claim "upon the broadest possible basis instead of quibbling over small questions like that of the Chinese promise and the failure of our financial interests to respond to the British invitation."[76] But the Conger agreement of 1904 was too good to be ignored, and the instruction to Fletcher insisted on its validity. Nonfulfillment would be tantamount to the evasion by China of a solemn obligation and a poor return for America's unvarying friendship. At his discretion Fletcher might also point out that, since likin was a security, the Hukuang loan involved serious political considerations. In such a situation China would benefit from having a staunch friend in a position to exercise an influence equal to that of the other Powers, a friend who would support her efforts to carry out reforms.[77]

Fletcher believed that Conger had put a stronger construction on the Chinese assurances than the documents themselves would justify. Nevertheless, since the Chinese Foreign Office did not question their validity, the legation proceeded on the assumption that they were binding.[78] The Chinese, already shaken by the American protest, were further disturbed by the new representations. Chang finally agreed to allow American participation in the loan if the banks would agree, but he was not willing to take the initiative in approaching them.[79] Despite the desire of the Foreign Office to defer the final agreement until American participation had been arranged, Chang nevertheless persisted in refusing to reopen the negotiations, even though the United States offered to waive its claim to a half share in the Hankow-Szechuan loan in return for a fourth share of the total Hukuang loan. Since the American demand involved the Hankow-Canton line, it put

75. Addis to Simon, June 14, 1909, FO 405/197/249.
76. DS 5315/251.
77. *FR, 1909*, 158-60.
78. *FR, 1909*, 152-54.
79. *FR, 1909*, 161.

Chang in an awkward position. He would now be accused of having paid a heavy price to buy out the Americans, only to let them
back in again.[80]

These developments so disturbed Jordan that he appealed to his
government to prevent any American action that might wreck the
agreement reached on June 6.[81] On June 14 the Foreign Office
responded by asking the United States not to put obstacles in the
way of the issue of the imperial edict approving the contract, and
it again held out the prospect of cooperation in future loans.[82] But,
as Reid noted, the American Group now controlled the situation
in China and could exact a guarantee of participation from the
other financiers or their governments before permitting the matter to be closed.[83]

He proved right. The Chinese Foreign Office was so seriously
embarrassed by having ignored the American claim that, to save
face, the bank representatives in Peking strongly recommended
to their principals that they be authorized to reach a settlement
with the Americans.[84] Chang nonetheless continued to insist that
it was too late to include the Americans in the financing of the
Hukuang project, but Liang, although now asserting that the Conger agreements were not binding, told Fletcher that, even so, his
government was trying to bring about a settlement because of its
friendship for the United States. After remarking that the situation was awkward indeed, Liang added that he might not be able
to restrain Chang much longer.[85] Again, Washington instructed
Fletcher to impress on the Chinese that the 1904 pledge was "absolutely binding" and that, if it were broken, the United States
would be forced to reconsider its established past policy of
friendly and practical cooperation with China. In addition, Huntington-Wilson authorized Fletcher to point out on his own initiative and at his discretion that President Taft might consider it
only just to recoup the loss caused by China's breach of faith by
discontinuing the remission of the Boxer indemnity.[86]

On June 17 and 18, 1909, during informal conversations with
Innes, Knox made it plain that he did not intend to withdraw his
protest until American capitalists got a share of the Hukuang

80. *FR, 1909,* 166-67; Jordan to Campbell, July 14, 1909, Jordan Papers.
81. Reid to Knox, June 14, 1909, Reid Papers.
82. *FR, 1909,* 160-61.
83. Reid Papers.
84. Telegram from Peking to Addis, June 16, 1909, FO 405/197/254.
85. Fletcher to Knox, June 18, 1909, DS 5315/263.
86. DS 5315/258-59.

loan. Innes now discovered that Grey's reply to Knox's note of June 9 had deeply wounded the Secretary's feelings. Innes tried to repair the damage by assuring Knox that Britain would value American cooperation and would respect American rights to participate; Britain's sole concern was to avoid any situation that might compel a renegotiation of the entire contract. Knox replied that the United States only wanted equal financial participation. He would waive the protest if the agreement were ratified in its present form and the European banks then transferred part of the loan to the Americans. Knox told Innes that he would not recede from this position, since the Department of State had already made public its intentions.[87]

Innes cabled Grey that if the United States Government "receives satisfactory assurances that arrangements have been made" for equal American participation, the Secretary would withdraw his protest against the signature of the agreement in its present form.[88] Grey replied that Britain would agree to American participation if the United States waived its protest against the agreement of June 6, and if it reached an agreement with the tripartite banks.[89] Grey's response hardly met the Secretary's terms. He informed Bryce that the United States found itself unable to change its instructions to the Peking legation

> or to admit that a third government, and much less that a group of foreign bankers, could expect to induce this Government to relinquish a right acquired for the benefit of its citizens through an official assurance from another government.
> ... As we all know, foreign bankers in China are quite dependent upon their home governments, and it is a corollary to this fact that it would be extremely easy for the Governments concerned to put an immediate stop to the present controversy. . . .[90]

Knox considered the issue too important to withdraw his demands merely because they inconvenienced other people. Two

87. Innes to Bryce, June 17, 1909, Bryce Papers; Bryce to Grey, June 22, 1909, FO 405/197/269; DS 5315/258-59; *FR, 1909,* 164-65. These were trying times for Innes. He detested Huntington-Wilson, and Huntington-Wilson's own account of one of their exchanges explains the strong feeling. When Innes intimated that it was rather humiliating for Great Britain to have the loan delayed, Huntington-Wilson replied "laughingly" that the humiliation had really come when Germany had stepped into the British Yangtze sphere and then condescended to let England share in the concession. Bryce Papers; Memorandum of conversation, June 28, 1909, DS 5315/307.
88. Quoted in Huntington-Wilson to Fletcher, June 19, 1909, DS 5315/258-59.
89. Grey to Bryce, June 21, 1909, FO 405/197/266.
90. *FR, 1909,* 164-65.

reasons account for his persistence. The economic benefits to be derived from this specific undertaking were, of course, one consideration; more important, however, were the long-term implications of participating in a loan guaranteed by revenue from provincial sources. The United States was concerned about China's development and in the maintenance of its political integrity "and primarily therefore in its financial affairs." Assuming, Knox wrote, that "the borrower is the servant of the lender, we propose in all cases to claim the right to proportional representation in the influence which attaches to the holding of the credits of the Chinese government, especially where their credits are secured by an hypothecation of Chinese revenues."[91] If there were even a remote chance of foreign intervention in the administration of Chinese finances, Innes wrote Bryce, Knox wanted his government to participate.[92] Grey might deny that the likin pledge would involve any interference with Chinese administration and thus imply that the loan had no political implications, but Knox did not believe him.

On June 24 Bryce wrote Knox a conciliatory letter explaining that Grey was most anxious for the American Group to reach an agreement with the European bankers. The Foreign Minister had not intended to refer the Americans to the bank representatives in Peking but rather to suggest that they send someone to deal with the principals in Europe.[93] On the same day, Fletcher reported that the Chinese Foreign Office had informed the bank representatives that unless they settled with the Americans China would not conclude the loan.[94] In one more effort to persuade the Americans to withdraw their protest, the British made what Huntington-Wilson called the "curious suggestion" that the United States waive its protest in return for assurance from the British Government that satisfactory arrangements would be made.[95] Knox was not accepting any offer so vague nor was he taking anything on trust. He told Innes that when the European banks and the American Group reached an agreement acceptable to the Chinese, he would withdraw his protest.[96] Knox

91. Knox Memorandum, n.d., DS 5315/215.
92. Innes to Bryce, June 17, 1909, Bryce Papers.
93. *FR, 1909*, 165-66. Fletcher believed that Valentine Chirol, influential head of the London *Times* foreign department, was chiefly responsible for the British change of heart. *Ibid.*, 203-6.
94. *FR, 1909*, 166.
95. DS 5315/307.
96. Innes to Bryce, June 29, 1909, Bryce Papers.

had won his battle with the European governments on the principle of participation. Now it was the bankers' round to settle the terms.

The press, obviously at the department's suggestion, noted the importance of the China loan. The *New York Times* remarked that the syndicate's operations were expected to strengthen greatly American influence in China, political as well as financial. "The point is emphasized," it added, "that in the Far East the strongest financial influence was likely to prove the strongest political influence as well." To the *Boston Herald* the presence of American financial interests in China offered the best way to prevent the closing of the Open Door. The *Cincinnati Star-Times*, owned by Taft's brother, echoing Administration jargon, referred to the loan as an "opening wedge" of a much more general American participation in the affairs of the Far East. The *Wall Street Journal* was pleased with the change of policy, for until now the United States' Open Door policy in the Far East had meant that the United States held the door open for others to enter. The *Brooklyn Standard Union* probably summed up the prevailing opinion with its remark that China was the greatest uncut commercial melon in the world.[97]

The three European groups met in London on July 6 and signed interbank agreements covering their joint financial and railroad enterprises in China. Although none of them welcomed American participation in the Hukuang loan, the Germans, led by F. Urbig, opposed it most vehemently. Urbig confided to Addis that American participation even in future business was "very little attractive for me."[98] He accused the Americans of sending cables to Europe stating that the German Group had gladly welcomed American cooperation, with the purpose of affecting the decisions of the continental bankers. Officially, Urbig told Addis, the German Government had merely thanked the Americans for their good intentions and informed them that participation in the Hukuang loan was out of the question. Urbig offered a simple formula for excluding Americans: Tell them emphatically that their share of the loan would not be quoted on the European exchanges. This measure would effectively bar them from participation in the loan, in Urbig's opinion, because American banks had never yet been able to float a foreign loan in their own country. Soon

97. *Literary Digest*, July 3, 1909.
98. FO 405/197/256.

after issue "the loans have invariably emigrated to Europe down to the last dollar."[99]

Addis himself did not like the complications caused by American participation in this particular loan, yet he saw advantages in having Americans share in international loans in the future. Without them, he believed, it would be difficult to enforce "the shadowy loan guarantees" of earlier mortgages, and the pressure of United States diplomacy, added to that of the tripartite countries, would increase the security of Chinese loans by 1 or 2 per cent.[100]

As for the French, although both the Foreign Office and Minister of Finance Joseph Caillaux considered the American *demarche* unjustified, they were willing to allot the United States a fourth of the loan for the Hankow-Szechuan section of the railroad. The share would be only financial and would carry no rights to furnish materials or appoint engineers. The Americans might share in future business in the Far East with the Europeans, but no bond issue would be international. Each bank would have to quote its flotation on its own exchange. Simon, spokesman for the French Group, did not agree with his government, simply because he did not think the United States would accept such conditions. It was he who suggested that, to strengthen their position vis-à-vis the Americans, the tripartite banks sign their railroad and financial agreements before the American representatives joined the talks.[101]

Straight, whom the American Group had appointed as its representative, left for London on June 26. On July 7 he and E. C. Grenfell of Morgan, Grenfell and Company, the J. P. Morgan and Company agent in London, joined their colleagues at the conference table. Straight quite accurately judged the Europeans' temper. The British were the smoothest, not wanting to admit the Americans but putting the blame for their exclusion on the Germans, who were, Straight thought, the most hostile and intolerant. The French he considered "excitable but . . . tractable."[102]

At this stage Knox was willing to accept participation on the same terms as the French—25 per cent of the total loan and equal rights in furnishing materials. He was prepared to waive Ameri-

99. Urbig to Addis, June 18, 1909, FO 405/197/263.
100. FO 405/197/268.
101. FO 405/197/287.
102. Straight to Huntington-Wilson, July 15, 1909, DS 5315/unnumbered, follows /375.

can rights with regard to engineers and auditors in order not to delay the final settlement.[103] After the Europeans had advanced a more limited counterproposal, Straight and Grenfell suggested a compromise: 20 per cent of the total loan, with equal preference in regard to materials.[104]

The American Group, considering this a fair business proposition, was ready to negotiate on these terms, but Huntington-Wilson refused. In his view, yielding on any point whatever might damage the American position at Peking, and he tartly reminded the group that the loan's terms involved more than questions of mere business. If the group objected to cooperating with the department in the national interest, the Government would seek other agents who would be willing to carry out its policy. Although the bankers obviously had misgivings about the wisdom of such an inflexible position, they assured Huntington-Wilson that their chief motive in entering the China loan had been patriotism and that they wished to act only with the Government's sanction and approval.[105] Straight, sharing the group's anxiety, cautioned the department that the Germans and French were especially irate about the Americans' late entrance into the negotiations. Some American concessions, therefore, offered the only chance of bringing about an amicable settlement, thus ensuring cooperation in future enterprises.[106]

When the bankers did not reach an immediate agreement in London, Chang became impatient at the delay and urged the Foreign Office to conclude the loan contract promptly.[107] Fletcher's cable bearing this news received a quick response. On July 15 the President of the United States made a personal appeal to the Prince Regent for equal American participation in the Hukuang loan.[108] Although Taft's request was, in the words of one indignant observer, a "high-handed action" that ignored "all the conventions of diplomatic intercourse," it brought about the desired effect. The Regent called the Foreign Office into conference and instructed it to come to an arrangement with the Americans.[109]

103. *FR, 1909,* 162-63.
104. Croly, *Straight,* 292-93.
105. DS 5315/344; *FR, 1909,* 169-71.
106. DS 5315/400. A memorandum of the consultations, written by Urbig and E. Rehders, clearly reflected the Europeans' displeasure with the Americans. Urbig to Zimmerman, July 10, 1909, *GP,* 32, No. 11622, 19.
107. *FR, 1909,* 171-72.
108. *FR, 1909,* 178.
109. Hillier to Addis, July 23, 1909, FO 405/198/44; *FR, 1909,* 180.

Even before Jordan learned of Taft's message, he had accepted American participation as a foregone conclusion. The Chinese Foreign Office recognized that a government to which it was under so many obligations could not be ignored. Further, the Chinese were aware that from a political point of view, American participation was to their advantage. Jordan did not think the Foreign Office would back Chang if he applied for imperial authorization to sign, which he was not likely to get anyway.[110]

Hillier suggested increasing the loan by 12 ½ per cent to 6,000,000, which would give the Americans equal participation without reducing the share originally allotted to the Europeans. Chang, the banks, and Knox accepted this solution. But the Secretary coupled his approval with a new demand. Now he wanted absolutely equal rights in every particular—in engineers, materials, auditors, and in all other advantages accompanying full partnership.[111] The change in policy came with the State Department's tardy realization that the right to furnish materials might be practically contingent upon the right to name engineers.[112]

Liang, worried by the new complication, considered the Americans extremely unreasonable for taking advantage of China's weakness to put her in a humiliating position. At the same time, as Liang told Hillier, the Chinese could not forget that friendship with the United States was the key to their foreign policy. China looked to the United States for protection against Japanese aggression and could not afford to ignore its wishes. In an effort to break the deadlock, Liang appealed to Taft through Rockhill, who was on leave in Washington. Liang asked the former minister to explain China's difficult situation to the President and to urge him to withdraw the latest demand. The department refused to yield.[113]

The American claim, which the Europeans resented and which Hillier called "dictation," led to a long round of negotiations over who was to get how many kilometers of railroad to construct. Grey stood firmly on the Berlin compromise signed in May and insisted that the redistribution of engineering rights be confined to the Hankow-Szechuan section.[114] Hillier questioned the wis-

110. FO 405/198/16.
111. *FR, 1909*, 180-81; FO 405/198/44.
112. DS 5315/383A.
113. DS 5315/389; *FR, 1909*, 187; FO 405/198/44.
114. *FR, 1909*, 207-9.

dom of Grey's policy, especially at a time when tension was running high in both Germany and England. First, the Germans had exchanged their rights in the Hankow-Canton section for British rights in the Hankow-Szechuan line; now, Britain was calling on them to give up a part of their Hankow-Szechuan rights.[115] In October the United States, although unwilling itself to make concessions, strongly urged the Europeans to reach an agreement. The Germans ultimately gave way and accepted the State Department's compromise proposal to leave the southern trunk to British engineers and to divide the western road between Germans and Americans.[116]

The quarrel over engineering rights, however, was not the American Group's chief concern. What the bankers wanted was a definite understanding on the interchangeability of bonds between the American and the three European markets. The American Group did not ask that the foreign bourses be opened to them immediately, but they wanted the bonds to become international after a given period, on the ground that it would be bad policy to have such a comparatively small loan cut up into four slices.[117] Although the French Group finally accepted the engineering compromise and agreed to interchangeability after several years, the French Government refused to concede the latter point if the French did not get engineering rights equal to those of the Americans and Germans.[118] Now the quarrel between the British and the French prevented final settlement of the Hukuang project.

While the Powers continued their wrangling in Europe, events in China seemed likely to minimize the results, no matter what they were. The death of Chang Chih-tung on October 4, 1909, removed one of the last of China's elder statesmen and the only man who could control Hunan and Hupeh. While he was alive the provinces had offered little overt opposition to a foreign loan, but his death led to the anticipated revival of agitation. Foreign observers generally agreed that the central government had never been so weak and that it continued to exist only because there was nothing better to replace it. Fletcher was not at all sure that without Chang the central government would have either the courage or the strength to impose its railroad policy on the Hu-

115. Hillier to Addis, September 3, 1909, FO 405/198/129.
116. *FR, 1909,* 207-10.
117. J. P. Morgan & Co. (London) to Addis, November 8, 1909, FO 405/198/205.
118. Simon to Jamieson, November 15, 1909, FO 405/198/215; McKnight to Knox, December 23, 1909, DS 5315/650.

kuang.[119] Some doubts arose among the observers of China's internal and international affairs whether the central government could govern effectively in any area of the national life.

119. FO 405/195; Jordan to Campbell, November 11, 1909, Jordan Papers; DS 5315/563.

10

The United States
and the Neutralization Scheme

Exhortations by the Department of State for a settlement of the Hukuang contract arose from two developments in Manchuria. The Sino-Japanese negotiations, which had opened in January on pending Manchurian questions, had culminated during August and September in agreements that caused the department grave anxiety over the development of the Three Provinces. Then, early in October, Straight signed a preliminary contract with the Chinese for a railroad from Chinchow on the Gulf of Pechili to Aigun on the Amur River. This concession gave the United States a tangible interest in Manchuria that readjusted the balance of power, which Japan had tipped in her own favor.

In the negotiations the most important issue, one that involved the future control of Manchuria, was the definition of Japanese railroad rights. The northern extension of the Chinese Imperial Railways (the Hsinmintun-Fakumen line and its eventual extension to Tsitsihar) and the Antung-Mukden railroad were the two roads—both of them crucial—under consideration.[1] From the Japanese point of view, settlement of the rights to the Antung-Mukden road was urgent, for Japan wanted to link the Korean and South Manchurian rail systems.[2] During the Russo-Japanese War the Japanese—without any authorization from China—had laid a temporary, narrow-gauge military track between Antung and Mukden. Article VI of the additional agreement to the Komura Treaty gave Japan the right to rebuild the railroad and to operate it for fifteen years. The crux of the dispute was the status of the

---

1. Rockhill to Root, January 11, 1909, DS 5767/38.
2. Rumbolt to Grey, July 8, 1909, FO 405/191/24.

concession. On one hand the Chinese claimed that it was entirely distinct from the old Russian contract, which formed the basis for the South Manchuria Railway Company's privileges, and insisted that China must retain all powers of civil jurisdiction along the line. On the other hand the Japanese maintained that the railroad, by virtue of various agreements, was part of the S.M.R. system. Although no clear authority existed for the Japanese claim, China had greatly weakened her own case by allowing, without protest, the Japanese to police and administer the land along the railroad since the end of the war. When Japan refused to admit Chinese jurisdiction, China then insisted that reconstruction be confined to the existing track and forbade Japan to relocate the roadbed or widen the gauge.[3]

When months of negotiation brought no results, Japan acted. On August 5, 1909, she notified the British that she intended to proceed with reconstruction, with or without Chinese consent. An ultimatum to China on August 6 brought immediate results. The following day China yielded and on the nineteenth signed an agreement settling the technical questions in Japan's favor and leaving that of jurisdiction open for future discussion.[4]

Japan continued to exert pressure on China to settle the remaining Manchurian questions, and, since no support seemed forthcoming from either the United States or Great Britain, China again gave way. On September 4 she signed two agreements with Japan, one relating to the Sino-Korean border and the other to development of mines and railroads. During the negotiations China had tried to clarify the Japanese interpretation of the secret protocol of 1905. Since the Japanese had objected to the Fakumen line as parallel and competing with the S.M.R., the Chinese wanted to know exactly how far away Japan would require the Chinese Imperial Railways to locate their extension. Japan refused to commit herself but extracted the promise that China would consult her before undertaking construction of a railroad between Hsinmintun and Fakumen. China further agreed (in Article IV) that the mines along the Antung-Mukden railroad and the main line of the S.M.R. would be worked jointly by China and Japan.[5]

3. DS 5767/49, 52-56.
4. DS 5767/49, 52-56; MacDonald, Annual Report, Japan, 1909, FO 405/195.
5. *Foreign Relations, 1909*, 118-20.

The United States Department of State had been watching the situation closely, and E. Carleton Baker of the Division of Far Eastern Affairs expressed its attitude when he wrote that the Japanese intended "to secure such control of the mineral resources and transportation facilities of Manchuria, and possibly [of] Manchuria itself, as will enable her to exploit that country."[6] After studying the situation carefully, Knox decided that the large and indefinite mining concessions might provide the grounds for a protest by the United States Government, either in concert with the other Powers or alone.[7] Baker, to whom Knox assigned the task of examining the question, agreed with the Secretary. Baker held that the mining rights granted to Japan created a monopoly, which not only contravened the treaty rights of the Powers but also constituted a violation of the Open Door. An American protest, he believed, would check Japanese aggression and encourage Chinese resistance. If made jointly with the other Powers, the protest would be even more effective.[8]

In spite of the department's activity, the protest might well have died quietly but for the interference of the new American minister to China, Charles R. Crane. Crane, a Chicago businessman with a good deal of experience in foreign countries, had accepted the appointment to Peking after several other nominees had turned it down. After being briefed by the department, Crane was directed by Taft to talk freely about the situation in the Far East, and Crane did just that. He leaked the information about a possible protest to Sumner Curtis, Washington correspondent of the *Chicago Record Herald,* which carried the story on September 27, 1909. Although Crane was in San Francisco, en route to China, Knox was so furious that he recalled him to Washington for an explanation. The Secretary found Crane's answers unsatisfactory and, despite Taft's reluctance, insisted on his dismissal.[9]

Knox, qualified by experience to be an expert judge in such matters, ultimately conceded that the mining agreement did not, on its face, show intent to gain a monopoly and that Japan could deny maneuvering for a corner on mines merely by citing the text of the implementing arrangement.[10] As a result, the Department of State merely requested China and Japan to confirm the Ameri-

6. Baker to Knox, October 7, 1909, DS 5767/132½.
7. DS 793.94/158.
8. DS 5767/132½.
9. DS 20602/23; Philander C. Knox Papers.
10. Knox Papers.

can interpretation of Article IV, that is, that it did not create a monopoly but referred only to certain specific mines. On November 15 the department issued a statement that Japan and China had endorsed the American point of view.[11]

The perfunctory notes that achieved this undoubtedly reflected more than Knox's legal background; the Secretary had by this time conceived an entirely different approach to the Manchurian problem. On October 2 Willard Straight had signed a preliminary contract for American financing of the Chinchow-Aigun railroad, giving the United States for the first time a concrete, special interest in that area. Here was a base from which to operate, an important new element that Knox would try to develop as a political counterweight to Japanese encroachment.

The genesis of Knox's plan lay in Harriman's tenacious but frustrated efforts to acquire a railway in Manchuria. In 1905 and again in 1906 Japan had refused to sell him the S.M.R. In 1907 the financial panic had prevented his taking up Tang's offer, and most recently, in January 1909 Japan had firmly quashed his renewed effort to buy the S.M.R. But neither Harriman nor Kuhn, Loeb was willing to forego the profits of railway development in China. Harriman, moreover, was still thinking of a world-wide transportation system, which required a railroad linking some point on the Trans-Siberian to an ice-free port on the Pacific.[12]

Throughout the summer of 1909, while the department carefully watched developments concerning Manchuria, Harriman was working on his old scheme, but with a new twist. He was now going after a concession from China for a road beginning at Chinchow, crossing the Trans-Siberian at Tsitsihar and ending at Aigun on the Amur River. Although parallel to the S.M.R., the route lay over 100 miles farther west and for that reason was not, in Harriman's opinion, in competition.[13] He did not necessarily intend to build the road. The mere fact that he held the concession might induce the Russians to sell the C.E.R., and if they should, the Japanese and the S.M.R. would be forced into the system on whatever terms the international syndicate might offer.[14]

In the summer of 1909 Harriman went to Europe, still hoping to make a deal with the Russians. His contact was Eduard Noetzlin,

11. *FR, 1909,* 121-22.
12. H. Croly, *Willard Straight,* 280, 297.
13. The proposed Hsinmintun-Fakumen line was only about half that distance from the S.M.R.
14. Memorandum of conversation with Straight, June, 1910, FO 800/248.

who held offices in both the Banque de Paris et des Pays-Bas and the Russo-Chinese Bank.[15] Harriman suggested to the French banker the organization of an international syndicate to buy the C.E.R. In August, after the Russians indicated through Noetzlin that they would consider such a proposal, some correspondence developed between Harriman and Kokovtsov on the subject. Illness interrupted Harriman's participation in the discussions, and on September 10 he died. Thereafter the American Group made no effort to continue the negotiations.[16]

After the initiation of the Sino-Japanese negotiations in January 1909, the viceroy of Manchuria, alarmed by Japan's growing aggressiveness, tried to neutralize her influence by reviving the railroad development scheme. In April he signed an agreement with Lord ffrench to build a railroad from Chinchow to Taonanfu and on to Tsitsihar; ffrench then went to Peking, hoping to work out the details with the central government. Despite the desire of George Pauling, head of a British construction firm, to keep the concession an exclusively British affair, ffrench soon abandoned the idea, realizing that, although the prolonged Japanese pressure had shaken the Chinese, they would not sign his final contract without talking first to the Americans.[17]

After the London conference in July 1909, Straight had set off for China to take up his duties as the American Group's representative. En route he visited Harriman in Europe and received a specific commission to negotiate a railroad contract with the Chinese Government. Straight arrived in Peking on August 19, the day the Chinese signed the Antung-Mukden railway agreement. They soon got in touch with him about reviving Tang's projects for a Manchurian development bank and a railroad connecting the Chinese Imperial Railways and the Trans-Siberian. Nothing came of the bank[18] scheme, but the railroad proposition was exactly what Straight was looking for. He accepted the validity of ffrench's concession, and the two men subsequently reached an amicable agreement whereby the British would build the entire road from Chinchow to Aigun and the Americans would finance it.[19]

This activity confirmed Jordan's unhappy premonition that Straight's reappearance in China meant a revival of the Fakumen

15. Simon to Addis, June 27, 1909, FO 405/197/287.
16. Willard Straight Papers; DS 2157/2.
17. DS 5767/88-89, 110-11; 893,77/1056.
18. Jordan, Annual Report, China, 1910, FO 405/195.
19. DS 5767/110-11; 893.77/1056.

project in a new and much less desirable form—an American-Pauling contract for a line from Chinchow to Taonanfu. Jordan deplored the project because it would place Great Britain in an extremely awkward position. Since the road from Chinchow lay over 100 miles west of the S.M.R. and opened up new territory, Japanese protests would not have the validity that they possessed for the Fakumen road.[20] That was, of course, what the Chinese had planned.[21]

The Japanese at first refused to state their position on the new concession, but when they finally did, the British Foreign Office shaped its policies to fit those of its ally. On July 20 Takaaki Kato, the Japanese ambassador in London, told Grey that, although Japan would not object to any lines feeding the S.M.R., she would oppose all railroads that tapped the main line at places like Tsitsihar and diverted traffic from it. Grey replied that, in his opinion, the Chinese would be wise to discuss with Japan the whole question of Manchurian railroads.[22] On August 17 Enjiro Yamaza, the counselor of the Japanese embassy in London, told George Pauling that if Japanese interests could participate in some form in the Chinchow-Tsitsihar line, his government would not oppose their inclusion. Pauling replied that he could not give the Japanese a share in the enterprise unless the Chinese asked him to do so.[23] Following this encounter Pauling asked the British Foreign Office for a promise that it would ignore a Japanese protest against his project. Grey answered that he would not accept any objections to the road as far as Taonanfu, but he thought that if the road connected with the Russian line at Tsitsihar, it might be considered competitive with the S.M.R.[24]

After receiving Pauling's answer, the Japanese suggested to China that she consult with Japan before making plans to construct any part of the railroad, even as far as Taonanfu. When the Chinese did not respond, Hikokichi Ijuin, the Japanese minister in Peking, asked Jordan to sound them out. Jordan thereupon explained Pauling's position to Hsü Shih-ch'ang, the former viceroy of Manchuria and now president of the Ministry of Communi-

20. Jordan to Campbell, June 22, 1909, John Jordan Papers; Jordan to Grey, July 14, 1909, FO 405/191/32.
21. E-tu Sun, *Chinese Railways and British Interests, 1898-1911,* 148.
22. Jordan Papers; Memorandum Respecting the Chinchow-Aigun Railway, February, 1910, FO 405/196.
23. FO 405/198/78.
24. Straight Memorandum, n.d., DS 5767/110-11. In view of Grey's remarks to Pauling, the department regarded Grey's later refusal to back the railroad to Taonanfu as a breach of faith.

cations, who was in charge of the negotiations. Hsü stated clearly that his main preoccupation was to exclude the Japanese from participation in any form.[25] Jordan believed that American support had much to do with Chinese intransigence.[26] On September 7 Grey relayed the information on China's position to Kato, who asked that Britain support the Japanese if China should proceed with construction. Grey replied that when the case came up he would tell China that, as long as Japan was willing to come to an agreement on railroad development in Manchuria, she and Japan should agree on terms that would safeguard the S.M.R. against unfair competition.[27]

During this time Straight was negotiating with the Chinese for the concession to build the line from Chinchow to Aigun on which he and ffrench had agreed. On September 4 he cabled J. P. Morgan and Company the outline of a proposal for a road from Chinchow to Tsitsihar and its eventual extension to Aigun—the so-called Chin-Ai concession. The Chinese offered very liberal terms, and, although they would not consent to Japanese participation, they were willing, in view of the political situation, to let the Russo-Chinese Bank have a small interest. Straight believed the Chin-Ai concession presented "a rare opportunity."[28]

From the day of his arrival in Peking, Straight had been openly proclaiming that his government would not tolerate Japanese opposition to American enterprise in Manchuria,[29] and he genuinely believed that Japan could be checkmated diplomatically without much difficulty. His program, with its accompanying elucidations, made American domination of northern China seem easily obtainable. Russian opposition to Chin-Ai would be eliminated by giving her a small financial share in the project. This done, the Russians could be induced to sell the C.E.R. by the *quid pro quo* of an entente with the United States similar to the Root-Takahira agreement. This accord plus certain diplomatic pressures on the Japanese "should render impossible any overt act of hostility or any very serious intrigue which could be . . . attributed to Japan."[30] Later, after Straight had signed the preliminary con-

25. Jordan to Grey, August 27, 1909, and September 1, 1909, FO 405/198/83, 134.
26. Jordan to Campbell, September 3, 1909, Jordan Papers.
27. FO 405/198/190.
28. DS 5315/483-86; in Jordan's opinion Pauling let Straight play the leading role in the negotiations so that if Japan objected, the Americans would have to deal with her. Jordan to Grey, September 2, 1909, FO 405/198/94.
29. Jordan, Annual Report, China, 1910, FO 405/195.
30. Croly, *Straight,* 306-8; C. Vevier, *The United States and China, 1906-1913,*

tract for Chin-Ai, his parting remark to the Chinese officials was, "Don't worry about Japanese and Russian objections."[31]

Although Washington was not quite so naive as the American Group's representative, both Straight and the Department of State shared a simplistic view of the power situation in the Far East. Despite Straight's eagerness, the Chinese would not close the contract at once. The agreements of September 4 had cooled their enthusiasm, for they felt that they must allow some time to elapse before resuming any negotiations that might give umbrage to the Japanese.[32] Straight then decided that by signing a preliminary agreement in Mukden he would force a decision on Peking, and he hurriedly left for Manchuria. Straight judged correctly the mood of the provincial officials; feeling the Japanese presence more directly, they were not so cautious as Peking. On October 2, 1909, Straight and Viceroy Hsi-liang signed a preliminary agreement for the construction of the Chin-Ai railroad in two phases: first from Chinchow to Tsitsihar, then from Tsitsihar to Aigun. Anglo-American interests would build and finance the line, and in no circumstances would persons of another nationality than British, American, or Chinese have any voice in its management or control without China's permission.[33]

Since neither the Viceroy nor Straight had been authorized to sign a contract, the agreement was not final or irrevocable. It would not become binding on the Chinese until an imperial edict ratified the action of the Manchurian authorities. On October 3, by secret edict, the Throne instructed the Foreign Office, the Treasury, and the Communications Department to discuss the concession and report their recommendations. Although the American Group took a sympathetic view of Straight's unauthorized signature and eventually even came to regard the Chin-Ai project as an important undertaking, it was not eager to pursue it until the bankers had reached an agreement on the Hukuang loan.[34]

Since the group was unwilling to proceed in Manchuria until the Hukuang contract was settled, the Department of State had offered its compromise proposal for the assignment of railroad

129-31.
31. Sun, *Chinese Railways,* 152.
32. FO 405/198/144.
33. Sun, *Chinese Railways,* 151-52; Croly, *Straight,* 303; DS 5315/530-33. The department wanted to keep the negotiations secret, but they leaked out through an indiscretion in Peking. Innes to Bryce, October 19, 1909, James Bryce Papers.
34. DS 5315/492-93, 581; Croly, *Straight,* 305.

mileage. Huntington-Wilson urged the British to accept, and he instructed Reid to emphasize at the Foreign Office the same point made to Mitchell Innes in Washington—the strong desire of the United States to wind up the Hukuang imbroglio in order not to affect adversely the success of Chin-Ai, which was "far more important" than the loan. Besides pressing for a quick solution to the current disagreement, the Americans also requested British backing for the new project.[35]

Lord ffrench's assurances to Straight that a strong American stand would be certain to command British support for Chin-Ai proved to be totally inaccurate. Huntington-Wilson's explanation that the intent behind the proposal to win British support was to divide the profits between England and the United States, with a small slice for Russia, made Innes suspicious. "I can't help wondering," he wrote Bryce, "whether the United States would not be glad to drive a wedge between us and Japan." An Anglo-American railroad enterprise in Manchuria, with Russia taking a minimal share, would be most effective.[36]

In any case, Grey did not intend to change his stand. He instructed Jordan to make his position clear if the Japanese raised the issue: He was maintaining his earlier stance; the British Foreign Office had had nothing to do with the Chin-Ai contract.[37] As he said to Reid, he knew that the Japanese would object to the proposed Tsitsihar railway as tending to divert traffic from the S.M.R. to the Trans-Siberian. Earlier, when Grey had told the Japanese that they could not expect on this ground to stop all railroad development in Manchuria, they had replied they had no desire to do so. Their view was that they should be compensated for the loss of through business by being allowed to participate in the proposed new line. Having thus intimated that the Japanese could be bought off, Grey asked if Knox intended to approve such participation; if approved, what did he consider a "fair share"?[38]

Jordan was unsympathetic to the Japanese, who seemed to him to be stretching their claims to the limit. Nevertheless, he resigned himself to Grey's policy. "But of course we must, I suppose, make some sacrifice of economic interests to political friendship." Yet he did not think the Chin-Ai had a promising future.

35. DS 5315/551A; Innes to Bryce, October 19, 1909, Bryce Papers.
36. Bryce Papers; DS 5767/110-11.
37. Grey to Jordan, October 6, 1909, FO 405/198/155.
38. DS 5315/559.

Even if Britain—and the United States as well—backed Japan's request for participation, Jordan thought the success of the project doubtful, since it was essentially a political rather than an economic undertaking. In Chinese eyes the *raison d'être* of railroads in Manchuria was to limit Japanese expansion, and at the moment anti-Japanese feeling was running high in China.[39] To construct a railroad for these purposes and in the existing political climate seemed to him to be folly.

Knox, however, welcomed Grey's inquiry, for the Secretary had been at his home at Valley Forge, considering this very question of multinational participation in Chinese economic affairs.[40] He concluded that the aim of American policy was to secure the sympathetic and practical cooperation of the Great Powers in maintaining the political integrity of China by making it profitable for them to support such a policy. Knox believed that where nations invested their capital, there they would be intent on preserving peace and promoting the development of the natural resources and the prosperity of the people.[41]

About a week after receiving Grey's inquiry, Knox submitted to Henry P. Davison of the American Group his plan for promoting international financial cooperation and for preserving Chinese integrity where it was most threatened. It was his famous scheme for the neutralization of Manchurian railroads. Without hinting at the nature of the plan, Taft confided to Bernstorff in mid-November that Knox would soon submit to the Powers a proposal aimed at bringing the Open Door policy closer to realization.[42]

The Secretary's neutralization scheme proposed that all Powers who were parties to the Open Door agreement should lend China the money to buy the C.E.R. and the S.M.R. and to build the Tsitsihar line. Although conceding that his plan was somewhat visionary, Knox believed that it could be carried through and would result in a permanent settlement of the Manchurian question. With its adoption China would own the railroads, and all the Powers would be involved in their financing. Knox argued that China would welcome the idea and that Japan would have to bow to it.[43] Later, Knox included an additional advantage: Neutraliza-

39. Jordan Papers.
40. Knox to Hoyt, October 8, 1909, Knox Papers.
41. DS 893.51/288.
42. Davison to Straight, November 6, 1909, Straight Papers; *GP,* 32, No. 11668, 67-68.
43. Davison to Straight, November 6, 1909, Straight Papers.

tion of the railroads would in effect establish a buffer state between Russia and Japan and preclude the possibility of a conflict
between them.[44]

Knox did not pull these ideas out of thin air. Willard Straight,
too, had reached the conclusion that some measure of financial
cooperation among the Great Powers must replace the scramble
for concessions. Further, Straight claimed direct authorship of
the neutralization scheme, noting that he had outlined the same
idea in a memorandum of November 1908, written for Jacob
Schiff, the financier, in connection with the possibility that
Russia could be persuaded to sell the C.E.R.[45] The concept of international control, however, had been suggested earlier by others.
On March 31, 1905, Conger wrote Hay apropos of the settlement
that would be made after the end of the Russo-Japanese War: "If
it were possible in the adjustment to induce or require Japan to
transfer this [South Manchuria] railway to the Chinese government under some international guarantee of payment and protection, a most formidable barrier, impassable to either Russians and
[*sic*] Japanese, might be created, permanent peace be established
between them and an open door assured to the trade and commerce of the rest of the world."[46]

Just a year later Huntington-Wilson wrote to Root from Japan
that the military leaders expected Russia to launch a war of re-
venge against Japan. In preparing for it they wanted to exclude
all foreigners from Manchuria and have a free hand there themselves. "They do not seem to . . . realize that vested foreign interests in Manchuria, especially American and British, would
probably go far as a buffer against aggression from the north."[47]

Although the bankers would have preferred to work out the
financial arrangements for neutralization before any political
steps were taken and they regarded any diplomatic move now as
premature, they did not try to interfere with the department's
action. On November 6 Knox answered Grey's inquiry about Japanese participation in the Chin-Ai project. Now that China had
signed and ratified the Anglo-American Chin-Ai concession by an
unpublished imperial decree, the United States was prepared,

44. Rosen to Izvolsky, December 28, 1909, Baron von Siebert, ed., *Graf Benckendorffs diplomatischer Schriftwechsel,* I, 208; *GP,* 32, No. 11670, 72.
45. Croly, *Straight,* 320.
46. Quoted in A. Vagts, *Deutschland und die Vereinigten Staaten in der Weltpolitik,* II, 1245.
47. Huntington-Wilson to Root, March 15, 1906; quoted in Vagts, *Deutschland,*
1242-43.

Knox informed Grey, to cooperate with Britain in support of that project.[48] Subject to Chinese approval, the United States was disposed to include all interested Powers who supported the Open Door and Chinese territorial integrity. But Knox asked Grey to consider first two alternative and more comprehensive proposals. The first, the neutralization plan, would obviously benefit Japan and Russia, for it would permit them to shift their responsibilities and expenses to the combined Powers. If neutralization turned out to be unfeasible, however, Knox had another suggestion that would do much to ensure Chinese control over Manchuria. England and the United States should invite the interested Powers to share in the financing and construction of the Chin-Ai line, plus all railroads built in the future. The participating countries would also lend China the money to buy any existing railroads that might be offered for inclusion in the Chin-Ai system.[49]

As Secretary Knox noted in his memorandum to Foreign Minister Grey on November 6, neutralization required the cooperation of the five Powers most vitally concerned. He expected China to welcome this cooperation, ignoring the fact that the same arguments that militated against Chin-Ai were also valid for his more sweeping proposals. Too, he assumed British support, apparently oblivious to the reality that the international situation on the Continent was forcing Britain to put her political interests in Europe ahead of her economic interests in the Far East. But his cardinal mistake was in thinking Russia would consent to join the other Powers, for he was counting on Russia's participation to force Japan's acquiescence. There were, in truth, a few signals that encouraged his belief that Russia might cooperate. The C.E.R. was known to be a financial liability, and the Russians had already demonstrated their willingness to sell it. But Russia's attitude toward Far Eastern matters hinged on her relations with Japan, and it was in his judgment of those relations that the Secretary erred. Accepting the signs of Russo-Japanese hostility, he ignored the indicators pointing to a *rapprochement.*

Opposition to the 1907 agreement existed in both countries but

48. Davison to Straight, November 6, 1909, Straight Papers; memorandum of conversation with Straight, FO 800/248, June 26, 1910. To say that China had signed and ratified the contract by an unpublished decree was disingenuous. Both Frederick D. Cloud, consul general in Mukden, and Henry Fletcher had made the project's status clear. Before the contract became binding another imperial decree ratifying the action of the Manchurian authorities was required. DS 5315/581; *FR, 1910,* 232.
49. *FR, 1910,* 234-35.

was much stronger in Russia, especially in certain military circles and in some sections of the press and public opinion.[50] By early 1909 this opposition had become more vocal, and the Sino-Japanese agreements in August and September fed its fears and suspicions. *Novoe Vremya,* a leading St. Petersburg newspaper, suggested an informal arrangement between the United States and Russia to check Japanese ambitions.[51] Russian officials also brought up the subject with Rockhill, recently transferred from Peking.[52] It was against this background of undoubtedly genuine and often publicly expressed fear and suspicion of Japan that the United States approached Russia with the neutralization scheme.

On November 6, 1909, Foreign Minister Alexander Izvolsky told Rockhill that Russian policy aimed at restraining Japanese ambitions in Manchuria. However, Russia, vulnerable to attack by Japan, could not afford to confront her openly while the other Powers tacitly acquiesced in her advances. Without protest from any of the Powers, Izvolsky declared, Japan had forced from China the most humiliating and excessive concessions under the September agreements.[53] And certainly from a strategic point of view, Russia might well be concerned. The Antung-Mukden line would link the Korean and south Manchurian railroad systems. The Changchun-Kirin extension, obviously of little commercial value, would reach into northeast Korea to connect with a projected Korean line. When completed, it would permit Japan on short notice to throw large numbers of troops into north Manchuria. The trans-Manchurian branch of the C.E.R. lay only a short distance north of the Kirin extension; by stationing forces athwart that railroad, Japan could cut off the southern Ussuri regions from Harbin.[54]

Izvolsky had another grievance: the agreements concerning Harbin. He indignantly pointed out to Rockhill that no one had objected to the regulations issued by the South Manchuria Railway Company, which had staked out a much greater claim to

50. E. B. Price, *The Russo-Japanese Treaties of 1907-1916 Concerning Manchuria and Mongolia,* 29.
51. DS 8594/3.
52. Rockhill to Knox, October 2, 1909, DS 8594/4. French Ambassador Louis emphasized to Pichon his belief that the Russian Government was uneasy over Japanese intentions. *Documents diplomatiques français, 1871-1914,* Series 2, 12, 497-98; hereafter cited as *DDF.*
53. DS 4002/255.
54. W.H.S., Memorandum on Manchuria, December 31, 1910, FO 405/196.

political predominance than did the Russian proposals for Harbin. Yet the Powers were opposing the Russian plans.[55] There was much truth in Izvolsky's charges about Harbin, and, since it was a point on which he seemed genuinely bitter—he referred to it frequently as an indication of the United States' hostile feeling toward Russia—a short examination of the dispute here will help to clarify the Russian attitude.

In December 1907 the Chinese Eastern Railway Company began trying to enforce new regulations for the municipal administration of Harbin, maintaining that under the Sino-Russian Treaty of 1896 the railroad company had received the right to govern the settlements along the railroad. The Russians wanted to establish a municipal council with jurisdiction over all residents, regardless of nationality, not only in ordinary municipal affairs but also with regard to taxation and police. They argued that the administrative changes were necessary to provide the law and order the Chinese had failed to maintain. On February 4, 1908, the Russians asked the Powers to support their plan, noting that the Japanese had already given their approval.[56]

The United States refused. The essence of its position was that the 1896 agreement did not give any private corporation the power to exercise extraterritorial jurisdiction and that no agreement between China and a railroad company could deprive Americans of their treaty rights. Municipal ordinances, therefore, needed the approval of the United States Government before they could be enforced against Americans. At the time, Huntington-Wilson described the plan as a project for making the ordinary control of railroad property into a political administration, which was a point-blank infringement of China's territorial and political integrity and thus an interference in the Powers' treaty rights. Both Henry Fletcher and William Phillips warned that, if Russia succeeded, Japan would ask for the same privileges in south Manchuria.[57] The American-Russian controversy over Harbin dragged on until May 10, 1909, when Russia and China signed a preliminary agreement regulating their differences. They also exchanged notes in which Russia recognized China's complete sovereignty and the treaty rights of the other Powers in the railway zone. Still maintaining that the arrangement infringed its

55. Rockhill to Knox, November 6, 1909, DS 4002/255.
56. DS 4002/2-10.
57. DS 4002/2, 36-42.

nationals' rights, the United States refused to recognize it as binding.[58]

State Department officials labored under the misapprehension that Japan would defer the establishment of administrative systems in her railroad areas pending definition of the Russian position. As a matter of fact, Japan's domination over southern Manchuria had been officially established under regulations for the administration of Japanese railroad settlements promulgated in August 1906 and February 1907, which boldly proclaimed the omnipotence of the railroad administration. Without any reference to China they conferred wide powers of enforcement on the Japanese railway authorities, including arbitrary taxation and forcible expulsion regardless of nationality. Japanese administration of southern Manchuria was as definitely, if not so elaborately, organized as Russia's proposals for her jurisdiction at Harbin. The Japanese ordinances recognized neither China's sovereign rights, nor Chinese participation in matters concerning her own subjects, nor the rights of subjects of the treaty Powers. While negotiating the September agreements, China made an effort to get from Japan an admission of her sovereignty over Manchuria similar to that in the May agreement with Russia, but she failed completely. The Japanese arrangements attracted little attention because their railroad settlements were much smaller and did not affect foreign interests to the same degree as the Russian. In August 1909, for example, the British consul general in Mukden reported that, so far as he knew, no European or American had ever lived in Japanese railroad territory.[59]

The State Department would not admit the Russian contention, insisting that the S.M.R. was practically a government enterprise and therefore subject to different regulation that the C.E.R. Moreover, there was no evidence that the C.E.R. had been allowed to exercise any political rights or that any American had ever registered complaints of this nature.[60] Fletcher deflated this argument by reminding the department that, since there were few if any Europeans in the Japanese settlements, they attracted little attention, and the question of taxation, for example, was therefore never raised, as in the case of Harbin.[61] Such was the background for Izvolsky's complaints.

58. *FR, 1910,* 209-13; DS 4002/185.
59. Sun, *Chinese Railways,* 145; FO 405/191/54, 75; London *Times,* November 9, 1909.
60. *FR, 1910,* 227-28; DS 4002/257.
61. DS 4002/256.

After the Foreign Minister had aired his irritation over the United States' failure to support his country's demands at Harbin, he added that it was now too late for the United States to make proposals for settling the issue. The Japanese Government had already suggested an understanding on Far Eastern matters. With the Harbin problem still unsettled, Izvolsky could not put off the Japanese, although, he confided, the conclusion of such an arrangement was contrary to his Manchurian policy.[62]

The interview was an exercise in diplomacy. Izvolsky, who did not believe that Japan wanted war, favored a *détente* with that country in order to strengthen Russia's position in the West.[63] At the moment he did not possess sufficient influence to impose this policy on his own government, but he was only waiting for changes in circumstances and public opinion to give him the opening he needed.[64] Knox, however, interpreted Rockhill's report of the interview as confirmation that the threat of Japanese aggression would be a strong motive for Russian acceptance of the neutralization plan. Telling Rockhill that this was "a rare moment" to further American policies, Knox instructed him to advance the ideas in the neutralization memorandum as if they were his own and to encourage Russian cooperation in the plan. Neutralization, Knox observed, would provide Russia with a dignified means of escape from the acute situation likely to confront her again in Manchuria. Rockhill was also to try to forestall any arrangement between Russia and Japan contrary to the spirit of the project.[65] A week later, Rockhill, who regarded the neutralization plan as "a good scheme if it can be carried through," explained it to Izvolsky. Rockhill got the impression that the Foreign Minister liked it in principle. Izvolsky agreed that the plan had many advantages, although he added that he needed to study carefully its effect on the economic, political, and especially the military interests of Russia.[66]

Rockhill believed that he could strengthen the American argument for neutralization by telling the Russians about the Chin-Ai contract, but Knox refused him permission to divulge this information until the British had replied to the note of November 6. At the end of the month the Secretary got his answer. The general principle of the neutralization plan "entirely commends" itself to

62. Rockhill to Knox, November 6, 1909; DS 4002/255.
63. DS 19038/7.
64. *DDF,* Ser. 2, 12, 558-60.
65. Knox to Rockhill, November 9, 1909, DS 5315/574A.
66. DS 5315/584.

His Majesty's Government, wrote Grey. Yet he thought it advisable to defer consideration of any further loans to China until the Hukuang business was settled. As for the alternative, Grey expressed pleasure that it called for cooperation among the interested Powers. He suggested as a preliminary step that the United States and England work together to persuade China to admit Japanese participation in the Chin-Ai railroad, since Japan was the most interested party.[67]

The Americans were not eager at the moment to press forward with Chin-Ai, nor did the Chinese show any desire to conclude the contract.[68] The Japanese had notified the Chinese Foreign Office that they expected China to keep them informed, "as they might be obliged to oppose the railway if the agreement were concluded without their being consulted."[69] On November 24 the three Chinese ministries that were considering the proposal memorialized the Throne against it. After Hsi-liang, viceroy of Manchuria, restated the political arguments in favor of construction, however, the Throne again referred the question to the ministries.[70]

The department at first concurred with the British that it would be inexpedient to broach the neutralization scheme until the bankers had agreed on the Hukuang contract. But negotiations during the first two weeks in December showed no signs of producing a speedy settlement. Fearing that continued publicity about the Chin-Ai loan might prejudice the Chinese against neutralization, the department decided to acquaint all the interested governments with the neutralization plan and its alternative. The instructions to this effect, issued on December 14, also made the point that the British had approved the general principle involved.[71] In St. Petersburg Rockhill, assuming that the prohibition against disclosure of the Chin-Ai project was still in force, presented only the neutralization scheme to Izvolsky.[72]

Despite the fact that the department was acting ahead of schedule, the timing seemed opportune. In Russia the scare of war with Japan had reached such proportions that the government felt impelled to issue an official and categorical denial of the rumors

67. *FR, 1910*, 235-36.
68. Jordan to Grey, November 30, 1909, FO 405/198/232.
69. FO 405/196.
70. Sun, *Chinese Railways*, 153-54.
71. *FR, 1910*, 236.
72. *FR, 1910*, 238-40; DS 5315/652.

of an impending break between the two nations.[73] The most important and insistent source of these rumors was the extreme right, which opposed Izvolsky's Far Eastern policy.[74] The Foreign Minister, convinced of Japan's desire for peace, was so disturbed by the agitation that he asked the British if some steps might be taken in London and possibly in Tokyo that would quiet the alarm in Russia.[75] The Japanese promptly gave assurances in London that there was no danger of a Far Eastern war, the Japanese ambassador pointing out to Grey that such rumors had received credence only in Russia. Grey too had the impression that they had been circulated by opponents of Izvolsky's policy.[76]

Knox, unaware that the furor stemmed in large measure from an internal Russian quarrel, explained to Baron Rosen, the Russian ambassador, that the United States' plan had three objectives: the neutralization of Manchuria under the control of the Great Powers, the safeguarding of China's rights in Manchuria, and the establishment of a buffer state between Russia and Japan.[77]

The reaction of the concerned governments to Knox's proposal ranged from coolness to hostility. In Berlin, the only capital not diplomatically involved in the Far East, Chancellor Theobald von Bethmann-Hollweg advised the Emperor that Germany should follow England's example of agreeing to the neutralization scheme in principle. Although it would be advantageous to have Russia entangled in the Far East, Bethmann-Hollweg saw little possibility of this eventuality. Rather, he viewed Manchuria as a subject on which Russia and Japan could completely agree, even to the point of an entente; if that entente developed, the Powers would have no trouble dealing with a weak China. Therefore, from the political point of view, Germany should welcome neutralization for, if Russia and Japan knew that the United States and particularly England would oppose their plans, they might act with restraint. From a commercial point of view, the Chancellor asserted, the scheme deserved an even warmer welcome. Since Germany and the United States were the only Powers whole-heartedly in favor on the Open Door and the preservation of China's sovereignty and integrity, they should therefore work

73. Schuyler to Knox, December 15, 1909, DS 8594/5.
74. Louis to Pichon, December 23, 1909, *DDF,* Ser. 2, 12, 558-60.
75. *BD,* VIII, 475.
76. *BD,* VIII, 473-75; Siebert, Benckendorff, I, 190-91.
77. Rosen to Izvolsky, December 28, 1909, *GP,* No. 7, 10-11.

together. Bethmann-Hollweg had grave doubts that either Japan or Russia would agree to neutralization, but since England had done so in principle, Germany must do the same. Further, Taft had expressed his desire to work as closely as possible with Germany on Chinese questions. If Germany did not now demonstrate her willingness to cooperate, she would drive the United States into England's arms. With this reasoning the Kaiser agreed.[78]

China indicated her willingness to approve the neutralization scheme in principle but wanted more time to study the Chin-Ai project.[79] When Fletcher and Jordan called at the Foreign Office on New Year's Eve, Liang informed them that China intended to proceed with the plans for Chin-Ai, but that there remained some details that required clarification. China had not yet decided whether other Powers should participate. Russia and Japan might be allowed to join if they accepted neutralization or yielded some *quid pro quo* in Manchuria.[80]

From Paris came word that, since the issues raised by the United States concerned primarily Japan and Russia, France's position would probably depend on Russia's decision.[81] The Japanese and Russian foreign offices waited for over a month to send their replies, and at first Thomas J. O'Brien was, at least officially, quite optimistic about the Japanese reaction.[82] Either he had not gauged the situation accurately or preferred to report what Washington wanted to hear, for Komura's immediate comment was the epitome of offended pride: "They are asking us to internationalize what is our own property, acquired by us at the cost of much treasure and many lives." On December 23 Kato told Grey that his government could not accept the proposal for neutralization. It would be quite contrary to the position that Japan had secured under the Treaty of Portsmouth.[83] On January 8 O'Brien informed Washington that Japan would decline to participate.[84]

Izvolsky, on the other hand, paid scant attention to neutralization; he was incensed over the plans for the Chin-Ai line, espe-

78. December 23, 1909, *GP,* 32, No. 11668, 65-68. The Kaiser must in fact have provided the department with one of its few cheerful moments by referring enthusiastically to the "real statesmanship" displayed by the Americans. Hill to Knox, January 3, 1910, Knox Papers.
79. Sun, *Chinese Railways,* 154; *FR, 1910,* 240.
80. FO 405/196.
81. Bacon to Knox, January 7, 1910, DS 5315/674.
82. *GP,* 32, No. 11670; No. 11690, 97-98.
83. FO 405/198/259, 266; FO 405/196.
84. *FR, 1910,* 245.

cially because Russia had not been informed about the negotiations at the same time as the other Powers.[85] Izvolsky maintained
that because the railroad so vitally affected Russia, economically
and strategically, the United States should have consulted Russia
even before signing the contract. The whole plan, added to the
Americans' attitude on Harbin, he told Rockhill, demonstrated
their hostility toward Russia.[86] When Rockhill mentioned that
Britain would support the project diplomatically, Izvolsky remarked that there were existing agreements that would have to
be considered. He was referring to the Scott-Muraviev agreements of 1899 by which the British bound themselves not to seek
railroad concessions north of the Chinese Wall or to obstruct Russian efforts to do so; the Russians had promised the same with
regard to British enterprises in the Yangtze Valley. Izvolsky now
charged that the United States had ulterior political motives; otherwise why would it give diplomatic support to a railroad of
which a considerable part—from Tsitsihar to Aigun—had no
value other than strategic? To Izvolsky the Chin-Ai line was not
only a vehicle for Chinese aggression; it also opened up for Japan
a third line of attack against Russia's exposed flank. He never
referred to British support for the proposal. "For him, it is a
purely American scheme, and conceived in no spirit of friendliness to Russia."[87]

Later, in March 1911—that is, after the signing of the Russo-
Japanese accord—Kokovstov spelled out for ffrench the precise
reason for Russia's opposition to the Chin-Ai project. In the event
of another Russo-Japanese war Chinchow, a port on the Gulf of
Pechili, would be vulnerable to capture by the Japanese. From
this strategically advantageous position Japan could throw troops
along the railroad to Tsitsihar, cutting the Chinese Eastern and
thus isolating Harbin and Vladivostok. What was the use of building railroads in southern Manchuria anyway, Kokovtsov asked,
when the area was destined inevitably to fall to Japan?[88]

Izvolsky was not taking any chances on the British defecting to
the support of the other Powers. On December 28 the Russian
Government sent a formal reminder that it considered the Scott-

85. Nicolson to Grey, December 25 and 27, 1909, FO 405/202/7-8; Siebert, *Benckendorff*, I, 219-22. Fletcher had kept the Russian minister in Peking quite well informed of the Chin-Ai negotiations. Müller to Campbell, February 13, 1910, FO
800/245.
86. Rockhill to Knox, December 21, 1909, DS 4002/270; FO 405/196.
87. Rockhill to Knox, January 20, 1910, DS 5315/731.
88. Buchanan to Grey, April 5, 1911, FO 405/204/191.

Muraviev notes of April 1899 still binding.[89] Sir Arthur Nicolson, the British ambassador in St. Petersburg, stressed in his report to Grey the importance that Izvolsky attached to the Chin-Ai project and his deep suspicion of it, which the invitation for Japanese participation had greatly increased.[90]

When the American press broke the story about neutralization on the basis of telegrams from St. Petersburg, the Department of State decided to make public the general outlines of the plan. In an interview on January 6, 1910, Knox briefly reviewed his China policy. He defended his vigorous demand for participation in the Hukuang loan as essential if the United States were to have the necessary influence in China to support urgent fiscal and administrative reforms. But there were stronger and broader grounds for participation: "The [neutralization] proposition . . . discloses the end towards which American policy in the Far East has been recently directed." This end was cooperation among the Powers—the best way to maintain the Open Door and Chinese rights in Manchuria. The Secretary spoke optimistically about the prospects of the plan. Great Britain, Germany, and China had "cordially" approved it, and France had signified her acceptance. It would be advantageous to the two remaining Powers to do likewise but, he conceded, "the hitch, if any is to come will be with Russia or Japan, or both."[91]

Reaction to the plan in the American press was cool. According to the *New York Tribune,* most observers felt that neutralization was impracticable because Japan would not receive a benefit proportionate to the sacrifice entailed. The Japanese press confirmed this impression; for example, *Kokumin Shimbun,* the semiofficial Japanese newspaper, asked France and Germany if they would be willing to neutralize the Shantung and Yunan provinces.[92]

Initially, the department had put no pressure on China to ratify Straight's contract for Chin-Ai, made in October.[93] Now, convinced that formal approval would strengthen the broader Manchurian proposals, it urged China to act.[94] Fletcher got no help from Jordan in his task, for Grey had instructed the British Minis-

89. FO 405/198/277.
90. Nicolson to Grey, December 31, 1909, FO 405/198/284.
91. *New York Times,* January 7, 1910.
92. *New York Tribune,* January 9, 1910.
93. Jordan to Grey, November 30, 1909, FO 405/198/232.
94. *FR, 1910,* 245.

ter to take no further steps until the Foreign Office learned the attitude of Russia and Japan toward the Chin-Ai line.[95] Liang temporized: China wanted to reserve her decision on that project until she saw what happened to the neutralization proposal. Although Japan had now informed China that she did not object in principle to Chin-Ai and was willing to participate in the neutralization plan, Fletcher did not at first succeed in winning approval from the Chinese.[96] But suddenly the mood in Peking changed. On the fourteenth of January Fletcher called again on Liang and read him a paraphrase of his latest instruction. Not only did Liang now change his mind on ratification; the presidents of the two other ministries involved also agreed to approve the project, with reservations on objectionable provisions.[97]

Very shortly the Chinese Foreign Office, the Board of Finance, and the Board of Posts recommended ratification, with reservations, of the preliminary contract for the Chin-Ai line, proposed on October 2. On January 20 the Throne officially gave its approval.[98] Liang informed Ijuin that, since he had expressed the wish to be consulted on the Chin-Ai agreement, Liang wanted to notify him that China had decided to approve the preliminary contract with the Americans.[99]

China's action preceded by one day the delivery of the Russian and Japanese replies to the Knox plan. On December 18—three days before Rockhill gave the complete American proposal to the Russians—Izvolsky and the Japanese ambassador in St. Petersburg agreed that their two governments should consult before answering the United States. By January 18 each had approved the other's reply.[100] Both rejected the neutralization scheme and its alternative; neither was definite on the Chin-Ai project alone.

The Russian Government blandly remarked that at the moment nothing seemed to be threatening the Open Door and Chinese sovereignty in Manchuria and that consequently it saw no need to consider the questions addressed to it by the United States. As for neutralization, since this would seriously affect very important Russian interests, public and private, Russia could not ap-

95. Grey to Jordan, January 11, 1910, FO 405/202/87.
96. Fletcher to Knox, January 10, 1910, DS 5315/773.
97. DS 893.77/800. Later, ffrench wrote that the central government kept stalling on the edict until Fletcher "practically assured the Chinese government that America would see them through in the matter." DS 893.77/1056.
98. *FR, 1910*, 246.
99. Fletcher to Knox, January 24, 1910, DS 893.77/840.
100. Siebert, *Benckendorff*, I, 219-22.

prove it. The Russians reserved their decision on Chin-Ai but expressed readiness, in principle, to study the question whenever the United States furnished more information.[101] For their part, the Japanese stood on their rights as granted under the Treaty of Portsmouth. In their view, conditions in Manchuria were not so exceptional as to require a system different from that existing in the rest of China. The objections to the neutralization scheme applied equally to the second alternative. As for Chin-Ai, since this project was not germane to the subject of Knox's note, the Japanese merely indicated that they were willing to participate.[102]

Almost simultaneously with its note to the United States, Japan authorized the South Manchurian Railway Company to float a loan for the development of the Antung-Mukden line and the improvement of shipping facilities at Port Arthur. This step, occurring at this moment, might have been mere coincidence, but circumstances made it seem significant in Japanese-American relations.[103] In the Diet on February 1, Komura "had no hesitation in making known his expansion policy." As a result of the war, he told the legislators, Japan had become a continental Power. If it wished to expand its influence in the face of the more populous nations around it—China, Russia, and America—its population must not only increase but must be concentrated. Therefore, the Japanese Government intended in the future to channel emigration to Manchuria and Korea.[104]

The rejections of its proposals in the Far East brought further criticism of the State Department from the domestic press, this time involving not only its policy but also its diplomacy. The *New York Journal of Commerce* expressed the general reaction: "The definite declination by Japan of the American proposal . . . suggests the question why Secretary Knox published his plan to the world without first consulting the two powers whose adhesion to it was absolutely essential."[105]

In diplomatic circles Knox and his scheme took a sound drubbing. The diplomatic corps was astonished by the plan, which Jordan described as "a scheme so vast and fantastic as almost to

101. Rockhill to Knox, January 22, 1910, *FR, 1910,* 248-50. The Russians made no distinction between the Chin-Ai project *per se* and Knox's second alternative to it.
102. *FR, 1910,* 250-52.
103. *New York Tribune,* January 23, 1910; MacDonald, Annual Report, Japan, 1910, FO 405/201.
104. O'Brien to Knox, February 10, 1910, DS 893.77/792.
105. *New York Journal of Commerce,* January 24, 1910, editorial.

stagger the imagination." It sounded as plausible in words as it would be impracticable in execution, a scheme of "grandiose simplicity."[106] From Tokyo MacDonald reported to Grey that the United States Government had "electrified" the Japanese with its neutralization note. The Ambassador could only register surprise that a proposal so obviously predoomed to failure could have been put forward.[107] The German ambassador in Tokyo, Baron Mumm, expressed himself as being unable to understand how the United States could defend the Monroe Doctrine with great energy, yet propose that Japan surrender her Manchurian railroads, which, along with Port Arthur and Korea, were the political and strategic pillars of her domination in northern China. In his opinion, the Americans were asking Japan to commit suicide.[108]

O'Brien put the department in an even worse light. Washington had sent him no background material to brief him on the reasoning behind the proposal; his only information, and Fletcher's as well, came from the dispatches. The proposal had aroused Japanese suspicions, and although O'Brien believed these would dissipate, he was aware that the Knox scheme had hurt the United States. "One would suppose," the Ambassador wrote Fletcher, "that the first move would have been to confer with Japan and then if proper with Russia, since these powers had the property to keep or to sell." O'Brien left no doubt what the result would have been: The first conference would have ended the plan, and no one need have been the wiser.[109]

Washington tried to cover up the extent of its defeat, the department making known that it regarded rejection of the neutralization plan as "closing the incident," but only temporarily. Moreover, it maintained that the Secretary of State had considerably strengthened the American position in the Far East for, by placing a disinterested proposal before the Powers, Knox had forced the two most interested to state their positions. Thus, the semiofficial position the department presented to the public became: Knox had wanted to elicit from Japan and Russia an exact statement of their present position with regard to the Open Door

106. Jordan, Annual Report, China, 1909, FO 405/195.
107. MacDonald, Annual Report, Japan, 1909, FO 405/195.
108. *GP,* 32, No. 11683, 84-88.
109. O'Brien to Fletcher, January 14, 1910, Henry Fletcher Papers. "Knox has managed to get his head punched in China . . . ," wrote Henry Adams. "He will have us in whole tubs of hot water if he keeps on another six months like the last, and he hasn't a man to depend on. . . ." Adams to Mrs. E. Cameron, January 24, 1910, Henry Adams Papers.

and to find out what their previous declarations in its favor were worth in a practical test, and he had succeeded.[110] Back in December, when he still believed that Russia would accept neutralization, Knox had told Bernstorff that the plan would smoke Japan out; she would have to avow her principles.[111] When the Kaiser asked, "With British smoke!?!" his question was to the point, and Britain's refusal to meet American expectations irritated the Taft Administration. The various countries' responses to the plan had clarified their policies in the Far East, and Knox expressed satisfaction for having achieved this end.

At first Knox and Taft had regarded the British answer of November 25 as promising some degree of support; only later did they realize that it was a rejection of their plan, at least until all opposition had been overcome.[112] Knox bitterly attributed the failure of his scheme to the untimely publicity it received in St. Petersburg and to the ill will it encountered in England.[113] After remarking that he would "so much" like to keep the door open, Taft added, "I wonder what England expects to get from Japan for helping them [sic]."[114] "Thoroughly disgusted" with Britain's attitude, Huntington-Wilson wanted to frighten the Foreign Office into cooperation. He recommended that Knox send for Bryce and talk to him in such terms that he would cable home the information that the Americans seemed to think that Britain was sacrificing everything to the Japanese alliance. The Ambassador should be given to understand that the British attitude was making Anglo-American cooperation difficult, in contrast with the attitude of Germany. The British attitude in this matter was tending to force Germany and the United States into special relations in the Far East.[115]

Straight, who had always been confident of British support, now began to change his mind. Although he admitted that the British position vis-à-vis Japan was delicate, he protested that, instead of trying to lead the Japanese along the right path, Britain seemed only to acquiesce in the dicta of the Japanese Foreign Office. Straight concluded that the Americans must rely wholly on their

110. *New York Times,* January 22, 1910; London *Times,* January 24, 1910.
111. *GP,* 32, No. 11670, 71.
112. *GP,* 32, No. 11681, 83.
113. Pichon Circular, November 18, 1910, *DDF,* Ser. 2, 13, 58-59.
114. Quoted in Bernstorff to Foreign Office, January 21, 1910, *GP,* 32, No. 11681, 83.
115. Huntington-Wilson to Knox, January 1910, Huntington-Wilson Papers. Knox did not follow this advice. In March Bryce reported to Grey that he had never discussed Chin-Ai with the department. Sir Edward Grey Papers.

own efforts with regard to Chin-Ai, using the Pauling interest to prevent Britain from going too far in her "Japomania."[116]

Certainly the British did not intend to help the United States carry through the neutralization scheme. To Bilby F. Alston, head of the Far Eastern Department of the Foreign Office, the reasons for American advancement of the plan were both "difficult to discern" and "not intelligible." That it was an impracticable financial scheme was of secondary importance. Its real significance was political; it was in fact a proposal to modify the Treaty of Portsmouth, a manner of procedure scarcely consistent with the traditions of diplomacy. By suggesting that neither Russia nor Japan was fulfilling its pledges under the treaty, the Americans appeared to be gratuitously interfering in a matter that primarily concerned Russia and Japan. Japan was absolutely within her rights in standing on the treaty, and Russia could hardly concur in a proposal to change it without appearing to want a resumption of hostilities. As for Britain, the Preamble to the Anglo-Japanese Treaty of 1905 pledged each signatory to respect the territorial rights and special interests of the other. Japanese possession of the S.M.R. would seem to be a special right in the sense of the treaty, and therefore Britain could not agree to the neutralization proposal without Japan's previous consent.[117] The truth of the matter was that a wide divergence of views existed between the State Department and the Foreign Office on the Manchurian situation. Knox believed that continued Russo-Japanese control of the C.E.R. and the S.M.R. would destroy the Open Door policy, thus violating the Treaty of Portsmouth. Grey thought the retention of leases that Russia and Japan had acquired before Portsmouth could hardly be construed as inconsistent with the Open Door. Before such a charge could be made, Russia and Japan would have to give preferential rates to their own nationals on Manchurian railroads.[118] In view of the reluctance of the Great Powers to complete the agreements basic to the neutralization scheme and the possibility of opposition from Russia and Japan, Knox ceased his active promotion of the plan and turned to other means for furthering U. S. aims in China.

116. Straight to Davison, January 12, 1910, DS 5315/763.
117. Alston, Memorandum Respecting the United States and the Far East, January 31, 1910, FO 405/196.
118. Grey to Bryce, February 10, 1910, FO 405/202/88.

11

The United States and the
Chinchow-Aigun Railroad

No amount of face-saving could hide the fact that neutralization was a lost cause; the department now fell back on the Chinchow-Aigun railroad as a vehicle for its policies in China. Japan had indicated that she was ready to participate in this project. True, when China ratified the preliminary agreement, Ijuin's government had instructed him to notify the Foreign Office that Japan must approve the detailed contract before final signature, since, by paralleling the S.M.R., the Chin-Ai line would vitally affect Japanese interests. Ignoring Japan's interests in the negotiations would cause serious trouble. Ijuin, however, softened the effect of this warning by explaining to Fletcher that Japan did not intend to oppose the railroad; she just wanted more information about it.[1]

The Russians, in their note of January 20, 1910, had promised to consider the project further, but Izvolsky's earlier remarks to Rockhill indicated that the United States could expect little encouragement from that quarter. On February 2 Russia echoed the Japanese caveat, pointing out that military considerations gave Russia a special interest in the Chin-Ai railroad. If China made any final decision without Russian approval, undesirable consequences might ensue.[2]

At the same time, Russia informed the United States that the American invitation to participate in the project and her own promise to examine the question on receipt of further details

1. *Foreign Relations, 1910,* 257; DS 893.77/891.
2. *FR, 1910,* 255-57.

committed the United States not to proceed without Russian consent. Russia therefore expected that the loan would not be concluded until she had a chance to express her views.[3] Nor were the Russians above using a little blackmail. On February 4 Nicolson telegraphed to his chief the gist of his conversation with Prime Minister P. A. Stolypin. The railroad would affect Russia's economic and strategic interests, the Prime Minister had declared, and he hinted that any British action supporting it would hurt the Anglo-Russian entente.[4] Grey immediately instructed Max Müller, the *chargé* in Peking: "Warn Chinese government of the impossibility of ignoring Russian and Japanese interests and arriving at final arrangement without consulting them." Müller followed this instruction on February 7.[5]

The British warning to China jolted Knox and angered him still further. He had finally grasped that Britain would not support the Americans' plans for the Chin-Ai line, but he believed that, had the English remained neutral, the Chin-Ai negotiations would have gone through. Now, however, the British had intervened actively to prohibit China from using Anglo-American capital to develop her own territory, for to the Chinese the word "warn" meant "prohibit" when the British used it.[6] Knox therefore instructed Reid to get an explanation of the change in Britain's attitude. Reid was also to find out as definitely as possible what the British intended to do with regard to the project and Russian demands for consultation. The United States favored ultimate participation by Russia and other interested Powers, but, since such participation was provided for in the agreement itself, there seemed no reason to stop the present negotiations.[7] Reid should discuss the matter plainly with the Foreign Office but without giving the impression that the United States was more concerned than Great Britain. Knox concluded, "You need not conceal my surprise that Great Britain has taken the action reported at Pe-

3. *Novoe Vremya* reflected another angle of the Chin-Ai affair by noting that consent would not be given until the Americans stopped meddling in Harbin. DS 893.77/818.
4. FO 405/202/92.
5. FO 405/202/80; *FR, 1910*, 257; DS 5315/776. On February 18 the French Minister in Peking advised the Chinese Foreign Office not to conclude any arrangement without previous agreement with Russia and Japan. Enclosed in Fletcher to Knox, April 13, 1910, DS 893.77/930.
6. Innes to Grey, November 11, 1910, FO 405/200/152.
7. The United States of course denied that by inviting Russian cooperation it had in any way bound itself not to take any steps in regard to the proposed railroad without consulting Russia. *FR, 1910*, 260.

king without previous deliberate consultation with the United States upon this joint project."[8]

To Reid, Grey expressed regret at not having forewarned the United States of the action contemplated at Peking—Britain had merely applied to Russia the policy she had followed toward Japan, of which the Americans had been advised at the outset. Repeating his conviction that the Tsitsihar line did indeed interfere with the S.M.R., the Foreign Minister added that the Japanese had grounds for asking compensation. In Russia's case the English had thought themselves warranted in assuming that the 1899 agreement had lapsed by mutual consent because of the Russian request for participation in the Hukuang loan.[9] Thus, Grey confided to Reid, he had been rather taken by surprise when the Russians, on the basis of that agreement, objected to the Chin-Ai line. They maintained that there was a marked difference between the Aigun project and the Yangtze development, and Grey confessed himself that the Russian view had some merit.[10]

Grey also refuted the charge that Britain had told China she could not construct a railroad on her own territory without consulting Russia and Japan. He had intended only to make clear to the Chinese Government that, if it pressed on with Chin-Ai without any regard for Russian or Japanese interests, those two countries would certainly oppose the railroad. China could not expect British support against their protests. Britain was still favorable to the Chin-Ai project in principle but "could not take any action in support of it until the Japanese and Russian interests had been taken into consideration."[11]

The Chinese had made informal inquiries of Russia and Japan about the terms for their participation but had received no answer. After the British warning Liang told Müller that China was anxious to receive suggestions from Russia and Japan, and he asked if Britain could expedite them.[12] Shortly thereafter Japan indicated her terms for support of the Chin-Ai project: participation in financing and providing materials and engineers; construction of a branch line connecting Chin-Ai to the S.M.R.[13] Thus, as Sun points out, Japan was trying in effect to make the Chin-Ai railroad a part of the Japanese rail system.[14]

8. Knox to Reid, February 8, 1910, DS 5315/754A.
9. Whitelaw Reid Papers.
10. Reid Papers; Reid to Knox, February 16 and 18, 1910, DS 5315/776.
11. Grey to Reid, February 19, 1910, DS 893.77/819.
12. London *Times*, February 11, 1910; FO 405/202/83.
13. FO 405/202/90; DS 5315/762, 772.
14. E-tu Sun, *Chinese Railways and British Interests, 1898-1911*, 161.

Knox, pleased with this sign of cooperation, welcomed the Japanese conditions. He told Baron Yasuya Uchida, the Japanese ambassador in Washington, that the United States favored connecting the two railroads, since the resulting economic development of Manchuria would benefit everyone.[15]

Russia, however, refused to join in this international enterprise, flatly rejecting Chin-Ai as exceedingly injurious to her interests, both economic (Chinchow to Tsitsihar) and strategic (Tsitsihar to Aigun). In 1899 China had promised that if she needed foreign capital to build railroads north and northeast of Peking, she would not give the contract to any country other than Russia. Russia would overlook this pledge only if a projected railroad would not threaten her interests. A satisfactory alternative and one that promised to be profitable for the investing capitalists would be a line through Mongolia from Kalgan via Urga to Kiakhta on the Russian frontier, with Russia controlling the Urga-Kiakhta section.[16] Rockhill appealed in vain to the Minister of Finance, whom Washington had always considered the Russian official most sympathetic to American objectives. Kokovtsov showed a solid front with Izvolsky, however, and Rockhill did not believe it possible to change his mind.[17]

Knox was now in an awkward position. Since China had ratified the preliminary contract for the Chin-Ai line, he felt that the project was secure. If Britain withdrew completely, however, he would need to consider whether he too should abandon Chin-Ai or whether he should continue with the help of others—specifically, the Germans.[18] The Secretary now tried to find some common

15. *JFO*, Tele Series, Reel 123. In this same conversation Knox tried to impress on Uchida the great benefits Japan would derive from neutralization—more, in fact, than any other country. Uchida informed his chief that he had made the proper expressions of gratitude in reply.

16. *FR, 1910*, 261-62.

17. Rockhill to Knox, March 5, 1910, DS 893.77/24-25. The American Associated Press correspondent in St. Petersburg had reported an interview with Kokovtsov in December 1909 that seemed to indicate that the Finance Minister was willing to compromise on Harbin and even sell the Chinese Eastern. Izvolsky, however, told Nicolson that the correspondent had entirely misunderstood Kokovtsov's remarks and greatly exaggerated them. There was no question of parting with the railroad, and the Harbin question remained unchanged. Nicolson to Grey, December 29, 1909, FO 405/202/9.

18. Bernstorff to Schoen, recvd. March 4, 1910, *GP*, 32, No. 11692, 99-100. Schoen instructed Bernstorff to avoid any act that might encourage Knox to try to involve Germany in Chin-Ai against the other Powers. *GP*, 32, No. 11693, 100. The documents in *GP*, 32, Chapter CCL demonstrate the Germans' anxiety lest Knox make a specific proposal for German-American cooperation in Far Eastern affairs. Such a proposal the Germans were prepared to reject tactfully; they could afford neither to accept it nor to alienate the United States. There is no evidence that Knox ever made such a proposal.

ground between the American and English positions, since, in his opinion, they were not irreconcilable.[19] Grey dashed this slim hope on March 23 when questions in the House of Commons forced him to declare publicly that England could not support the United States in its Chin-Ai plan because of the Anglo-Russian agreement of 1899. Displaying his utter misapprehension of British foreign policy, Reid concluded that Grey was not likely to recede from this declaration without a fresh lease of power or the excuse of new circumstances.[20] The well-informed "Day in Washington" columnist reported that, although the State Department refused to comment, Knox and his associates regarded England's position as unwarranted, on the grounds that the Treaty of Portsmouth superseded the Scott-Muraviev accord.[21]

Knox informed the British that he regarded the Russians' objections as unjustified. The 1899 agreement between England and Russia was not binding on China, and the Secretary was resolved to "go ahead" with the project.[22] Bryce tried to explain that Britain must consider the interests of Japan and the susceptibilities of Russia; because of the delicate situation in Persia, England must avoid friction with Russia, a most sensitive government.[23]

In spite of the Russians' refusal to participate in Chin-Ai, the department told Straight that it saw no reason why he should not complete the contract with the Chinese. From the beginning the United States had favored "proper" Russian and Japanese participation, and the final agreement could be drawn so as to provide for revision to include them, if necessary.[24] In mid-March Straight opened negotiations with the Chinese; at the outset he expected their completion at an early date, in the belief that the Russians were only bluffing. At this point Straight was still defending Knox and his neutralization scheme, but less than two weeks later, either wiser or more candid, he had joined the critical chorus.[25] He approved of the direct assault but complained that people were trying to make horseshoes out of cold steel, and he concluded that there seemed to be hell to pay all over the place. Although he believed that the Chinese political situation was

19. Knox to Reid, March 11, 1910, Reid Papers.
20. Reid to Knox, March 25, 1910, Reid Papers.
21. *New York Tribune,* March 25, 1910.
22. *GP,* 32, No. 11697, 106-7.
23. Bryce Memorandum, March 31, 1910, James Bryce Papers.
24. McKnight to Knox, February 28, 1910, DS 893.77/821.
25. Willard Straight Papers.

progressively deteriorating and expected that "one of these days" the growing ferment would boil over, Straight was not yet ready to quit. He still disliked and distrusted the Japanese as heartily as ever, but he respected them. If China alone were at stake, he would be inclined to let Japan proceed with her plans, but the United States must be true to its own ideas, and for its own sake should try to save China, not only from others, but from herself. He viewed the United States' protection of China's integrity essential to the logical and inevitable growth of the United States into a world Power.[26]

The negotiations with the Chinese Government, related to the Chin-Ai line, finally convinced Straight that the Chinese would not try to save themselves from the rapacity of the Powers. They were so obviously reluctant to conclude an agreement because of Russian opposition that he suspected them of not acting in good faith. His suspicions were correct. The Chinese Foreign Office believed that negotiations with Straight over contract details should wait for a prior settlement with Russia and Japan, who fully understood China's objective of strengthening her position in Manchuria through Chin-Ai. Hsi-liang, arguing that Russian and Japanese opposition was not unexpected and that China must not be intimidated, did open the talks, but with the promise that he would make no firm commitment to Straight without approval from the Foreign Office.[27]

By the end of April Straight felt that he could accomplish nothing more at the moment in China. Under existing political conditions he believed that, even if the four banks reached an agreement on the Hukuang loan among themselves (as seemed imminent), it would be not only unwise but dangerous to press the central government to coerce the provinces to cooperate at this time. Furthermore, convinced that China would not budge on Chin-Ai unless the Russians came around, Straight decided that he might change the Russians' attitude by going to St. Petersburg. He left Peking on the twenty-eighth of April, but the Chinese caught up with him at Shanhaikuan, where, on April 30, he signed a draft loan agreement for the Chin-Ai railroad with the Viceroy's representatives.[28]

On April 15 the German Foreign Office cabled Bernstorff that,

26. Straight to "Dear Excellency," March 23, 1910, Straight Papers.
27. H. Croly, *Willard Straight*, 324-25; Sun, *Chinese Railways*, 162.
28. Straight to Morgans, April 22 and 30, 1910, DS 893.77/914, 924; Straight to Schiff, April 24, 1910, Straight Papers.

according to its secret information, Russia would abandon her opposition to Chin-Ai if the Americans offered her a share in the concession. Knox too had heard plausible reports that the Russians would abandon their objections to the line and participate in its financing, since they did not believe in the feasibility of a lasting entente with Japan. He therefore had definite hopes for an immediate start on the first section of the line.[29] The conciliatory answer to Russia's note of February 24 reflected the Secretary's convictions. The United States welcomed the proposal for the Kalgan-Kiakhta line as a sign that the Russians wanted to cooperate in promoting China's economic development. On this basis the State Department advanced Chin-Ai as a practical vehicle of collaboration. Although the department denied any Russian right to veto American enterprise in any part of China, it promised to urge the American Group and the Chinese to consider any modifications of the contract Russia might propose. Knox's memorandum concluded with the request that the Russian Government withdraw its protest, thus enabling the Americans and British to sign a contract for at least the first stage of the railroad.[30]

After an interview with the Minister of Finance, Rockhill reported that Russia would not withdraw its protest until it had received a report from the surveying party sent out from Harbin to examine the proposed Chin-Ai route. The report would probably be ready some time in July. Kokovtsov's reference to the surveying party was certainly not meant to be ironic, but the turn of events made it so, for the new entente between Russia and Japan was to be signed in that same month. The entente had originated, however, in October 1909 when the Japanese Government, learning that Kokovtsov was planning a trip to the Far East, made arrangements for Prince Ito to meet him in Harbin for a discussion of Russo-Japanese relations.[31] Ito and Kokovtsov met on October 26 and spoke privately for a short time. They never resumed their conversation for, as Ito was reviewing a company of railroad

29. Stemrich to Bernstorff, April 15, 1910; Bernstorff to Foreign Office, April 21, 1910, *GP*, 32, 107-8.
30. *FR, 1910*, 264-66.
31. *FR, 1910*, 267; DS 19038/2; Malevsky-Malevitch to Izvolsky, October 12, 1909; Siebert, *Benckendorff*, I, 143-44; Louis to Pichon, October 14, 1909, *DDF*, Ser. 2, 497-98. In Peking the conviction was strong, especially among the Chinese, that the aim of the meeting was to bring about an understanding between the two countries to safeguard their interests in Manchuria. Fletcher shared this belief. Fletcher to Knox, October 30, 1909, DS 4002/260.

guards, he was shot and fatally wounded by a Korean national-ist.[32]

Korostovetz, the Russian minister in Peking, who had attended the meeting, returned to his post on November 1. In discussing the Harbin dispute with Fletcher on the following day, the Minister intimated that continued opposition of the Powers to Russian policy might drive Russia to make common cause with Japan. Fletcher could say in reply only that American opposition would persist whether the principle of political status for a railroad company were advanced by just one Power or by two.[33]

Nevertheless, when the Japanese in that same month made their first definite overture to Russia regarding a *rapprochement,* the Russians did not respond. The neutralization proposal offered the Japanese an occasion to return in full force to the subject, and by the middle of January they were so insistent on starting negotiations that the Russian ambassador in Tokyo, Nicholas Malevsky-Malevitch, asked Izvolsky for instructions.[34]

With the delivery of the notes on neutralization, however, both Russia and Japan apparently took time out from the effort to cooperate so that each could play her own game on Chin-Ai. Although the Russians were prepared for the possibility that Japan might pursue an independent course, they were not aware as late as February 21 that Japan had agreed to participate. Equally interesting was the Japanese reaction to Russia's proposed Kalgan-Kiakhta railroad, which Komura communicated to H. G. M. Rumbold at the British embassy on March 4. Japan promised to give "moral support" if Chinese refusal to grant the new concession did not prejudice Japanese participation in Chin-Ai and if the new line were built with international cooperation.[35]

But China made no move to include Japan in the Chin-Ai project and the United States gave no serious consideration to the Kalgan-Kiakhta alternative, so on March 8 Komura again broached the subject of an agreement to Malevsky-Malevitch. He suggested that the new convention cover the maintenance of the *status quo* in Manchuria, the definite demarcation of the special Russian and Japanese interests, and their protection against ag-

32. Kengi Hamada, *Prince Ito,* 230-31.
33. DS 4002/261.
34. E. B. Price, *The Russo-Japanese Treaties of 1907-1916 Concerning Manchuria and Mongolia,* 51-52; Siebert, *Benckendorff,* I, 216-18.
35. Nicolson to Grey, February 21, 1910, FO 405/202/111; Rumbolt to Grey, March 4, 1910, FO 405/202/120.

gression by a third Power. In mid-April Itschiro Motono, the Japanese ambassador in St. Petersburg, back at his post after a leave, sounded the Russian Government on an entente. The response being favorable, he received instructions to open negotiations.[36] The course of the discussions apparently was not smooth, and Prime Minister Taro Katsura was disturbed at reports in the newspapers early in May that the agreement had been signed or would be shortly. He issued an official disclaimer and at the same time impressed on the Russians the need for haste. By mid-May Komura was telling French Ambassador A. Gérard that the accord would probably be concluded, although there were not yet any definite arrangements. As a matter of fact, until that time Izvolsky and Motono had held only one general conversation about the alliance. The Russian Foreign Minister was very uneasy about Japanese intentions in Korea and may have delayed, in the fear that Japan's annexation of Korea was imminent.[37]

Nevertheless, on May 23 Post Wheeler, *chargé* at St. Petersburg, who had been reporting rumors of the agreement for two weeks, informed the department that the understanding between Russia and Japan was approaching concrete form and would probably be published within the next few weeks. On May 24 the department told the legation in Peking that it seemed no more than equitable for American residents in Harbin provisionally to pay ordinary municipal taxes as did all other citizens, pending adoption of satisfactory municipal regulations. Concerning these, the department reserved all American rights.[38] The department also instructed O'Brien to make inquiries at the Japanese Foreign Office about the rumored entente.

Since the United States Department of State had now completely reversed its policy on Harbin, the question arises whether the change was intended to forestall the Russo-Japanese accord or to secure Russian approval for Chin-Ai. At the end of February Korostovetz had asked Fletcher if he thought there were any possibility of settling the Chin-Ai and Harbin questions together, and he hinted that the United States might modify its position at Harbin in return for Russia's consent to Chin-Ai. Fletcher was noncommittal, but promised to report the conversation to Wash-

36. Siebert, *Benckendorff,* I, 253-54; *BD,* VIII, 478-79; *DDF,* Ser. 2, 760-63. For some reason, the Japanese kept insisting to everyone that Russia was making the overtures. FO 410/55/87; DS 761.94/47.

37. Gérard to Pichon, May 14, 1910, *DDF,* Ser. 2, 12, 760-63; Nicolson to Grey, May 13, 1910, FO 410/55/107.

38. DS 76194/12; *FR, 1910,* 230-31.

ington. When Bernstorff asked Knox point-blank if he had not shifted his position in order to induce the Russians to consider Chin-Ai favorably, Knox smilingly conceded that he had. The Russians, however, interpreted the concession on Harbin to mean that the Americans had finally realized they were driving the Russians into the arms of the Japanese, as officials in St. Petersburg had warned.[39]

Whatever the motive, Knox's change of policy did not affect the course of events, either on Chin-Ai or on the entente. On June 20 Russia and Japan put into final form the public and secret agreements, which they then communicated to Britain and France; their representatives signed the documents on July 4.[40] In the secret treaty in 1907 the two countries had pledged themselves to maintain the *status quo* by all the peaceful means in their control. Now, however, the two signatories publicly announced that they would defend the *status quo* by whatever steps they might, after consultation, deem necessary. Furthermore, the new secret treaty interpreted the *"status quo"* and "special interests" as synonymous.[41] These special interests arose chiefly from the exploitation of the C.E.R. and the S.M.R. and the mines the railroads served. In Gérard's opinion the aim of the new conventions was to safeguard the railroads, which implied maintenance of the *status quo.* This being the case, he believed that Russia would never accept the Chin-Ai project and Japan would, by treaty, support Russia's opposition to it.[42]

A number of factors had contributed to bringing the new accords into being. Japan wanted an understanding with Russia that would define their interests in China, as did that part of the ruling circle in Russia whose policies were oriented toward Europe and the Middle East; settlement of the questions in the East would free their attention for matters in the West. And no doubt the adamant American protest against the Harbin regulations played a part in bringing the two recent enemies to agreement. Certainly the American position increased Izvolsky's hostility toward the United States, which dated back at least to the Russo-Japanese War. Izvolsky complained indignantly to Curtis Swenson, like Izvolsky a member of the diplomatic corps in Copenhagen at the time, that the United States was pro-Japanese and hostile to

39. DS 893.77/892; Bernstorff to Bethmann-Hollweg, July 1, 1910, *GP*, 32, 111-12; G. N. Trubetzkoi, *Russland als Grossmacht*, 75.
40. *BD*, VIII, 480-81; Price, *R-J Treaties*, 113-14.
41. Price, *R-J Treaties*, 42-44.
42. *DDF*, Ser. 2, 12, 808.

Russia. And again, when Taft saw Izvolsky in St. Petersburg in December 1907, the Russian remarked, "You helped the Japanese to ignore us. How do you like it now?"[43] His anti-Americanism and his suspicions of the United States were brought sharply into focus when the Taft Administration inaugurated its forward policy in Manchuria. Few voices disputed the theory that Knox played a large part in bringing about the entente.

In St. Petersburg the semiofficial *Novoe Vremya* of July 7 described the *rapprochement* with Japan as the fruit of the whole Far Eastern situation. But certainly the foreign policy of the United States had given the treaty its last and decisive impulse. Therefore, the paper added graciously, Mr. Knox deserved Russian gratitude. Mr. Knox must also be thanked for the provision in the agreement for combined action by Russia and Japan in cases threatening the Manchurian *status quo.* Grey minuted that the policy adopted by the United States in China hastened, if it did not bring about, the Russo-Japanese treaty. Gérard too assigned an especially important role to the Knox neutralization memorandum in bringing the agreement to fruition. The Russians and the Japanese gladly gave Britain credit for her assistance and publicly thanked their ally for her help in fending off the Americans. The *North China Daily News* of Shanghai, the most reliable and influential English-language paper in China, offered its own succinct and brutal opinion of the treaty's effect: "No diplomatic language can cover up the fact that Manchuria is to all intents and purposes lost to China."[44]

The State Department, however, registered no alarm. On May 26, in response to O'Brien's inquiries, Komura had confirmed the discussions with Russia but told the Ambassador that the press reports were inaccurate. As far as Japan was concerned, no new agreement with Russia was needed; diplomatic action was being taken chiefly to calm the suspicion and alarm of the Russian people. When William J. Calhoun reported in mid-June that the Chinese were very uneasy over what might be brewing, the department informed him that the press accounts were incorrect. Washington did not believe that any agreement that might be reached would be prejudicial to China.[45]

43. DS 893.102H/280; quoted in Bernstorff to Foreign Office, January 21, 1910, *GP,* 32, 83.
44. Enclosed in Wheeler to Knox, July 7, 1910, DS 76194/32; *BD,* VIII, 485; *DDF,* Ser. 2, 12, 523; enclosed in Wilder to Huntington-Wilson, July 11, 1910, DS 761.94/48.
45. DS 761.94/18, 27.

The calm continued in Washington even after Huntington-Wilson had looked over a copy of the Russo-Japanese treaty left at the department on July 11. He concluded that the agreement seemed fairly harmless, apparently a codicil to the 1907 convention. He remarked that, "since the provisions . . . are all subject to the Open Door Policy and the rights of other Powers, and since Russia and Japan cannot bargain away rights held from China by others, one reaches the conclusion that the bark, or moral effect, is the main thing about this Convention, rather than its bite, or legal force." Huntington-Wilson then wired Calhoun that a careful analysis of the text and specific assurances from both the Russian and Japanese governments, as well as the views of the British Foreign Office, confirmed the department's opinion that the agreement would not be prejudicial to China. The Americans' conclusion that the treaty contained nothing inimical to China caused more amusement than satisfaction at the Chinese Foreign Office.[46]

Straight had persevered in his determination to go to St. Petersburg to see if, by personal conversations, he could sway the Russians to approve the Chin-Ai project. He arrived on June 20, the day the treaties were put in final form. A series of interviews with government officials over the next five days convinced him that the Russians would never willingly consent to construction of the railroad. Straight therefore recommended that the American Group avoid both the one extreme of urging China to build the road all the way to Aigun and the other of abandoning Chin-Ai for Russia's proposed Kalgan-Kiakhta line. Instead, he proposed a middle course that would alienate neither Russia nor China. The financial group should immediately begin constructing the first section of the Chichow line to Taonanfu. This action would eliminate having to take Japan into consideration, since Grey had given assurances that, so long as the road did not go beyond Taonanfu, Britain would not allow the Japanese to participate or interfere. The group should also make arrangements to cooperate with Russia on the Kalgan-Kiakhta line and assure Russia that it had no intention for the present of extending the Chichow railroad past Taonanfu. Straight was sure his plan would work, since

46. Huntington-Wilson Memorandum, July 11, 1910, DS 761.94/30; Huntington-Wilson to Calhoun, July 12, 1910, DS 761.94/28. Grey told Reid that he believed that the newspaper reports of the agreement were substantially correct. Reid to Knox, July 6, 1910, DS 761.94/22; Müller to Grey, July 27, 1910, FO 405/200/48. C. Vevier, *The United States and China, 1906-1913,* 157, claims that Russia wanted to cooperate with the United States.

the Russians themselves admitted that they could not prevent construction, and as for Izvolsky, "I am under the impression that most of his conversation was 'bluff'." Although the Russians might be unable to stop the project, both Kokovtsov and Izvolsky threatened reprisals if China permitted it.[47]

Straight's next two suggestions were his most interesting because they demonstrate so clearly his utter failure to grasp the political realities confronting the financial group and the State Department. From Harbin, China was to operate a steamship line on the Sungari River. The "threat" of constructing a railroad from Taonanfu to Petuna on the Sungari to connect with the steamer service, "together with the threat" of extending the Taonanfu railroad to Tsitsihar and then Aigun, would give the group a lever, while building the first section, to remove Russian opposition to the whole line and to persuade Russia to sell the C.E.R. to China. The State Department could help by instructing the embassies at St. Petersburg, Tokyo, Berlin, and Paris to keep those governments in a good humor and ignorant of the broader significance of the plan. One feels that the friend who commented of Straight, "It is perhaps superfluous to add that he is a confirmed optimist," was indulging in British understatement.[48]

Straight's tactics were no better than his strategy. In talking with Izvolsky, he annoyed the Foreign Minister by maintaining, on the one hand, that the United States had no political aims in Manchuria and, on the other, repeatedly referring to the political significance of the situation. Of course China wanted to be her own master in Manchuria, he told Izvolsky, thus confirming the latter's belief—and fear—that the Americans' aim was to direct future Chinese policy. Another of Straight's comments to the Foreign Minister moved one diplomat to remark, "Language like this does not naturally tend to disarm opposition."[49]

Although at the end of June Knox was insisting to Bernstorff that he would not yield to Russian pressure and that he was counting on the construction of the Taonanfu section of the railroad, the department did, in fact, on June 28 veto any action. When the financial group inquired what the department's attitude would be

47. Straight to Morgans, June 28, 1910, DS 893.77/1011; Nicolson to Grey, February 21, 1910, FO 405/202/111.
48. Straight to Morgans, June 28, 1910, DS 893.77/1011; Kidston, Memorandum of conversation with Straight on June 26, 1910, FO 800/248.
49. Wheeler to Knox, June 29, 1910, DS 893.77/1013; Jordan to Grey, January 2, 1911, FO 405/204/31.

on construction up to Taonanfu, Huntington-Wilson replied that nothing should be done until Rockhill had returned to his post in St. Petersburg.[50] The truth was that the State Department was not willing to proceed without backing from the British Foreign Office. Not that the banking group itself was anxious to push ahead; it had become involved in political power-plays that it found distasteful, and it was unhappy over the considerable expense incurred in connection with the Hukuang loan, which still seemed to offer little hope of profitable conclusion.

Following Chang's death in October 1909 and during all the months that the bankers haggled in Europe, agitation in the Hukuang for local financing and control of the railroads had continued to increase, and the provincial assemblies, which had first convened also in October, provided a forum for the expression of discontent among the Chinese. By February 1910 pressure on the central government from the provinces became so great that Peking granted the Hupeh gentry the right to form a railway company and issue stocks for the construction of the Hupeh section of the Hankow-Canton railroad. On the grounds that this action was a breach of the June 6 agreement, the French, German, and British governments decided to protest the edict. The United States abstained, with the statement that it was not a party to the June understanding.[51]

A compromise on the assignment of engineers satisfactory to the French was also accepted by the Americans and the Germans. To the department's annoyance, the British continued to resist all demands that meant giving up part of their share of the mileage. "In the deliberate opinion of the [American] Government it therefore now rests with Great Britain . . . to decide whether or not there is to be any finality to these negotiations." Grey agreed that the outlook was not promising but had different reasons for thinking that the whole scheme might vanish into thin air. Reports to the Foreign Office showed that the Chinese central government's control was steadily weakening and the independence of the provinces and their hostility to foreign concessions steadily increasing. Yet, England did not seem in any great hurry to reach an interbank agreement. Reid, who sympathized with Grey's stand

50. Bernstorff to Bethmann-Hollweg, July 1, 1910, *GP*, 32, 111-12; Huntington-Wilson to Morgans, June 28, 1910, DS 893.77/988.
51. Sun, *Chinese Railways*, 117; Addis to Campbell, February 1, 1910, Grey to Bryce, February 7, 1910, FO 405/202/66, 83. The tripartite governments did not send their notes until April 22, 1910. FO 405/202/176.

on the loan, thought there was a limit to what the government at Peking could do—it was in an extremely weak political position. Straight did not share Reid's view. He was convinced that soon after the United States entered the loan picture, the British Foreign Office had seen a chance to wreck the enterprise and thus keep the Germans out of the Yangtze Valley. In Straight's opinion it might very well have been a deal cooked up between the British and the French, with the British chiefly responsible.[52]

By April Reid and Straight were agreeing on at least one facet of the problem. Although Britain and France were close to solving their disagreement on distribution of mileage, this slight step probably would not bring a consummation of the loan. Reid believed that if the Peking press stories were accurate, there was no cause to rejoice over success in Europe. As for Straight, he seemed ready, if not to junk the whole business completely, at least to postpone it indefinitely. Even if the bankers reached an agreement with the Chinese Government, it would be not only unwise but, he thought, dangerous to urge Peking to coerce the provinces into their settlement. Serious riots had already occurred in Hunan, and unrest was spreading in the Yangtze Valley, where a state of active or suppressed excitement prevailed. Pressure to force the loan might bring on a serious revolt.[53]

As a matter of fact, the battle of the kilometers soon ended; the four banks signed an agreement in Paris on May 23, 1910, that gave the victory to England. Grey now suggested that the four governments present identic notes to China, requesting final consummation of the contract. Knox agreed, but noted that, in the State Department's judgment, the timing for bringing pressure on the central government was questionable, since such serious conditions prevailed in the involved provinces.[54]

In mid-July the foreign ministers in Peking presented their notes to the Chinese Government, although Calhoun was not enthusiastic about joining the representations. Müller predicted that unless the department instructed Calhoun to change his attitude, the other Powers could not count on much help from the

52. Huntington-Wilson to Reid, March 5, 1910, DS 893.77/826C; Reid to Mrs. Reid, March 12, 1910, Reid Papers; Straight to Marvin, March 15, 1910, Straight Papers. The view that the British were deliberately trying to wreck the loan was commonly held in Peking and apparently shared by Fletcher.
53. Reid to Phillips, April 20, 1910, Reid Papers; Straight to Morgans, April 22, 1910, DS 893.77/924; Straight to Schiff, April 24, 1910, Straight Papers.
54. *FR, 1910,* 280-81; Reid to Knox, June 8, 1910, and Knox to Reid, June 21, 1910, DS 893.77/952.

Americans. Calhoun in fact went beyond reluctance; twice he tried to convince Müller that the moment was "singularly inopportune" for any pressure. Calhoun seemed entirely oblivious to the fact, Müller remarked, that, but for the United States, the railroad would already be under construction.[55]

Calhoun's reports reflected his deep pessimism. Except in north China, he informed Knox, "a general seething" existed that seemed ready at slight provocation to burst into sudden violence. The greatest danger lay, he thought, in the declining powers of the central government vis-à-vis the increasing strength of the provincial gentry. Rear Admiral John Hubbard, Commander-in-chief of the Asiatic Fleet, confirmed Calhoun's fears. He believed a revolution possible, almost probable, in the not remote future and wanted his fleet reinforced to cope with such an eventuality.[56]

Because of the difficulties over the Hukuang loan and more particularly the diplomatic entanglements over Chin-Ai, the American Group at this point was becoming distinctly uneasy over its China undertakings. Henry P. Davison intimated to Fletcher that, while it was all right to make history, a banker's business was to make money, and he expressed some doubt about the group's continued operations in China. Fletcher urged him to stand fast. The State Department was exerting every effort to bring negotiations to a successful conclusion, but such undertakings always proceeded slowly. Although Fletcher was not entirely sympathetic with impatient businessmen, in private he frankly confessed that the department might as well acknowledge that the prospects for success in the Chin-Ai situation were unpromising. Fletcher suggested that the group either lend China the money to build whatever railroads she liked or take the Germans into partnership as a counterweight to Russia and Japan.[57]

Both Straight and Calhoun were dissatisfied with the department's "wait-and-see" policy. Straight warned that, after all the big talk about supporting Chinese rights in Manchuria, a meek retreat before Russia and Japan would be fatal to the American position in the Orient. Calhoun echoed Straight. He believed that unless the department soon found a way to break the stalemate, American prestige would suffer a serious blow. The Chinese were

55. FO 405/203/24.
56. Calhoun to Knox, July 5, 1910; Hubbard to Secretary of the Navy, July 26, 1910, DS 893.00/422, 432.
57. Miller, Memorandum of conversation with Fletcher, July 14, 1910, Philander C. Knox Papers.

so agitated by the recent entente—the viceroy of Manchuria was reported to be panic-stricken—that Calhoun urged some reassurance. Would the department, he asked, support construction of the line as far as Taonanfu—300 miles of track requiring eighteen months to build?[58]

Huntington-Wilson and Miller drafted an instruction for Calhoun, which Knox approved, deprecating any undue panic on the part of the Chinese Government. China should help itself, in the department's opinion, by promptly instituting strenuous measures regarding currency and tariff reform, since from revenue comes governmental strength. The United States was ready to cooperate cordially in the implementation of such efforts. As to Calhoun's specific question about the railroad and the related subject of Chin-Ai, the department thought the banking group must make the decision. The department's own views would be determined in due time and after considering Britain's position, the attitude of the other Powers including Russia, and perhaps also German participation on a large scale.[59]

This less than enlightening instruction mirrored the State Department's embarrassment and uncertainty about the situation in China. Huntington-Wilson's reflections on Chin-Ai and American policy in the Far East clearly demonstrated that the depths of the question were impenetrable. He anticipated the Japanese resistance to Chin-Ai to be perfunctory, but certainly the Russians were unalterably opposed to the Americans' enterprise in China. Although admitting her inability to stop the project, Russia nonetheless warned China that construction would bring unpleasant consequences. The United States faced the dilemma of offending Russia or—much worse—losing China's confidence and thus losing face everywhere by abandoning what was the first practical test of its much-vaunted Far Eastern policy. Yet, if the United States compelled China to offend Russia, China might then turn against the United States. If the State Department's China policy were to succeed, Huntington-Wilson conceded, the United States needed strong and sincere support from England and Germany. Such being the situation, Huntington-Wilson mused, the thought "naturally occurs to one" that an opportunity might arise to tear down the Anglo-Japanese alliance and bring

58. Straight to McKnight, July 20, 1910, Straight Papers; Morgan, Grenfell to Morgans, July 21, 1910, DS 893.77/1029; Calhoun to Knox, July 14, 1910, DS 761.94/29.
59. Huntington-Wilson to Knox, July 15, 1910, Knox Papers; Huntington-Wilson to Peking Legation, July 19, 1910, DS 893.77/1016.

about a "fresh alignment" of Germany, Great Britain, and the United States in the Far East. For the moment, however, the department could do little in this unusually difficult situation, except perhaps quietly sound out Britain and Germany. The Far Eastern Division meanwhile could study the problem, in the hope that ultimately the best course for the United States might become clear.[60]

Huntington-Wilson asked Reid if he could confirm his statement of March 12 that Britain would support construction as far as Taonanfu. Reid could not. Since such a line avowedly would be extended beyond its presently stated terminus, Grey held that the same conditions applied to it as to Chin-Ai. In Reid's opinion England's refusal to cooperate with the United States resulted partly from Britain's "chronic invertebracy" and partly from her desire to preserve the Russian entente. Although granting that Anglo-Russian friendship was a real as well as a moral counterpoise to Germany in the Near East and elsewhere, Huntington-Wilson was convinced that England was infatuated with the Japanese alliance and morbid with fear of Germany.[61]

Britain's unwillingness to support the United States effort to promote Chinese development led Huntington-Wilson to ponder the Far Eastern question more deeply. The United States had a good excuse to drop the Chin-Ai project, since from the beginning Knox had made American support contingent on British cooperation. Even with a legitimate excuse, however, it would be difficult to differentiate a decision to cease negotiating for the project from complete admission that the Open Door policy was a dead letter in northern China. But Huntington-Wilson did not yet abandon hope of British collaboration; it might come with a change of ministry or with a change of heart on the part of the existing government caused by the increasing opposition of public opinion to the existing English policy in China.[62]

At a meeting with the banking group early in August, Huntington-Wilson discussed two possible courses of action. Chin-Ai could be abandoned and Britain blamed for the loss of United States prestige in the East, for certainly American prestige would suffer. The other alternative was to get substantial financial and diplo-

60. Williams to McKnight, August 9, 1910, DS 893.77/1068A; Huntington-Wilson to Knox, July 15, 1910, Knox Papers.
61. DS 893.77/1016, 1039; Grey to Reid, July 30, 1910, FO 405/203/23; Huntington-Wilson to Knox, July 27, 1910, Knox Papers.
62. Huntington-Wilson to Knox, July 27, 1910, Knox Papers.

matic support from the Germans, either without British participation or ultimately with it, the second possibility being one of
great political importance. For the present the department would
encourage China to keep the Chin-Ai opportunity open, and the
group should quietly do the same by showing no signs of retreat.
Meanwhile, all concerned should wait patiently and maintain the
status quo, pending development of the ultimate attitude in England and consideration by the department of overtures to Germany, to be made either through diplomatic channels or through
the bankers.[63]

Taft learned indirectly that the banking group was now proposing to abandon all participation in Chin-Ai because of Russian
opposition and because Knox had failed to get support from the
other Powers. The President took the news so seriously that he
asked Knox to talk to the group before it took the step that would
completely defeat the international purposes of the United
States. Failure to insist on the American's right to carry through
the concession would severely damage United States prestige.
Knox agreed to meet with the bankers, although he regarded reports of the group's demoralization as exaggerated.[64]

The bankers had already arranged to confer; on September 1
they met in New York to thresh out the circumstances and the
resolution of their involvement in China. The First National Bank
and the National City Bank favored withdrawing from all agreements, whereas J. P. Morgan and Company and Kuhn, Loeb
wanted to proceed. After much discussion they voted to continue
their China projects but at the same time decided that they could
not act as a tool of the State Department. "They did not want it
said with even the remotest degree of plausibility that the promotion of their interest as investment bankers was pushing the
American nation into war with any European or Asiatic country."
To make their position clear, the bankers took two steps: They set
up a conference with Knox to work out the group's future relation-

63. DS 897.77/1068A; on October 15, 1910, Uchida reported to Tokyo a conversation
with Huntington-Wilson in which the latter brought up the possibility of an
American-German understanding if France, England, Russia, and Japan continued to resist all suggestions. To Uchida's query if such an understanding would
not violate the principle of eschewing entangling alliances, Huntington-Wilson
replied that of course it could be called an understanding, "but it is coming to that
very rapidly with us." JFO, MT Series, Reel 48.
64. Taft to Knox, September 1, 1910, and Knox to Taft, same date, William Howard
Taft Papers.

ship to Far Eastern policy, and they sent a telegram on September 2, 1910, to their Peking representative, D. A. Menocal. "We cannot now go any further until our own Government and the other Powers are agreed upon the construction of the Chinchou-Aigun road in its entirety." That it was really, as Taft had heard, Chin-Ai and its international complications that troubled the bankers is clear from the fact that, on this same day, the group decided to undertake negotiations with the Manchurian viceroy for a $20,-000,000 development loan.[65]

After meeting with the group on September 4, Knox drew up a statement on future policy that he claimed had the bankers' approval. "Schiff, Davison & [sic] Straight assure me that [the telegram of September 2] means that in view of objections by other powers arising subsequent to the launching of the project they will await the assurance of this Govt. [sic] that it has or has not reached an understanding with the powers and if it has not they are ready to go on with assurances of Govt. support." Croly asserts, however, that although Knox tried to get the bankers to support any policy he might decide on, the group informed him that it was not interested in serving as "the instrument of an exclusive and aggressive American policy in China." The group threatened to withdraw from China unless the Administration changed course, and it gave Knox to understand that it would serve as the department's financial agent only if it were not asked to undertake projects that aroused the unbending opposition of the other Powers.[66]

The investment group was not the only object of the department's displeasure; irritation with Great Britain reached a climax in the summer and fall. The list of international projects for whose failure or delay the British were held responsible was an impressive one: the Hukuang loan, the neutralization scheme, Chin-Ai, the Harbin regulations, abolition of likin and tariff increase, the opium conference, the fur-seal fisheries, cooperation in the Japanese immigration question, "and doubtless . . . many other questions," as Samuel Heinzleman put it.[67]

65. Croly, *Straight,* 342-43; Williams to Huntington-Wilson, August, 1910, DS 893.-77/1046; Morgans to Menocal, September 2, 1910, DS 893.77/1074; Straight Memorandum of the History of the Currency Loan Negotiations, September, 1910, to January, 1911, DS 893.51/325.
66. Knox, Memorandum, n.d., DS 893.77/1074; Croly, *Straight,* 343-44.
67. Heinzleman to Fletcher, February 18, 1910, Fletcher Papers.

By mid-August Bryce was sufficiently concerned about Anglo-American relations to suggest that the Foreign Office take steps to soothe American feelings. He picked this moment because Huntington-Wilson, now having second thoughts about the Russo-Japanese treaty of July, 1910, was indulging "in language of unbecoming strength" both in regard to the convention itself and what he considered Britain's part in it. Huntington-Wilson was saying that the entente violated the Treaty of Portsmouth and reduced the Open Door to a dead letter and that he could not understand why Britain would adopt an attitude hostile to its own commercial interests merely to meet Russian wishes.[68]

Grey defended Britain's position on Chin-Ai and drew up his own list of grievances against the United States. American Far Eastern policy had put Britain in a very difficult position, according to Grey, and the only apparent result of that policy had been to draw Russia and Japan closer together and make preservation of the Open Door increasingly difficult. The neutralization scheme, Grey said in effect, violated the Treaty of Portsmouth. Furthermore, while claiming British support, the Americans had not reciprocated. The United States had reversed its position on Harbin, for example, without consulting London. Not that it was a matter of great importance, "but it shows an absence of purpose, coupled with a disregard of us." Yet Grey, too, believed that good relations with the United States were extremely desirable and he wanted to work with the Americans in the Far East "as far as circumstances permit." England wanted to maintain the *status quo* in Manchuria, where any change the United States feared would hurt the British equally. Innes, who did not think the situation was serious, placed the blame for whatever irritation existed on Huntington-Wilson, "that pestilential beast."[69]

But the department did not fret much longer about how to extricate itself from the Chin-Ai mess, and as that project faded into the background, American displeasure with the British receded as well. Another even better opportunity to help China help herself had arisen. By mid-November Knox was telling the banking group that the department did not object to a new suggestion made by ffrench: abandon the Chin-Ai route and replace it with two other

68. FO 405/200/67.
69. Grey to Bryce, September 22, 1910, FO 405/200/176; Innes to Grey, November 2, 1910, FO 800/248.

lines. Knox did however have one reservation about the new project and its implementation. He preferred that the group not approach China or Britain until the loan for currency reform and Manchurian development had been arranged.

12

The Currency Loan

Since the Chinese proposal for a combined loan for currency reform and the development of Manchuria seemed to offer a productive escape from the current sterile policy, the State Department grasped it eagerly. But the new course proved no more successful than the old, and ultimately the Taft Administration learned its lesson: Power politics had sealed off Manchuria to American influence and enterprise.

China intended to use the money from the new loan to reorganize her fiscal and financial system and to strengthen Manchuria against foreign encroachment through colonization and the development of resources. As to the other part of the program, there was no question about the currency's need for reform. Although the Chinese had been talking for several years about remedying their chaotic financial situation, their first real step in this direction came with the reform edict of May 1910. The department greeted the news warmly, since it regarded the currency reform not only as desirable in itself but as offering a good opportunity to push another project that it had been urging on China for some months—the appointment of a foreign financial adviser. In spite of reports from Peking, such as Fletcher's remark that "there is a pronounced unwillingness, if not, indeed, hostility to the employment of foreign advisers and assistants," the department never seemed to grasp the depth of China's aversion to foreign supervision over her fiscal affairs. In mid-July, at the time of Chinese panic over the Russo-Japanese Treaty, Huntington-Wilson returned to the charge. In his opinion financial reforms were vitally important to China, and the necessity for expert foreign advice in carrying them through apparent. Calhoun, however, shared Fletcher's belief that the Chinese would not respond favorably to the suggestion.[1]

The department was urging China to appoint a foreigner—not necessarily an American—as financial adviser, and in mid-August the Chinese suggested an American for this position. They assured Calhoun that if Liang Tun-yen, who was about to leave for the United States, succeeded in negotiating a large loan for currency reform, they would hire an American expert to advise them on financial and currency reform. But instead of working directly with the bankers through Liang, China on September 22 approached them through the American legation. After Huntington-Wilson discussed the proposal with the banking group, Knox cabled Peking on September 29 that the bankers were ready to undertake the loan, provided that the Chinese appointed an American adviser at an early date. Actually, it was not the bankers but Knox who stipulated the condition.[2]

The bankers had scarcely accepted the invitation to take the currency loan when China proposed merging it with the Manchurian loan for which the American Group was negotiating with the Viceroy. Claiming that the Tang memorandum had committed the Viceroy to borrow the money for Manchurian development from the American Group, the New York bankers strove to get the business away from their European competitors. The Europeans, also insisting on a prior right to the loan, based their claim on the loan contract that the Viceroy had signed in November 1908 with the Hongkong and Shanghai Bank and its French and German colleagues. The agreement included a stipulation

1. G. C. Allen and A. G. Donnithorne, *Western Enterprise in Far Eastern Economic Development, China and Japan,* 102-4; *Foreign Relations, 1912,* 88-89; Fletcher to Knox, February 25, 1910, DS 893.51/104; Calhoun to Knox, July 31, 1910, DS 893.51/114. In 1903 the United States tried to put China on the gold standard when Mexico and China both complained of the fluctuations in the price of silver in relation to that of gold. Charles Conant of the Morton Trust Company submitted a plan, as did Cornell University's Jeremiah Jenks. Both plans called for the presence in China of foreign advisers with strong control over all Chinese finances. Jenks and Conant traveled in Europe in 1903, trying to convince the Europeans of the feasibility of their plans, but the Europeans did not want to admit the United States to controls in China. Jenks then proceeded to China, but there he experienced no greater success. (We are indebted to Professor Lloyd Gardner for calling the above incident to our attention. See C. Conant, "Putting China on the Gold Standard," *North American Review,* November, 1903; DS Misc. Letters, 1903-1904.)

2. DS 893.00/429, 437; *FR, 1912,* 89-90; DS 893.51/122, 127. Liang had another mission besides the loan. China wanted to get mutual declarations from Germany, Austria, and the United States that would reaffirm the Open Door policy. He arrived in the United States in late December and had several conversations with Knox, who rejected his request for the statement. DS 893.00/429.

that the bank would have first refusal in case the Viceroy borrowed additional funds during the life of the loan.[3]

The Chinese now suggested a loan of $50,000,000—$30,000,000 for currency reform and the rest for Manchuria. They were anxious to settle the matter quickly, fearing that if the other Powers learned of the negotiations, they would try to interfere. The Chinese also told Calhoun that if the loan went through, they would appoint an American adviser, to serve in a purely consultative capacity. When the American Group agreed to accept the loan if the Viceroy dropped his separate negotiations, the Chinese consented. On October 27 the group's representative signed the preliminary agreement, which the Emperor approved the following day. The terms provided that the Americans would negotiate and sign the final loan contract, after which they could dispose of the bonds in whatever market they wished.[4]

On October 31 the United States informed London, Berlin, St. Petersburg, Tokyo, and Paris of the signature to the agreement for the currency loan but, oddly enough, made no mention of the fact that part of the loan would be used for Manchurian development. The department merely noted that China would spend most of the money on currency reform, for which the United States asked the Powers' cooperation. In addition, the department confidentially told the heads of the missions that the United States was requiring as a condition of the loan that China employ an American adviser with a measure of real authority.[5]

In May 1910 three European banks had invited the American Group to join their syndicate and share equally with them in all future business in China. Although the invitation was repeated on several occasions, the group would not negotiate until it had a loan contract securely in its own hands. Now it indicated its willingness to join the consortium if the banking agreement provided for the internationalization of all bond issues and a quarter share

3. Davison to Morgan, Grenfell, September 24, 1910, DS 893.51/136; Straight Memorandum, DS 893.51/325; Calhoun to Knox, September 14, 1910, DS 893.51/118.
4. Calhoun to Knox, October 2, 1910, DS 893.51/134. The efforts at secrecy were successful. Although the European bank representatives in Peking were usually well informed, they were unaware that the negotiations were in progress. DS 893.51/481; Morgans to Grenfell, October 5, 1910, DS 893.77/1086; Straight Memorandum, DS 893.51/325, *FR, 1912,* 91.
5. DS 893.51/175B. On November 3 Rockhill told the Russians that China wanted a loan for currency reform and Manchurian development. Siebert, ed., *Graf Benckendorffs diplomatischer schriftwechsel,* I, 384-85. Apparently the French Foreign Office first learned of the Manchurian angle when Knox mentioned it to French Ambassador Jusserand around November 18. *DDF,* Ser. 2, 13, 58-59.

for each member of the syndicate. If the Europeans accepted these terms, the Americans were ready to make the new loan a joint venture. Although China had stipulated that the Americans must negotiate and sign alone, the group did not regard financing the loan as exclusive. The original London agreements of July 6, 1909, provided that if one bank undertook business under conditions which prevented the admission of the others, the original party could proceed alone, making provision in the contract for the other banks to issue the bonds jointly. At the end of October the four banking groups arranged a conference to work out the details of American participation in the consortium.[6] Since this question of financial cooperation had important ramifications for American political cooperation with the European Powers, the subject deserves some discussion at this point.

Although the diplomatic complications of the Chinchow-Aigun railroad had led to the American Group's rebellion against being used by the State Department as a political tool, the bankers were nevertheless willing to continue strictly financial operations in the Far East. The group had begun the Manchurian negotiations entirely on its own initiative; in response to the bankers' request the department backed their claim to exclusive rights in the matter. When the Viceroy suggested that the two competitors share the loan equally, the Hongkong and Shanghai Bank was prepared to settle on those terms, but the American Group refused, persisting in its demand for the entire loan. Once it had the contract, it would then be willing to share with the consortium banks. This attitude puzzled Morgan, Grenfell, who pointed out that competition meant only delay and friction, with the Chinese ultimately reaping the advantage. "If you are willing [to] make quadruple agreement, would it not be better to do so before competing . . . over this Manchurian loan?"[7]

There is no indication that the bankers were moved by any but financial considerations, for they had already decided not to pursue an independent policy.[8] The United States Government was depending on the group to float loans abroad to promote American influence in China, something the group could not do if it were limited to the American market. Internationalizing the bonds was a prerequisite to success. The imbroglio over the Hukuang loan

6. *FR, 1912,* 88; Straight Memorandum, DS 893.51/325.
7. Morgan, Grenfell to Morgans, October 1, 1910, DS 893.77/1082.
8. H. Croly, *Willard Straight,* 350.

had soured the Europeans, and in their resentment they might close their markets to an issue of Chinese bonds from which they did not profit. But if the group offered to admit the consortium to share in a purely American enterprise, the Europeans might then prove hospitable.

Although Straight realized the practical banking difficulties, he was torn by conflicting considerations. He wanted the group to act alone although, he conceded, this would mean that China was getting European money through American bankers. If obliged ultimately to admit the Europeans to the loan—a combination he considered scarcely consistent with past American policy—the group might then find it desirable to make a definite agreement with them for all future Chinese loans. If such an arrangement became necessary, he believed that, by standing on the Tang memorandum, the group should be able to set the conditions for European cooperation. Straight's objective was to secure European support for American supremacy in Manchuria; he would cooperate with the Europeans if he must, but on terms that set the United States in a predominant position. For several years and in spite of many bitter disappointments Straight clung to his dream, but finally even he recognized the inevitable. As his biographer notes, "it proved impossible to reserve for the American Group special privileges and responsibilities in any particular region which the other members of the Consortium would in practice permit their American associates to exercise."[9]

Calhoun, on the contrary, favored genuine cooperation with British, French, and German capitalists, either members of the consortium or independents, his point being that to cite the Tang memorandum would provoke the accusation that the United States was pursuing monopolistic designs in Manchuria at the same time that it was proclaiming the Open Door policy. When the currency loan came up, Calhoun conceded the advantages of negotiating the entire loan but nevertheless urged cooperation with European financiers. As long as the United States followed a go-it-alone policy, warned the Minister, it could expect concerted opposition from the treaty Powers, which might put the United States in the position of being unable to sustain its role as China's friend. "Although the advantages of isolation may present a more dazzling prospect, its dangers are likewise far greater. Our substantial interests here would not seem at the present stage to be commensurate with the risk entailed from

9. Croly, *Straight*, 350-52; Straight to Morgans, December 13, 1909, DS 2112/98.

following such a course. . . ." In view of public opinion in the United States and the limited American interests in China, America could speak with more authority and security while working in close cooperation with the other capitalist Powers than while acting alone. "While at first glance," the Minister wrote, "it might seem that we were abandoning our position of independence as a friend of China, it must be obvious that single handed we are in no position to effectively assert such sympathy except at a cost out of all proportion to its value for us." The United States could better manifest its real friendship for China by joining a combination of Powers in which "we would naturally take the lead."[10]

Calhoun's pleas for cooperation were not received sympathetically at the department, since Knox did not share Calhoun's trust in human nature. Whether the Americans handled the issue themselves or shared it with the Europeans, Knox intended to see that the contract provisions gave the United States a decisive voice in Chinese financial affairs. Knox was very much aware that Americans still had no bona fide interest in China, and the United States needed the Manchurian loan and currency reform if it were to acquire its long-sought economic leverage against other Powers.

During an interview with French Ambassador J. J. Jusserand in mid-November, Knox frankly admitted that $50,000,000 was more money than China needed for currency and administrative reforms. The United States really wanted this money to build railroads and to penetrate Manchuria economically, thereby creating an obstacle to Russian and Japanese domination. Taft voiced the same idea, saying that he had strongly urged the loan because through it he hoped to set a firm foot in China. There was even some talk that an independent loan might enable the State Department to force European support for Chin-Ai. To ensure this American predominance, Knox was insisting upon an American adviser in China as a condition of the loan. It was not enough to help China borrow the money, he argued; the United States was morally bound to ensure that China used the proceeds of the loan wisely and effectively.[11]

The British did not learn of the American efforts to place an adviser in China until December 8—information that came from

10. Calhoun to Knox, October 1, 2, 11, 1910, DS 893.51/134, 198-99.
11. *DDF,* Ser. 2, 13, 58-59; Siebert, *Benckendorff,* I, 386-88; Bernstorff to Benthmann-Hollweg, November 5, 1910, *GP,* 32, 163; Morgans to Grenfell, September 2, 1910, DS 893.77/1063; Knox to Calhoun, October 6, 1910, DS 893.51/138.

the Paris embassy. American insistence on the point put the British in an awkward position. For political reasons generally they did not want to quarrel with the United States over the issue; on the other hand, they agreed with the French that an American adviser would give the United States an undue advantage in Chinese financial matters. Grey complained that the American demand could hardly be reconciled with the principle of absolute equality that the Foreign Office assumed the quadruple banks had approved at their meeting in London on November 10.[12]

By the time of that conference the Europeans of course knew about the preliminary agreement that gave the Americans the exclusive right to negotiate and sign the final loan contract. Hostile and suspicious, they were in no mood to make concessions when it came to drawing up the regulations governing the four-bank consortium. Since France refused to permit internationalization of bond issues, the American Group received the option of floating its share of any issue at home or in Europe, but if it chose the latter, it could work only through the tripartite banks. As for the currency loan, the European banks resisted the demand, made by the American Group, with strong department backing, for the continuance of the original tripartite provision that accorded any group the right to negotiate and sign alone. If the Americans could not get China to permit quadruple signature, or if for any reason the European banks refused to participate, the Americans would be free to issue the bonds in Europe through their own channels. In that event any group could withdraw from the syndicate, and the French, German, and British banks would revert to their position under the agreements of July 1909, thereby disrupting the four-bank consortium.[13]

The Europeans, confident that the American Group could not float the issue alone and that it would be forced to admit them to the loan, saw no reason why they should pay for the Americans' "diplomatic plumage." Pichon considered it a mistake to allow the United States to gain the advantage attached to the prestige of signing alone, especially since the United States would be promoting its own policy with Europe's money. He also opposed letting the Americans negotiate the conditions of the loan because he was afraid that some of the money might be used for projects

12. FO 405/200/200; John Jordan Papers.
13. Addis to Foreign Office, November 11, 1910, FO 405/200/127; Straight, Memorandum, DS 893.51/325; *FR, 1912,* 92.

in Manchuria, which would displease the Russians and Japanese. When the British and Germans joined Pichon in urging that all four groups sign the agreement with China, Knox pointed out that he had to take China's wishes into consideration. He promised, however, to do his utmost to convince China that all the Powers should participate in the agreement. He would not discuss the subject with China, however, until the contract with the European banks was in final form.[14]

Although Knox gave way on joint signatures with China, he would not budge from his determination to negotiate alone. Thus, when the contract was ready to be signed, the Europeans would face an accomplished fact: an American would hold the post of financial adviser to the Chinese Government. Knox was so insistent on this point that he even refused to continue negotiating until China had made the appointment. And Knox would not rest with the mere appointment; the adviser must be given effective authority. Calhoun believed that the discussions would be fruitless until a currency reform plan was devised that was acceptable to both Chinese and Americans; then the adviser's services would be limited to seeing that the proceeds of the loan were applied as specified in the contract. The department must recognize, Calhoun insisted, that China would never sign an agreement giving a foreigner the right to impose a plan that she had not approved beforehand. Knox would have no part of such a procedure. The Chinese must appoint the adviser and then consult with him and get his approval for the reforms, the plans for their execution, and the expenditures of funds.

A stalemate resulted, and by the end of January Straight confessed that he was "pretty darn well licked," since Knox refused to yield, even at the risk of wrecking the whole program. As Straight pointed out to J. P. Morgan and Company, everyone knew that if the American Group did not admit the Europeans to the loan, China would not get a satisfactory price for the bonds. By insisting that appointment of the adviser must precede the negotiations, the State Department appeared intent on gaining advantages over the European banks.[15] Straight accused the de-

14. Straight to "Dear Excellency," January 29, 1911, Straight to Davison, February 21, 1911, Willard Straight Papers; *DDF,* Ser. 2, 13, 58-59; FO 405/200/153, 160, 203; *GP,* 32, 166.
15. Straight to Morgans, January 23, 1911, DS 893.51/290; Calhoun to Knox, December 19, 1910, DS 893.51/292; Knox to Calhoun, January 13, 1911, DS 893.51/274; Croly, *Straight,* 384, 390.

partment of lacking finesse and of wasting golden opportunities through maladroit diplomacy, and his disillusionment encompassed the Chinese as well. Once he had been eager to champion the "deserving Chinese [but] I do not feel this as keenly now."[16]

In Straight's opinion, however, the real blame for the deadlock rested with Russia and Japan. Practically from the moment of his arrival in Peking, late in November, Straight was convinced that Russia and Japan were engaged in an intrigue against the consummation of the loan.[17] Straight was not mistaken. In mid-September the Russian minister in Peking reported hearing that the Chinese wanted to borrow abroad for general administrative purposes. What were St. Petersburg's views on the subject? Although the new chief of the Foreign Office, S. D. Sazanov, believed that such a loan would run counter to Russia's interests, he did not think Russia could prevent its issue on the American market. He therefore weighed other alternatives, among them Russian participation in the loan. Kokovtsov rejected this course, arguing that Russia's share would be too insignificant to increase her influence in China and that participation would be interpreted as approval of the loan by the Russian Government. Furthermore, unlike Sazanov, he did not write off Russia's ability to frustrate the Sino-American project. True, the Russians could not bring direct pressure on the United States, but they could exploit the Americans' lack of export capital. Without the cooperation of British and French financial circles, the Americans could not float the loan, and Russia was in a position to exert a certain amount of pressure against cooperation in London and Paris.[18]

On November 3 Rockhill informed the Russians that China wanted an American loan for currency reform and Manchurian development. Later, he told them also that the bankers would insist on placing an American in the Chinese Ministry of Finance. The United States would be pleased, Rockhill assured Sazanov, if Russian capital participated in the loan. Sazanov and Motono reached the obvious conclusion that the United States Government intended to use money raised in Europe to influence not only Chinese currency reform but also general Chinese policy. Frankly expressing dissatisfaction over the increasing penetra-

16. Straight to Davison, January 2, 1911, same to "Dear Excellency," January 29, 1911, same to Marvin, January 11, 1911, Straight Papers.
17. Croly, *Straight,* 373.
18. Sazanov to Kokovtsov, September 14, 1910, Kokovtsov to Sazanov, October 11, 1910, Siebert, *Benckendorff,* I, 358-59, 370-71.

tion of foreign capital into China, Motono suggested that Russia and Japan together float a similar loan. Sazanov demurred; he pointed out that China probably would not want to increase her dependence on the two countries. But he noted that if the United States cited its obligations to China under the 1903 treaty, Britain and Japan could do the same and also ask to appoint an adviser. Russia would then make a similar claim on the basis of her 1895 loan and the Boxer indemnities.[19]

In November, when Straight offered Noetzlin a 5 percent participation for the Russo-Asiatic Bank, Noetzlin refused, for at this point Russian activity was concentrated, as Kokovtsov had suggested it should be, on frustrating American efforts to float the loan. The Russians sought—and received—assurances that France would not permit the quotation on the Paris Bourse of loans with political objectives harmful to Russian and Japanese interests.[20] In a direct approach to the problem, the Russian Government informed the Chinese that if they appointed an American adviser they must also name a Russian. While pointing out that the quadruple agreement in November foreshadowed international control of China's finances, the Russians added that, in view of their stake in China, they must have an equal voice in any operation whose objective was China's financial rehabilitation.[21]

Japan, however, preferred to participate in the loan rather than to obstruct it. Ijuin made representations to the Chinese Government similar to those of Russia, and the Japanese Government also approached the bankers directly. In mid-November Korekiyo Takahashi informed the Hongkong and Shanghai Bank that the Japanese were now ready to take up the British offer, made in 1907, to let Japanese capitalists share in Chinese loans. Addis replied for the bank that the consortium could not admit Japan unless she could contribute some project to the syndicate—as the Americans had the currency loan. Further, if the other groups declined to participate in business accepted by Japan, the European markets would be closed to her and she would have to float the entire loan at home. The Japanese reply, "a polite species of blackmail," in Addis' view, mentioned that although Japan's capi-

19. Sazanov to Kokovtsov, November 19, 1910, Siebert, *Benckendorff*, 384-85.
20. Straight to ffrench, February 7, 1911, Straight Papers; Neratov to Izvolsky, March 15, 1911, F. Stieve, *Der diplomatische Schriftwechsel Iswolskis 1911-1914*, I, 42-43.
21. Hillier to Addis, January 11, 1911, FO 405/206/11; Jordan to Grey, January 11, 1911, FO 405/204/16.

talists had never competed for loans in the past, they might well find it necessary to do so in the future. Shortly afterward Schiff received an appeal from Takahashi, asking him to use his influence to get Japan into the consortium, to which he replied early in January that the Americans would do their best to win the Europeans' consent.[22]

Pichon, worried by the Russian and Japanese representations against the loan, instructed Paul Cambon, the French ambassador in London, to inform the British that the French Government was not yet sure how the money was to be used. If it were to be spent in Manchuria and Mongolia in a way displeasing to Russia and Japan, the French Government would insist that the French banks decline to participate. Could the British prevent the United States from working against Russia and Japan? Nicolson told Cambon that he had no details of the loan, but if Russia and Japan wanted to appeal to Grey, Grey would probably be willing to ask the United States if the proceeds were really meant for currency reform. If not, the English banks could scarcely participate if their government withdrew its support. Nicolson added that he considered unilateral American negotiations inexpedient and that the British Cabinet was not sympathetic to them. But Grey did not agree with Nicolson, for he felt that even if the Chinese refused to allow joint signature, the Foreign Office could not forbid the British Group to participate. Grey maintained that such a ban was impractical, since the Government could not thereby be sure of stopping the loan or even of preventing other British banks from assuming it.[23]

Pichon also instructed the French ambassador in Tokyo to make the French position known to Komura. On November 23 Gérard informed the Japanese that his government consented in principle to the participation of the French Group in the currency loan. However, if the funds were to be spent in a way inconsistent with the special interests of Japan and Russia, the French Government would take immediate steps requiring its group to withdraw. In short, France's attitude was the same toward the loan as

22. Calhoun and Straight knew of the Russian and Japanese representations. Straight, Memorandum, DS 893.51/325; Croly, *Straight,* 382; Takahashi to Townsend, November 14, 1910, same to Schiff, November 29, 1910, Schiff to Takahashi, January 5, 1911, JFO, MT Series, Reel 215; Addis to Campbell, November 16, 22, 1910, FO 405/200/142, 155.
23. Kato to British Foreign Office, November 30, 1910, FO 405/200/167; Etter to Russian Foreign Minister, November 23, 1910, Siebert, *Benckendorff,* I, 387-88; Campbell to Jordan, December 24, 1910, Jordan Papers.

it had been toward the neutralization scheme.[24]

Both Russia and Japan now approached the Americans. In December the Russian Government notified the United States Department of State that if China concluded any loan that might lead to some measure of foreign control over her financial affairs, Russia intended to share the foreigners' responsibilities. The Russians also asked for information about the guarantees of the loan and the purposes for which the funds would be used. From Tokyo came the report that, although the Japanese were piqued at having been excluded from the London conference, they would nevertheless accept with pleasure an invitation to participate in the financing plans. The Russians received a noncommital reply, and the department informed the Japanese that at the proper time it would urge the admission of Japanese bankers to the loan. What the Japanese were not told was that their participation, like that of the Russians, would be urged on the same basis as any other nonsignatory to the quadruple agreement—without the right of joint signature.[25]

The department paid no further attention to the Russians and the Japanese until it received Calhoun's telegram of January 23, 1911. Japan was using the spectre of the consortium to arouse fear in Chinese circles—especially in the National Assembly—that the foreign banks intended to control Chinese finances; and the Russians were abetting Japan's efforts to frighten China. To thwart these designs, Calhoun suggested that the department obtain assurances from Britain, France, and Germany that if their banks were admitted as signatories to the loan contract, they would then agree to the appointment of a single adviser—not necessarily American—and would either oppose Russian and Japanese participation or agree to their admission on the basis that they waive any right to appoint an adviser.[26]

More than two weeks elapsed before the department instructed Calhoun to "carefully sift reports of Japanese and Russian intrigues" and report by telegraph their basis and the "explanations, if any, of the Japanese and Russian Ministers." Straight visualized himself and Calhoun going to Kumataro Honda, in charge of the Japanese legation, and to Korostovetz and asking, "Have you perchance done aught to interfere with our altruistic

24. Confidential Memorandum, n.d., JFO, MT Series, Reel 215.
25. DS 893.51/335, 270, 245A.
26. Calhoun to Knox, January 23, 1911, DS 893.51/287.

plan?" And they would reply, "Naughty, naughty, *how* could you have thought it!" Was Washington thinking, Straight wondered, that the diplomats in Peking were playing kindergarten games instead of gambling for an empire?[27]

Calhoun and Straight continued to work toward a compromise, in full estimate of the stakes in their game, and finally devised a formula acceptable to the Chinese. China would allow quadruple signature and appoint an adviser nominated by the United States. Although his nationality was unspecified, he would be an American if the other Powers agreed, a neutral if they did not. Calhoun predicted that the currency matter could now move very fast, for both Finance Minister Duke Tsai Tsê and Shêng Kung-Pao of the Communications Ministry, admitted to Calhoun that it was the urgency of the Manchurian situation that made them submit on these two points. The German *chargé* belived that China wanted the contract signed because this would meet halfway the lively American desire for currency reform and would add to the economic interests of the four Great Powers in Manchuria as security against foreign appetites there.[28]

But the department did not intend to admit an alternative to the nationality of the adviser. It informed London, Paris, and Berlin that China would consent to joint signature and supervision of expenditures if the European governments would not raise the question of joint advisers. "In view of the concessions made by the United States in order to get joint signature of Hukuang loan," the United States Government hoped that the Powers would support its legitimate claim for the appointment of one financial adviser, an American. "Such finesse!" commented Straight, "When the mere mention of Hukuang is like a red rag to a bull to these European Foreign Offices! But for us the line would now be being built by them!"[29]

Yet just five days later, on February 23, Knox was indicating to Bernstorff and Bryce that he would by no means insist that the adviser be an American; he would be glad eventually to name a neutral to the post. The department's about-face was the result of Straight's report to J. P. Morgan and Company on February 15 of

27. Croly, *Straight*, 389.
28. Calhoun to Knox, February 11, 18, 23, 1911, DS 893.51/299, 301, 761.93/28; Luxburg to Bethmann-Hollweg, April 17, 1911, *GP*, 32, 172-73.
29. Croly, *Straight*, 392. Straight wrote to Davison that his telegrams had perhaps seemed very bitter against the State Department; the state of his mind, he confessed, had been more so. Straight to Davison, February 15, 1911, Straight Papers.

a rumor that the Russo-Asiatic Bank had combined with an English house (the London City and Midland) and a powerful Belgian group to lend money to China. Grenfell confirmed the formation of the new syndicate, which, in his opinion, might mean trouble for the currency loan. Grenfell had also learned that the new group apparently did not intend to do business in China proper but, rather, proposed to operate in Manchuria and Mongolia. On February 24 Knox formally notified the tripartite governments that if they objected to the appointment of an American, he would suggest a neutral.[30]

The department had been forced to retreat from its earlier position and from its attempt to garner prestige, Chinese gratitude, and subsequent benefits by playing a lone hand. Calhoun's policy of genuine cooperation with the tripartite countries became the department's policy because there was no alternative but failure and/or withdrawal. The banking group's relief was apparent.

> We take this opportunity, in behalf of the American group, of expressing their appreciation of the broad-minded statesmanship shown by the Department in waiving insistence on the appointment of an American adviser in the interest of the less obvious but, we hope, more far reaching and enduring advantage which will result from complete harmony among the Governments and the banking groups of the great lending nations. . . . [31]

The British and the Germans accepted the department's offer to name a neutral. The French Foreign Office instructed Jusserand to agree to cooperate in the loan if the other Powers did so, and if the loan contract would not apply to Manchuria under conditions to which Russia and Japan objected. Later, France added the condition, which Knox accepted, that the bankers must name the adviser.[32]

On April 15, 1911, the four bank representatives signed the currency and Manchurian development loan agreement with China, Manchurian revenues guaranteeing one half of the loan, revenues from China proper the other. On the day of signature China was to give the banks a detailed program of currency reform, a list of specific enterprises planned for Manchuria, and the estimated cost of each item in both programs. The banks would

---

30. *GP*, 32, 169; DS 893.51/312, 350; *FR, 1912,* 94.
31. Morgan & Co., to Knox, February 24, 1911, DS 893.51/310.
32. DS 893.51/323, 329, 346.

have six months to approve or reject the plans. If China needed additional foreign capital to continue or complete these projects, she was obliged under Article 16 of the agreement to let the banks make the first tender. Should the principal parties disagree on terms, China would be free to borrow elsewhere. China received the option of asking the consortium to advance £1,000,000 for Manchurian industrial development and an equal amount for currency reform. Although theoretically the contract was in its final form, it left many points open to future negotiation.

By now Straight was reconciled to American cooperation with the Europeans on equal terms. He regarded Article 16 as offering the four banks the opportunity of a preferential position for later expanded activity—even for railroad building—in Manchuria. He was convinced, however, that the consortium must move with the greatest caution and discretion. But no amount of optimism could overcome the practical obstacles. There were the assurances that France had given to both Russia and Japan in November. And by February the Russians had embarked on a new policy, as Grenfell had reported. The Russians' objective now was not merely to frustrate the currency loan but to split France from the four-Power consortium by bringing the French Group into the recently created Russian financial syndicate and perhaps including the Japanese as well. The Russian plan strictly delimited the spheres of activity, with American, British, and German capitalists financing industrial loans in China proper and the Russians and their colleagues lending money for similar enterprises north of the Great Wall. Each consortium would share equally in all Chinese financial-political loans. To carry out this policy, Russia had formed the banking group that drove Knox to withdraw his insistence on an American adviser.[33]

In Paris and St. Petersburg the Russians discussed the consortium's operations with the French, and both the French Foreign

---

33. *FR, 1912,* 95-96. Calhoun described the negotiations as "the most tortuous and nerve racking with which I ever had anything to do." Calhoun to Knox, April 27, 1911, DS 893.51/470; Izvolsky to Foreign Minister, April 21, 1911, Stieve, *Izvolsky,* I, 74; Luxburg to Bethmann-Hollweg, April 17, 1911, *GP,* 32, 172-73; Addis to Campbell, February 17, 1911, FO 405/206/14. The financiers distinguished between "financial" and "industrial" loans. The proceeds of *financial* loans were intended for nonproductive purposes, and the promoters realized their profit from floating the bonds. The currency and the later reorganization loans fell into this category and were also classed as political loans, since the monies were destined for administrative reforms. *Industrial* loans, used for railroads and similar productive enterprises, gave the financiers a profit not only from floating the loan but also from the concomitant purchases of construction materials and similar items.

Office and its representative gave the desired assurances. France would participate only if the legitimate interests of its friends were protected and Russia's wishes—not only those expressed in the past but also those which she might bring up in the future—respected. But the Russians' suspicions boded ill for the consortium's future success; they believed not only that Article 16 gave the syndicate a monopoly on Chinese financing but also that the currency loan under discussion was merely the first of a series.[34]

On April 19 Izvolsky, now serving as Russian ambassador in Paris, inquired at the French Foreign Office about the details of the loan agreement, and these were sent him the following day. The French Foreign Minister tried to reassure the Russians, pointing out that France had no grounds for assuming that China intended to spend any of the money on the Chin-Ai railroad. The consortium knew that Russia objected to the road and that on this question the French Government stood by its ally. France could not believe that the bankers would ignore these objections and thereby run the risk that the loan would not be quoted on the Paris Bourse. When the Chinese presented their outline of proposed expenditures to the bankers, France would pass it along to Russia for examination. Since the four groups had six months to study China's program, the Russians would have plenty of time to shape and voice their objections.[35]

Even these assurances did not calm Russian apprehensions. Acting Foreign Minister A. A. Neratov told Motono of his fear that China, greatly strengthened by the loan, would attack the C.E.R. Motono did not share Neratov's anxiety over Chinese aggression; he foresaw danger only from the United States, whose Pacific Fleet would be so strong after the Panama Canal was finished that the Japanese fleet could only defend itself, not attack. In Motono's opinion the Russians and Japanese must attain a favorable settlement of their position in Manchuria before the canal opened.[36]

At the moment the Japanese seemed to think that participation in the consortium would help to strengthen their position in Manchuria. After their failure in November to get any support from the British, they had, as noted earlier, turned to Schiff. Schiff

34. Stieve, *Izvolsky*, I, 42-47.
35. Stieve, *Izvolsky*, I, 74, 80-81.
36. Siebert, *Benckendorff*, II, 87-88.

found the Europeans indisposed to admit the Japanese, on the ground that they would contribute no financial strength to the combination. In early January 1911 Schiff promised the Japanese that he and his partners would use their influence to arrange Japan's participation, and in March the Yokohama Specie Bank, in response to a government inquiry, agreed to represent Japan if she were invited to join the consortium. Japan's sensibilities, always delicate, seemed seriously offended by her exclusion from the currency loan, and the sharp comments in the Japanese press reflected this resentment.[37]

Impelled by this reaction in Japan, the department discussed with the American Group the desirability of allowing the Japanese to participate. Although the consortium was not enthusiastic about admitting Japan, the department was aware that Japan's treaty rights gave her a claim to moderate financial participation in enterprises in China. Furthermore, since the success of the currency reform program depended on the cooperation of all the Powers, the department strongly favored the widest possible participation. But the inclusion of Japanese capital was a question for the banks to resolve, and the department believed that the consortium would not consider giving Japan more than a small share that carried no voice in the management.[38]

In May the Russians made an unexpected overture to the consortium. Two circumstances explained their sudden friendliness. The London City and Midland Bank announced that it was not associated with any syndicate formed to do business in China. Furthermore, the Russo-Belgian group was now afraid that it might have trouble getting its bonds quoted on the Paris Bourse. On May 5 De Hoyer, who represented the Russian-Belgian syndicate in Peking, suggested to Straight that the two groups work together. Straight agreed—feeling that the consortium should try to conciliate Russia—in order to quiet Russo-Japanese distrust concerning the Manchurian features of the loan. The four bank representatives in Peking also recommended an understanding with Russia regarding specific Mongolian and Manchurian projects. They reasoned that in these areas the Russians could not get concessions from the Chinese without the political neutralization that cooperation with the consortium would bring; at the same time Russian exclusion would evoke enough opposition to prevent

37. Schiff to Takahashi, January 5, 1911, JFO, MT Series, Reel 215; Morgans to Knox, March 13, 1911, DS 893.51/343; O'Brien to Knox, April 22, 1911, DS 893.51/391; Jordan to Grey, May 5, 1911, FO 405/204/242.
38. DS 893.51/391.

the consortium from securing concessions there either.[39]

The American Group consulted the department to determine its willingness to consider the proposed Russian participation without including a similar provision for Japan. Knox decided that if the Japanese wanted to join, they must be included. In his view, Japan had quite as much right as any other country to expect a share of the loan, both because of her interest by treaty in currency reform and her involvement in Manchuria particularly and in China generally. To the group's question about the participation of additional countries, Knox replied that, in his opinion, Japan and Russia would exhaust the list of those vitally interested, especially since the Russian Group seemed to include the Belgians. The department informed Japan's representative that, although the decision regarding her participation rested finally with the bankers, it was prepared to support her application on an equal footing with others not included in the London agreement.[40]

But the problem of who was to participate in the loan was momentarily overshadowed by China's request on May 6 for an immediate advance of £400,000 for Manchurian development. At the same time she presented a statement listing projects for which she would use the money. France consulted Russia, who objected to the advance, on the grounds that it would mean automatic approval of the loan contract by the banks and their governments even though it had been concluded without Russia's knowledge. Russia also wanted to know how the loan funds would be spent, since part of them were intended for Manchuria and certain Manchurian revenues would serve as guarantees. The advance of funds thus opened up the possibility of foreign interference, perhaps also of foreign control, in the internal affairs of that area.[41]

When the British, German, and American governments approved the advance and showed a readiness to proceed even without the French, France tried to bring pressure on London to refuse the advance and advised the Russians to do the same. Grey did not question the right of the French to withhold approval of the advance until satisfied that the Chinese would not use the money to

39. Jordan to Grey, May 10, 1911, FO 405/206/70; Straight to Morgans, May 8, 1911, DS 893.51/465; Morgan, Grenfell to Morgans, May 9, 1911, DS 893.51/414; Straight to Morgan, Grenfell, May 6, 1911, DS 893.51/421. German *chargé* R. Luxburg, reporting on the De Hoyer approach, noted that Russia had neither capital for foreign investment nor a market for Chinese bonds. Obviously her motive in joining the four groups was purely political. *GP,* 32, 174-76.
40. DS 893.51/414-15; *FR, 1912,* 96.
41. Stieve, *Izvolsky,* I, 92-93.

hurt Russia's interests, but the program that China had laid out in her request of May 6 seemed quite unobjectionable to Grey. Nor was it at all clear to him why France now required the consent of a third Power to China's appropriation of her own Manchurian revenues. Finally, on May 23 the French relented and, over Russian objections, agreed to pay their share of the advance funds.[42]

Grey warned Knox, however, that international difficulties connected with the loan had been only temporarily overcome. Japan was apprehensive over future Manchurian projects; Russia was afraid that the money would be used for Manchurian railroads; France was worried about her relations with Russia. Grey thought that if the consortium and China could draw up an overall Manchurian program that did not include railroads, all diplomatic difficulties would disappear. Knox accepted this suggestion, noting that the amount of money earmarked for Manchuria was not large. He was prepared to insist that China use the funds strictly for the enterprises specified.[43] Grey therefore proposed to China that she formulate her statement.

At this point the Russians were reviewing their policy toward financial operations in Manchuria. In a letter dated June 4 addressed to his Prime Minister, the Russian Minister of Finance discussed the implications of the projected Manchurian loan and laid down the Russian policy, which harked back to his suggestions of October 1910. Kokovtsov agreed with Foreign Minister Sazanov that the loan had an undoubted political significance and that it should therefore be considered as affecting Russian interests. It was true that the consortium had not succeeded in securing the right to administer the revenue sources or to control their collection. Consequently, the governments behind the four-Power syndicate could say, strictly speaking, that the operation had an exclusively financial character and did not seek to injure the political interests of Japan and Russia. This explanation could not be accepted. Certainly, if the revenues of a region were earmarked as a guarantee of a financial operation carried through by foreigners, those foreigners would in fact obtain political influence in that area.

According to Russian information, the initiative for this undertaking had come from the Americans, who thought tripartite sup-

42. Stieve, *Izvolsky,* I, 100; DS 893.51/425, 441; Grey to Cambon, May 20, 1911, FO 405/204/237.
43. Grey to Bryce, May 30, 1911, FO 405/204/260; DS 893.51/462.

port necessary. Neither Russia nor, apparently, Japan had been informed of the project, and even now, when the contract had been signed, the details were still being withheld from them. Kokovtsov did not believe that Knox had the same goal in this operation as in the neutralization scheme. Previously, the objective had been to take away from Russia and Japan the railroads that were the chief instruments of their influence in Manchuria. Now it was a matter of creating, as counterparts to the Russo-Japanese interests, financial and economic interests of the four Powers and giving them the right to take part in the solution of all questions concerning Manchuria. The new plan seemed calculated to deprive Russia and Japan of their dominant position in Manchuria and, if it succeeded, of again bringing forward the question of the complete neutralization of that area as proposed by Knox. As a result, Russia could anticipate a sort of Manchurian protectorate of the four Powers, with the United States at their head.

Russian hostility had helped defeat the neutralization proposal, and Kokovtsov advocated the same attitude toward the currency loan, since he saw it as a first step toward the same goal—to weaken Russian influence in Manchuria. Had it been an isolated matter, it probably would have little importance, but the consortium was to be entrusted with all future financial operations in China. Further, the consortium intended to profit greatly from China's recent disposition to reorganize her government and modernize her army. The creation of such a powerful syndicate representing the four most interested countries constituted a share in China's internal affairs that could not be explained if the consortium's object was merely to carry through a relatively unimportant loan of £10,000,000. Certainly the bankers intended to lend China additional funds for her army, navy, industry, and railroads. The loan contract even contained a clause on this point: China agreed to borrow from the consortium if she needed more money to carry out her projects.

The Russian Finance Minister harped on the preponderant role that the United States was playing. It was a role that it would seek to perpetuate because the Americans obviously wanted to strengthen their influence in China. Kokovtsov thought the United States would try above all to carry through projects that promised to be most detrimental to Russia.

On the basis of all these considerations, Kokovtsov again rejected the suggestion that Russia join the consortium and share in the loan. For one thing, the Russian share would be only one fifth of the total, and this modest participation would not provide adequate protection to her interests. On the contrary, she would be contributing to the realization of an operation that would eventually be unfavorable to her. Even more important: Russian participation would implicitly sanction the entrance of other foreigners into Manchurian affairs and complicate any Russian protests in the future against harmful consortium projects.

The only way to end the conflict between Russian-Japanese interests on the one side and those of the consortium on the other was to transform the consortium with the help of Japan and France: Japan would follow the Russian lead because she did not want foreigners in Manchuria; France, because she habitually did so. A new group, which included Russia and Japan, would join the consortium on condition that the enlarged syndicate was subdivided into two groups: one with Russian, Japanese, and eventually French or neutral capital; the other with British, German, and American capital. To avoid competition, the groups would agree to delimit their spheres of influence, the Russo-Japanese group operating north of the Great Wall.[44]

In spite of all the difficulties over the currency loan, the month of May furnished the four banks and their governments with one piece of good news. On May 20 China signed the final loan contract for the Hukuang railroads. In July 1910 the four governments had sent China identic notes, pressing for conclusion of the loan. The Chinese made no reply until October, when they announced that the June agreement was not final and that some modifications were necessary to soothe public opinion and prevent serious trouble in Hupeh and Hunan. The State Department, still influenced by the gloomy forebodings of the legation in Peking, instructed Calhoun not to take the lead in urging China to sign. He was to act with his colleagues, however, in any representations on which the four governments agreed. Such a course went beyond the Minister's inclinations. In his opinion it was undignified and unworthy of civilized powers to attempt to force such a loan on an unwilling government. But he was willing to yield the point "to maintain that harmony of cooperation which appears so all important to the success of any future policy we might have in China."[45]

44. Copy in JFO, MT Series, Reel 216.
45. FO 405/203/54; *FR, 1910,* 291; Calhoun to Knox, October 25, 1910, DS 893.51/208.

Calhoun continued to be pessimistic over the internal situation and only reluctantly concurred in the identic notes presented by the ministers in late October and again in late November. When no response had arrived by the end of December, Calhoun agreed to accompany his colleagues to the Foreign Office to make personal representations, but he took no part in the discussion. He went along, he said, only because the Hukuang loan would have gone through long before but for American intrusion. Two weeks later Jordan was admitting that the concerted pressure on China had brought no results. The Chinese knew that the Americans were lukewarm, which was enough to undo all the others' efforts.[46]

Yet, the new year wore on and no uprising occurred in the provinces, even though the government in Peking had twice given them good grounds for protesting against foreign influence in their internal affairs. First, China had capitulated to Russia on Mongolia and then, to pacify the consortium governments, had agreed to joint signature of the currency loan. Since these events had had no untoward results in the threatened areas, Knox decided that the Chinese plea of opposition in the provinces no longer carried conviction and that the central government was damaging itself abroad by pretending an inability to withstand civil unrest. Consequently, he instructed Calhoun to urge an early signature to the Hukuang loan. This time Calhoun approved the action but assured Knox that "provincial opposition is not wholly threadbare. Unfortunately there is much substance to it."[47]

Now China yielded. On May 9 an imperial decree ordered the early signature of the Hukuang contract. At the same time the central government reserved for itself the construction of all trunk-line railroads, limiting provincial efforts to branch lines. Not only did the decree cancel the right that Peking had previously given local companies in Hupeh and Hunan to build their own railroads, but, by providing inadequate compensation for repurchase of provincial railroad stocks, the decree gave the shareholders a real grievance. Describing the government's action as "a step which cannot fail to have the most far-reaching consequences," Jordan predicted that it would either compel acquiescence or invite rebellion. Although later proved a mistaken prophet, he believed that after expressing loud pro-

46. DS 893.00/448—; FO 405/206/5; Jordan Papers.
47. DS 893.51/385A-86.

tests the provinces would soon yield to firmness.[48]

On June 15, 1911, the consortium issued the £6,000,000 Hukuang loan. That within two days the bonds were greatly oversubscribed Addis attributed to the fact that no matter what China did, "a perfect infatuation" persisted in England for bona fide Chinese securities. Although by mid-June serious opposition to the decree nationalizing trunk lines was becoming manifest in the provinces, the four Powers saw no cause for disquiet, since unrest in China was nothing new.[49] They continued to concentrate on the important business at hand, eliminating Russian and Japanese obstruction of the currency loan.

On May 25 Kato had mentioned to Grey that, according to reports current in Japan, China had given the consortium an option on future Manchurian loans. Surprised by Kato's comment, Grey remarked that he could understand if Russia and Japan felt strongly about being excluded forever from participation in industrial projects in Manchuria; he agreed that this exclusion would indeed be inconsistent with the Open Door policy. But China had responded to Grey's suggestion to include Russia and Japan in the financing, and the British forwarded to the two obstructing nations the outline of the Manchurian projects along with the loan contract. After conferring together, on June 26 Russia and Japan presented protests in London and Paris against Article 16, which, they contended, by granting a monopoly of financial and industrial undertakings in Manchuria, violated the Open Door policy. Japan was willing to accept an amended article; Russia offered no alternative: Article 16 must go. France indicated that she would not approve the loan until Russia and Japan were satisfied. In Peking De Hoyer was predicting triumphantly that the loan would never be floated.[50] In fact, after receiving Russia's protest of June 26, the French Foreign Office replied that the currency bonds would not be listed on the Bourse until the consortium solved the question of Article 16 to Russia's satisfaction. Still unhappy, the Russians informed French Foreign Minister de Selves that they wanted to create a special syndicate of Russian, French, and Japanese capitalists to operate in the Russo-Japanese spheres. Having prepared the ground in his dis-

48. E-tu Sun, *Chinese Railways and British Interests, 1898-1911,* 117-18; FO 405/206/61; Jordan to Campbell, October 30, 1911, Jordan Papers.
49. Jordan to Grey, June 20, 1911, FO 405/207/6.
50. *FR, 1912,* 99-100; Stieve, *Izvolsky,* I, 126; *DDF,* Ser. 3, I, 456-64; Grey to Rumbold, May 26, 1911, FO 405/204/252; *GP,* 32, 178.

cussions with De Selves and Caillaux, Izvolsky felt that the moment had arrived to present a concrete plan. In spite of French support, however, he anticipated that the execution of his plans would meet great obstacles and that it would be especially difficult to exclude the United States. He suggested a vigorous diplomatic effort to this end, since France now had special need of Russian support in solving the Moroccan question.[51]

Izvolsky also approached Simon of the Banque de l'Indo-Chine and frankly explained the Russian position. Simon promised to do his utmost to bring the actions of the French Group into harmony with Russian desires. Although little difficulty stood in the way of eliminating Article 16, the creation of a new syndicate presented greater problems, since both the United States and Germany would oppose it energetically. Sensing Simon's hesitancy, Izvolsky repeated to his superiors that no time should be lost in making a definite offer to the French Government.[52]

On July 11 the Russians and Japanese presented their protests to the American and German governments. Knox tried to convince Uchida that the Japanese were misinterpreting Article 16 and that the four Powers did not intend to monopolize Manchuria. After some amendments, Knox told the Minister, the article would satisfy Japan. Certainly Knox was sympathetic to complaints of monopoly, for after examining the draft agreement for the loan in the fall of 1910, he had himself raised this very point with the banking group. He had then expressed the opinion that no one could misinterpret the preference given to the group in furnishing additional money for currency reform; what could be misunderstood was the extension of that option to anything so indefinite as "certain industrial enterprises in Manchuria." The Secretary had informed the bankers that the United States would not necessarily construe Article 16 as binding it to support any project they might decide to undertake. He now sharpened his point by recalling the American reaction to the vague and indefinite mining rights conferred on Japan under the September 1909 agreements.[53]

Because of the difficulties created by Russia and Japan and the Secretary's desire to avoid all implications of exclusiveness, Knox and Grey decided to amend Article 16 by limiting the consortium's

51. Stieve, *Izvolsky,* I, 126-27.
52. Izvolsky to Deputy Foreign Minister, August 2, 1911, Stieve, *Izvolsky,* I, 129.
53. *FR, 1912,* 99-100; *GP,* 32, 179-81; Knox to Morgans, July 29, 1911, DS 893.51/518A.

financial options to specific enterprises and by disclaiming any monopoly. The bankers having accepted this clarification, Grey agreed to sound out Germany and France. Germany approved, but the French, although declaring themselves satisfied, doubted that the Russians would be. The French thought cancellation the better course but were prepared to withhold this suggestion if Britain would approach the Russians. Grey, who did not favor canceling the article outright, received the Germans' and Americans' consent to approach Japan as well as Russia, which he did at the end of August. At the end of September the bankers agreed that they would not insist on the execution of Article 16 but that Russia must ask China to suppress it.[54]

Not until October did Grey receive answers to his inquiries, and they did nothing to advance a solution of the problem, for neither Russia nor Japan had changed its position. Both observed that China's program of expenditures for Manchuria was so general in character that it created a practical monopoly in favor of the consortium. One could not exorcise a monopoly by denying its existence. Grey agreed with their complaint that the program was vague and suggested that China should outline specific undertakings, including the actual work contemplated and the monies budgeted in each case. A month later the other three governments had agreed to this approach, but now Grey believed that, owing to the confusion in China, further action was useless at the moment.[55]

54. DS 893.51/526, 536; *GP,* 32, 187-88; FO 405/205/76; *DDF,* Ser. 3, I, 456-64.
55. DS 893.51/596, 656.

13

The Revolution and the Reorganization Loan

Grey, in commenting on the confusion in China, was referring to the outbreak of the long-predicted rebellion in southern China. During the first half of September both Calhoun and Jordan were reporting serious disturbances in Szechuan over the railroad question, but the actual revolt came in Wuchang, the capital of Hupeh Province, on October 10. Willard Straight expressed satisfaction that the Hukuang loan had been profitably placed in the hands of unsuspecting bondholders before the revolution began. Yet he was not blind to the connection between the loan and the revolt; he did, in fact, observe that the conclusion of the large loan had been largely responsible for China's difficulties. Although the country was apparently ripe for rebellion, the protest of the Szechuan gentry against nationalization of the railroads and the Government's unfair compensation to the old shareholders had, in Straight's words, "started the applecart down the hill."[1]

Chargé E. T. Williams reported from Peking that, although the rebellion was undoubtedly the most serious since the Taiping uprising, foreign interests so far had been carefully respected. Knox expected Peking to quell the revolt temporarily, but because the movement was antidynastic, in the long run he was not sanguine about the central government's chances for survival.[2]

Knox's immediate concern was the safety of American lives and property, but he had another objective as well. He saw an opportunity to establish a pattern of cooperation on Chinese affairs among the Powers, thus making it more difficult for any one of them to pursue an independent course. Using the protec-

1. Straight to Kahn, November 27, 1911, Willard Straight Papers.
2. *Foreign Relations, 1912,* 48; Knox to Taft, October 13, 1911, DS 893.00/565A.

tion of foreign interests as a vehicle for joint action, the United States Department of State immediately sent circular notes to the European Powers and Japan. Did those governments, like the United States, contemplate advising their nationals to concentrate at the ports? Were additional cooperative measures needed to protect foreign interests? The replies varied, but Knox was on the whole reassured. In general the Powers agreed that no further steps to protect their nationals were necessary, except perhaps to call them in from the exposed districts.[3]

Announcing at the beginning of the revolt that their movement was not directed against foreigners, the rebel leaders promised to respect China's existing treaties and to protect foreigners. Although in the following years lives of some foreigners were lost and foreign-owned property destroyed, no serious incidents occurred and, consequently, no pretext for intervention.[4]

A few days after the Wuchang revolt the central government asked the consortium for an advance on the loan. Jordan opposed granting it, since he foresaw a demand by the consortium governments for some control over the money's expenditure. Inasmuch as China would undoubtedly ask for additional sums later, these loans might eventually place all Chinese finances under foreign control. Jordan took the position that the British would be better advised to conserve their resources and then lend money to whichever government survived the revolution. The French *charge* favored the advance for the same reason Jordan vetoed it —the hastening of international control. Williams strongly advised lending China the money because a refusal would endanger foreign interests. Furthermore, he reasoned, the four Powers had a moral responsibility to see the Chinese Government through the present crisis, which they had helped precipitate by insisting on signature of the Hukuang loan. Jordan thought Straight was largely responsible for Williams' views, since Straight wanted to bolster the central government in order to save the currency loan, on which his professional reputation depended.[5]

Both the American Group and the British Foreign Office asked the State Department's opinion about the advance of money, and both got the same noncommittal answer. The loan was a legitimate business proposition on which the bankers must make the

3. *FR, 1912,* 163—; Knox to Taft, October 17, 1911, DS 893.00/582A.
4. *FR, 1912,* 49.
5. DS 893.51/595, 610, 621; Jordan to Campbell, October 23, 1911, John Jordan Papers; Jordan to Grey, October 24, 1911, FO 405/205/164.

decisions. Since the Hukuang loan would compete with the currency loan on the markets, the group was "not very keen about it," although it agreed to abide by the decisions of the other banks.[6]

The department's views became clearer after Grey stated his position on October 23. Since the outcome of the revolution was still in doubt, Grey wanted no hasty decision, his caution induced in large part by the fact that three fourths of the British interests in China—lives and property—were in the south where the antidynastic feeling was strongest. When the time came to decide, the consortium governments, not the bankers, should set the course. If the governments of the United States, France, and Germany favored lending the money, Grey would insist that the terms include certain safeguards: foreign supervisory officers for expenditures, foreign audit of the finance department, and the establishment of a reform government by the strongest possible men, including, for example, Yuan Shih-kai.

At this point Knox wanted to abstain from any interference in China's internal problems or even from taking official cognizance of China's request to the banks. He considered it premature to discuss any scheme for the eventual control of China's finances and doubted the advisability of submitting Grey's terms to the Powers. Miller, in fact, told Innes that, according to his information, the consortium did not favor the loan, and Miller hoped their attitude would resolve the entire complicated problem.[7]

The Germans, both banks and government, favored a loan under certain conditions, lest the hostile attitude of the consortium drive the Chinese to find other backers—notably the Japanese—who might compel China to put up important state enterprises, such as railroads, as security.[8]

China greatly increased the pressure on the bankers to act when on October 28 she signed the so-called Cottu loan agreement with an Anglo-French-Belgian syndicate. Before the bankers met on November 8 to discuss this new development, the department informed the American Group of its opposition to any advances except those which would enable China to pay her existing obligations, including service charges on existing loans. Although Straight was pressing for the advance, the American Group, in

6. Miller to Knox, October 17, 1911, Philander C. Knox Papers; Miller Memorandum, DS 893.51/621.
7. FO 405/205/156, 166, 194; Miller Memorandum, October 24, 1911, DS 893.51/634.
8. M. Warburg to P. Warburg, October 28, 1911, DS 893. 51/636; GP, 32, 191-93.

view of the department's attitude and its own belief that the four governments might eventually have to intervene and protect the consortium's interests, decided not to instruct its conference representative. In Paris the bankers voted unanimously to continue the present policy: no money at all to China until there was a responsible government in Peking.[9]

In Peking the tottering Manchus recalled Yuan Shih-kai— whom they had summarily dismissed from office three years earlier—in an effort to save the throne. The British expected no decisive action from Yuan, both because he was an ambitious opportunist and because his own followers were urging him to recognize the hopelessness of the Manchu cause. Tang Shao-yi, who tried to persuade Prince Ch'ing to resign his office as Prime Minister, told Yuan in plain terms that he was not interested in joining a sinking ship. Afraid that the government troops would revolt or disband if not paid, Yuan immediately approached the bankers' representatives for a loan, and they agreed to advance the money, their governments approving. Now the State Department was sure of its stand; it refused to endorse any loan unless the interested Powers could agree on a plan that would enable China to meet her international obligations and perform the ordinary functions of government. China must not use the money for military purposes, and she must accept some form of foreign supervision over expenditures. Loans should be strictly neutral and be endorsed both by the South (the rebels) and the North (the central government). Also, since the objective of the loan was primarily to protect the Powers' common interests, Knox wanted the loans open to the nationals of all countries having important relations with China.[10]

Jordan worked to get both Chinese factions to a peace conference, but although the rebels accepted a truce on December 2, they would not consent to discuss peace until the Manchus abdicated. On December 6 the Prince Regent agreed to resign, thereby opening the way for negotiations. Believing that the conference would fail unless Yuan could find the money to keep his troops loyal, Calhoun urged the department to support the bank representatives' offer of a loan to Yuan. Convinced that Peking offered the best nucleus for a reconstituted central authority,

9. *FR, 1912,* 101; Morgans to Morgan, Grenfell, November 6, 1911, DS 893.51/648; H. H. Harjes to Morgans, November 8, 1911, DS 893.51/652.
10. *FR, 1912,* 101-2; Jordan to Campbell, November 17 and 19, 1911, Jordan Papers.

Straight too advised giving Yuan the money, as he had from the beginning of the crisis.[11]

But Knox was still not ready to approve a loan to the North, and the division of opinion continued among and within banking groups and governments over the advisability of lending Yuan money while the Chinese political scene was so murky. The Japanese and Russian ministers in Peking attended the discussions when they began in mid-December, and although their presence satisfied Knox's requirement that the loan have a broad international basis, it did not further a decision. To make the loan was to choose sides, which the governments were reluctant to do lest their action give the rebel leaders a pretext for attacking foreigners.[12] The loan negotiations therefore remained in abeyance until February 1912, when the Chinese seemed to have put their house in some order.During the stalemate on the loan, Knox was busy on the diplomatic front. The Powers had agreed to act together if the Chinese situation deteriorated, but by early December Knox was beginning to suspect that Japan was concocting plans of her own. From Tokyo the United States Ambassador reported that the government was considering sending troops to China, and the naval attaché that the British had consented to intervention by Japanese troops. And in truth Japan had broached the subject in London. On December 1 Grey learned from *Chargé* Yamaza that Japan wanted an end to the civil war and a limited monarchy set up. In the next few weeks the Japanese kept returning to the subject, but Grey wanted clarification of their intentions before stating the British position.[13]

A communication from the Japanese Government on December 21 reinforced American fears that Japan's intentions for China conflicted with those of the United States. Jordan had been instrumental in arranging peace talks between the South and Peking, which began in Shanghai on December 18 and in which he was playing an important role. During the discussions among the diplomats in Peking on intervention in China, the Japanese had hinted broadly that they would like to join Jordan in his conferences with Yuan and the rebels, and the British met their wishes. The department concluded from the Japanese note that the British and they had reached a "bilateral understanding" to

11. Jordan to Campbell, December 4, 1911, Jordan Papers; *FR, 1912,* 102; H. Croly, *Willard Straight,* 422.
12. *FR, 1912,* 106-7; *DDF,* Ser. 3, I, 555-57.
13. *FR, 1912,* 55; Grey to Jordan, December 1, 1911, FO 405/205/407.

facilitate the negotiations. Not soothed by assurances that Japan's assistance would be of a "merely benevolent nature," the department asked the British Foreign Office for more information and also instructed the ambassador to Russia, Curtis Guild, to discover the Russian attitude toward this new development.[14] Grey carefully explained the reasons for inviting Japan to join the talks, adding emphatically that Britain would adhere strictly to the policy of concerted action; she would take no step without the Powers' consent. When Guild reported Russia's attitude, which she had communicated to Japan, was that all countries should act together in China, Knox correctly concluded that Japan had wanted to intervene in China but had been unable to secure British support.[15]

Knox faced threats to his policy of international cooperation not only from abroad but at home. On February 12 the Manchu dynasty formally abdicated, and when Yuan Shih-kai assumed leadership of the new provisional government, the question of recognition came to the fore in the United States. After Senator William Sulzer introduced a resolution calling upon the administration to recognize the Republic of China, the Far Eastern Division drew up a substitute proposal that attempted to satisfy public sentiment both at home and in China without actually recognizing Yuan. The State Department proposed that the Congress of the United States merely congratulate the people of China on their assumption of self-government and express hope for their future liberty, happiness, and progress. Such a congressional resolution not only left the President free to recognize China at his own discretion; it enabled him also to maintain an entirely consistent attitude toward joint action with other nations.[16]

A Japanese memorandum delivered to Huntington-Wilson on February 23 brought the question of recognition of the Republic of China to a head, for the Japanese suggested that the Powers, acting jointly, base their recognition on two conditions. They should ask the new Chinese government to confirm all the rights, powers, and immunities enjoyed by foreigners, including those based on custom and legislative enactment as well as on treaties. Further, the Powers should require China to give formal engagements with regard to her foreign indebtedness.

The State Department drafted a reply to the Japanese memo-

14. *FR, 1912,* 53, 59; Guild to Knox, December 23, 1911, DS 893.00/810.
15. *FR, 1912,* 59-60; *GP,* 32, 247.
16. Far Eastern Division, Memorandum, February 19, 1912, DS 893.00/1146A.

randum that agreed in principle to multilateral recognition, but specified the agreement hinged on the understanding that this course entailed no delay. The loophole was deliberate in order that the President might act alone, if necessary, to prevent a delay "which might cause trouble in Congress." Nevertheless, the department thought it important to adhere to the principle of joint action. If the United States could follow that policy and also manage to gain China's good will by an early expression of sympathy to the new government, the United States might eat her cake and have it too. When Huntington-Wilson consulted the President, Taft approved both the reply to Japan and the draft congressional resolution.[17] On February 26 the House accepted the department's draft, and the next day the department replied to the Japanese note.[18] For the time being the Administration had quashed any desire in Congress for immediate unilateral recognition of China.

With the outbreak of the revolution, the consortium governments had suspended their attempts to reach an understanding with Russia and Japan on the advances for Manchuria under the terms of the currency loan contract. But to Russia the disturbances in China were apparently the signal for a renewed and more open effort to break up the four-power financial syndicate. In mid-November Izvolsky informed both Simon and the French Foreign Office that Russia and Japan would not tolerate consortium loans to Manchuria. Now claiming a preferential position, the Russians announced that they were creating a financial group to undertake 80 per cent of future Manchurian loans; the remaining 20 per cent would be handled by the consortium. The allocations would be reversed for business agreements in China proper.[19]

The adamant Russian stand, reinforced by Japanese support, now led the department to reassess its Manchurian policy, and although the United States kept up the façade of battling to maintain Chinese integrity, in early December it in fact gave up the struggle. Under the new policy, not clearly enunciated until the close of the Taft Administration, the United States abandoned its efforts to save Manchuria and Mongolia for China and limited itself again to an effort to maintain the Open Door policy for trade in the north and to preserve and strengthen the eighteen provinces of China proper.

17. DS 893.00/1119; *FR, 1912,* 69.
18. The department's draft was passed as a concurrent resolution of Congress on April 17, 1912.
19. DS 893.51/678-79; Campbell to Jordan, November 11, 1911, Jordan Papers.

Straight summed up the American dilemma: In view of the growing German threat, France and Britain were not likely to support the United States against Russia and Japan; since the British held the key position, the Americans had to agree with them. "We don't have the force so that we can talk. I only wish that we were strong enough to talk, and that we were not discredited bluffers as we are." But that was the way matters stood, and Straight conceded that the United States would have to resign as champion of the Open Door and allow Russia and Japan to participate in all Chinese business. He soon was making a much greater concession. Still concerned with keeping the currency loan intact, Straight now admitted that the price for maintaining it would be recognition of Russian and Japanese predominance in Manchuria. "In any case, and aside from the question of the loan, I am inclined to regard that recognition as inevitable in the settlement which must follow the upheaval." He was soon writing off Manchuria as "pretty well lost" to China, and in March his thinking evolved to the final step when he welcomed a partnership with Japan.[20]

Calhoun too had few illusions about America's ability to carry on an independent policy in China. Despite the cooperation of foreign diplomats in maintaining neutrality, the atmosphere in Peking was one of jealousy and suspicion, with the United States the object of the greatest—and universal—mistrust. The local diplomats and their governments assumed that the United States was pursuing an exclusive policy and that its professions of altruism were merely a blind for selfish ends. Calhoun spelled out for Knox the reasons why the Powers had come to this assumption. When the Americans forcibly injected themselves into the Hukuang loan, tried to neutralize the Manchurian railroads, proposed to build Chin-Ai, and secretly negotiated a preliminary contract for the currency loan, they were following a policy that was competitive with all other foreign interests in China if not actually hostile to them. As a result of these actions, America's motives came under general suspicion, and Calhoun foresaw a deliberate effort to checkmate American influence in China. The Chinese were friendly but impotent; knowing that the United States could give only sentimental and philanthropic support, they

---

20. Straight to Davison, December 18, 1911, same to Charles [?], January 16, 1912, same to H. Bonar, March 13, 1912, same to J. P. Morgan & Co., January 9, 1912, Straight Papers; DS 893.51/756.

dared not oppose either Russia or Japan. Diplomacy, no matter how astute, beneficient, or altruistic, would avail little if unsupported by force that commanded respect.[21]

Revision of American policy in the Far East became imperative; the first move toward a new policy came early in December of 1911, when Knox asked the American Group to propose to its colleagues that Russia and Japan be invited to join the consortium. England agreed with the suggestion only reluctantly. For the Germans, Urbig conceded that, politically, such a move might appear the proper thing; financially, "I should deem it disastrous." The French were pleased, believing that the American approach removed all serious obstacles to cooperation except "the individual whims and ambitions" of Russia and Japan.[22]

France urged the Russians to accept the invitation, arguing that Russia's solidarity with France and Japan, and in many negotiations even with England, would give her a decisive influence on the choice of projects. Kokovtsov sent the director of the Russo-Asiatic Bank to Paris to inform the French that Russia and Japan could not enter the consortium on the proposed basis of one sixth for each. Furthermore, since there was only one Russian member-bank in the Russian Group (the Russo-Asiatic), Russian capital would get merely one twenty-fourth of the syndicate's undertakings. The Russians also refuted the French argument that they would have English and Japanese support; in some cases those two Powers would pursue their own interests rather than supporting Russia's. But the arguments were only a matter of form; Russia was not in any case interested in participation. She maintained that the only acceptable solution was for France to withdraw from the consortium and join the Russian syndicate.[23]

The suggestion to withdraw piqued the French, who complained that their ally was not considering French interests, only Russian. They told the Russians that in the present circumstances they could not leave the consortium. Anglo-French interests had cooperated in China for many years, a working arrangement absolutely indispensable to the French bankers. By withdrawing, France would break this connection and thus exclude French banks from any further share in Chinese financing. But the French had another, more important reason—not divulged to

21. Calhoun to Knox, February 12, 1912, *FR, 1912*, 64-65.
22. Urbig to M. Warburg, December 8, 1911, DS 893.51/703; *GP*, 32, 199-201; *DDF*, Ser. 3, I, 456-64.
23. F. Stieve, *Der diplomatische Schriftwechsel Iswolskis, 1911-1914*, I, 196-99.

Russia—for refusing to break with the four-Power group: Such a course would thwart the policy that France had been pursuing in China for the last seven years to establish international control of China's finances. The current talk about reorganizing Chinese fiscal affairs made the achievement of this goal an imminent possibility.[24]

When Russia encountered this "unaccustomed resistance" to her demands, she used the Moroccan situation and the newly created Russian banking group in an effort to force a French surrender, but France would not yield. The French Government refused to sacrifice its interests in China for those of Russia— whereas in Morocco Russia had no interests to sacrifice. Further-more, the French reasoned, economic and political competition among the Western Powers would benefit no one but Japan. As for the rival banking group, it was powerless because all the big French banks were in the consortium, which controlled the money market. The French repeated that Russia and Japan could best defend their interests by sitting in on the councils of the consortium.[25]

In the next two months Knox reassured first Japan and then Russia about the American position in northern China. At the end of January, when the Germans began to suspect that Japan was readying troops for stations on the mainland, they urged the United States to issue a statement that in effect cautioned all the Powers against unilateral action. The Secretary, who in Bern-storff's opinion had become very cautious since his previous fail-ure in China, demurred; although he did not want Japan to inter-vene, he did not propose to offend any government, especially the Japanese. Knox did, however, suggest an alternative. If Germany were to inquire about the American attitude toward the Far East-ern situation, Knox would repeat to Berlin the replies sent by the Powers to the American circular note of October 14, 1911. He would then repeat to the other governments the answer he had given the Germans. This solution satisfied the Germans, and without taking the initiative, Knox was able to remind the inter-ested parties that they had committed themselves to cooperate in China.[26]

The background maneuvering that resulted in the American

24. Izvolsky to Sazanov, December 26, 1911, Stieve, *Izvolsky,* I, 196-97; *DDF,* Ser. 3, I, 456-64.
25. De Selves, Circular Instruction, January 9, 1912, *DDF,* Ser. 3, I, 456-64.
26. *GP,* 32, 250-57; *FR, 1912,* 63-64, 109.

notes to Germany and the Powers was in itself of no particular importance. The incident was significant because it led Knox, in a conversation with Uchida, to indicate to the Japanese that there had been a basic change in American policy. On instructions, but stating the alternative as his own opinion, the Ambassador told Knox that, although Japan had agreed to prior consultation, a threat to her special interests in Manchuria might force Japan to act alone. The Secretary assured Uchida that he was aware of those special interests and that of course they were outside the general principle he had proposed and were unrelated to it. He hoped, however, that those interests would need no protection.[27]

The assurances to Russia came the following month in the course of another effort to bring about Russian participation in Chinese financing. Russian intransigence had frustrated the attempt made in December at the department's suggestion to enlarge the consortium, an outcome that neither the British nor the Germans particularly regretted. Now, however, Britain began actively promoting Russian and Japanese membership because of Japan's intrusion into the Yangtze Valley. With no restraint from their government, Japanese banks had granted loans to the Shanghai-Hangchow Railroad, the Hanyang Iron Works, and the Chinese Merchants' Steam Company. All were Chinese-owned, and in each case a good share of the loan went to the rebel government rather than to the operating company. The British concluded that the Japanese had two objectives: to placate the rebels, angered by earlier Japanese opposition to a republican form of government, and to get a good foothold in the Yangtze Valley. They might also have recalled that Japan had warned that if she were excluded from the consortium, she would lend money independently. After noting that the last two loans gave the Japanese control over the only two big industrial enterprises in China, Simon added that Japan's policy was leading to a resumption of the old sterile competition in lending money.[28]

The British reacted quickly. The British bankers were convinced that if the four groups did not now voluntarily ask Japan to join the consortium, they would later be forced to issue the invitation. Jordan and Grey agreed, and they also decided that the

27. Grey to MacDonald, February 15, 1912, FO 405/208/207.
28. Calhoun to Knox, February 7, 1912, DS 893.51/753; Grey to MacDonald, February 5, 1912, Addis to Langley, February 17, 1912, FO 405/208/136, 220; Langley to Jordan, February 3, 1912, Jordan Papers.

consortium must advance China some money, since the Japanese were ready to meet the urgent needs of the Nanking government if the consortium banks stood aside. The last thing Britain wanted was a revival of the earlier competition for Chinese loans. She hoped to prevent it by making participation by the Russians and Japanese a condition of her approval for any loan.[29]

The United States Department of State, the French Foreign Office, and Yuan agreed with the British view; the American bankers were reluctant. It was of course the inclusion of Russia to which the American Group and especially Schiff objected. The German banks and government continued to oppose Russian and Japanese participation, and although they finally yielded, it was only for the duration of the existing crisis. They did not consider themselves bound to cooperate with Russia and Japan in future loans.[30]

But before England and France could approach Russia and Japan, there were two new developments in the Chinese situation. On February 27 Tang, now Prime Minister in the Peking government, asked for advances for April, May, and June, the money to go equally to Peking and Nanking. Tang also mentioned that in midsummer China would arrange for a large loan to repay the advances, reorganize the administration, and initiate a scheme of commercial and industrial development. China wanted the loan payments spread out in equal installments over a five-year period —actually a series of loans amounting to £60,000,000 and secured by the salt gabelle. The new transaction, later called the *reorganization loan,* was of course a distinct operation from the currency loan and the temporary advances. When the consortium agreed to an immediate advance for April in return for options on future advances and on the proposed reorganization loan, Yuan and the bank representatives exchanged the letters of agreement on March 9, and the banks immediately paid over the money. Five days later the news leaked out that shortly before getting the advance, the Chinese had contracted with a Belgian syndicate for a £1,000,000 loan, with an option on a further large loan. Although Tang had signed the preliminary agreement more than two weeks before Yuan wrote his letter of March 9, the consortium nevertheless regarded the Belgian loan as a clear breach of

29. FO 405/208/228, 236; *FR, 1912,* 110.
30. Morgans to Morgan, Grenfell, February 29, 1912, DS 893.51/784; Montgelas, Memorandum, March 1, 1912, *GP,* 32, 293-94.

contract and broke off negotiations. The Chinese and the bankers outside the consortium, on the contrary, considered the Belgian loan a good opportunity to frustrate the consortium's monopoly of the China loan market.[31]

The Belgian loan involved politics as well as finance. In addition to the Société Générale of Belgium, the syndicate included the Russo-Asiatic Bank, A. Spitzer and Company (French), and two London firms—the Eastern Bank and J. H. Schroeder and Company. British financial circles believed that the creation of the Belgian Group gave Russia a powerful instrument to bring pressure on the four-bank syndicate and to promote her own special political plans. De Hoyer, the Russo-Asiatic's representative in Peking, admitted that he had negotiated the loan with Kokovtsov's approval, because the consortium had advanced money without Russia's approval. He had not signed the contract, however, because his government did not want the Russo-Asiatic connection known.[32]

Despite the breakdown of the Peking negotiations, the English and French, acting on the consent given by the banks and their governments, prepared to approach Russia and Japan about sharing in Chinese financial operations. In view of the Germans' attitude, Grey decided that to bring up the question of enlarging the consortium was premature, so Russia and Japan were asked to share only in the advances and the reorganization loan. Japan had never concealed her desire to join the Western banks in their Chinese financial undertakings, but now for the first time Russia indicated that she too was considering the proposal favorably. The Japanese Government was the first to accept the banks' invitation and designated the Yokohama Specie Bank as its representative. The Foreign Minister added that Japan "naturally" expected that nothing connected with the loan would prejudice her special rights and interests in southern Manchuria. The United States and Britain agreed in interpreting the Japanese statement as referring to those rights and interests arising out of treaties.[33]

Although Sazanov would consent to share only in the temporary

31. DS 893.51/1024; *FR, 1912,* 117-18; C. F. Remer, *Foreign Investments in China,* 126.
32. *GP,* 32, 294, 305-6; Stieve, *Izvolsky,* II, 36; Jordan to Grey, April 3, 1912, FO 405/208/483.
33. Stieve, *Izvolsky,* II, 54-55; Buchanan to Grey, March 9, 1912, FO 405/208/349; *FR, 1912,* 122.

advances, he added that Russia would also participate in the reorganization loan if Britain and France promised to protect her interests in the Far East. He hinted that the lack of such a guarantee would distract Russia's attention from Europe; a reorganized China might turn into a militant China, against whom Russia would need to defend herself. To allay these fears, the British Foreign Office reminded Russia that, by participating in the loan, she would be in a position to protect her own interests, since the entente Powers and Japan would constitute a majority.[34]

Now the Americans stepped into the picture. On March 30 the Russian *chargé* in Peking reported to the Foreign Minister categorical assurances by Calhoun that there was nothing in his instructions to cause him to frustrate Russian activity in Manchuria or Mongolia. Calhoun also repeated the same assurances to Jordan, who remarked in a dispatch to the Foreign Office that he regarded American exclusion from the consortium as impossible "and indeed unnecessary now that the policy for which Straight and a few other young men stood has been tacitly dropped by the Americans." Huntington-Wilson's comment on a dispatch from Calhoun bore out Jordan's observation on American policy. "That Russia and Japan want to be fair to China," reported the Minister, "I do not believe. Therefore cooperation is impracticable, if not impossible." The marginal note reads: "If you can't get what you want you'll take nothing? H. W."[35]

On April 6 the Russians consented to share the loan, making their customary reservation about Mongolia and Manchuria and now including Turkestan. The Russians refused to accept the Anglo-American view that the reservation referred only to special rights and interests arising out of treaties and agreements with China, insisting that economic ties and geographical proximity to China and the secret conventions with Japan gave the Russians special privileges. Grey now indicated clearly what he meant by his interpretation of the Russian reservation; he reminded Benckendorff of their conversation on June 28, in which he had said that Britain would welcome the new secret agreements between Russia and Japan "so long as they did not impair the 'open door' in Manchuria for our commerce, which was our main interest." Grey repeated that by participating in the loan Russia would be

---

34. FO 405/208/401, 422; Siebert, *Benckendorff,* II, 327-33.
35. Siebert, *Benckendorff,* 365-67; Jordan to Langley, April 16, 1912, Jordan Papers; DS 893.51/981.

able to eliminate any undesirable projects.[36]

Although by the end of April both De Hoyer and Japan's Odagiri were attending the meetings of the Peking bank representatives, the four banks did not by this step commit themselves formally to accept the Russian and Japanese reservations. On their governments' instructions, the consortium admitted the two men solely to facilitate an agreement among the six banking groups at a meeting to be held in May. But French Minister Bruno J. de Margerie and Calhoun were pessimistic about Russian cooperation.[37]

In mid-April China was again forced to seek money from the consortium, for after a reprimand by the French and British governments to their nationals in the Belgian syndicate, that group would not advance additional funds. The Chinese having agreed to cancel the Belgian contract and not to use consortium money to repay that syndicate's advances, the negotiations were resumed. Not until a month later, however, when China reluctantly agreed to let a foreign auditor supervise expenditures, did the four banks advance any money. The insistence on supervision was understandable, for, as Calhoun observed, "Patriotism is not the only impulse that inspires the forces which are shaping the destiny of this country." Tang had remarked casually that the government had to compensate some people for sacrifices made in the revolutionary cause; no one knew, the Minister commented, just how many deserving patriots would be recompensed from the loan proceeds. Although the supervision did not go so far as the French wanted—Poincaré favored the strictest control not only of the loan funds but of "l'ensemble même des finances chinoises" —it was enough to arouse Chinese public opinion. Serious antiloan agitation spread throughout China in June.[38]

At a conference in London on May 15, the banks were unable to agree on six-Power participation in the reorganization loan because the Russian and Japanese representatives made demands that the consortium bankers were unwilling to accept: the Japanese that the loan funds not be spent in Manchuria and adjacent parts of Inner Mongolia; the Russians that the proceeds not be used for any projects detrimental to their interests in Manchuria,

36. Siebert, *Benckendorff*, II, 334, 340-41, 350-51; Foreign Office to Cambon, Memorandum, April 3, 1912, makes the point that Russia and Japan had not yet been invited to join the consortium, owing to German opposition. FO 405/208/487; DS 893.51/831; *FR, 1912*, 124; Grey to Benckendorff, May 6, 1912, FO 405/208/586.
37. DS 893.51/869, 1024; Jordan to Langley, April 16, 1912, Jordan Papers.
38. Calhoun to Knox, May 7, 1912, DS 893.51/919; Cambon to British Foreign Office, May 7, 1912, FO 405/208/587.

Mongolia, and Turkestan. The representatives also demanded the right to issue their share of the loan in the other groups' markets through their own agents rather than through the groups. This right would have made possible the independent operation of the Russian and Japanese groups in the British and French money markets in competition with consortium representatives. The British and French felt that the interbank agreement permitting the bankers of one country to issue in other countries through consortium members was liberal enough.[39]

On June 7 representatives of the six groups reconvened in Paris but made no headway. The differences over financial procedure could obviously be settled; the stumbling block was the political situation. The consortium bankers suggested including a statement (Clause VI) that China must have the consent of all six groups before undertaking any special project, thus giving Russia and Japan a veto. The newcomers insisted, however, that the agreement state explicitly that the loan would not injure their special interests in Manchuria, Mongolia, and Turkestan. In other words, their objective was not to prevent an attack on their privileges—of which there was no danger—but to force the consortium to recognize their position in general terms, so that later they would be sole judges of the extent and character of the rights thus recognized but not defined. After much discussion the four banks rejected the proposal, stating that such political declarations did not come within their competence. The meeting then adjourned until June 15, when the Russians and Japanese would have to state whether they would accept the conditions for joining the consortium.[40]

Davison and Schiff reported from Paris that, unless Russia came in, the French would probably leave the consortium. Even without the French, the British and Germans would very likely be ready to proceed if the Americans joined them. The two bankers expressed personal opinions that the group should decline to proceed under such conditions; indeed, they felt strongly that if the week ended with no settlement the group should authorize them to withdraw and release China from her commitment not to borrow elsewhere. Maurice Casenave, the Peking representative of the French Group, confirmed the French intention. He informed

39. Siebert, *Benckendorff*, II, 356-57; Sazanov to Motono, April 18, 1912, JFO, MT Series, Reel 219; DS 893.51/1024.
40. DS 893.51/913, 1024; *GP*, 32, 327-29.

Calhoun that, although France was reluctant to leave the consortium, the protection of the Russian alliance and the complicated state of affairs in Europe necessitated her withdrawal.[41]

On June 13 Japan proposed deleting Clause VI and adding a two-point statement in the minutes: (1) nothing connected with the loan would prejudice the special rights and interests of Russia in northern Manchuria, Mongolia, and western China and of Japan in southern Manchuria and adjacent portions of Inner Mongolia; (2) the banks were not competent to deal with political questions. To the Japanese proposal Knox added a significant statement: The banks were not competent to deal with political questions "without consulting their governments. [The banks], however, expressed the belief that *their governments would be entirely considerate of any such rights and interests reasonably related to existing treaties and conventions with China and compatible with the recognized principles of equality of opportunity and the open door."* [Italics added.][42] Knox, like Hay, had found himself in an untenable position and had had to retreat to a more defensible line.

At the same time the British made a public statement of their policy. Both Russia and France had been pressing Grey to support the Russian demands, and for political reasons he deemed it absolutely necessary to reach an agreement with Russia. In the House of Commons Grey declared that Great Britain recognized all Russian and Japanese special interests in Manchuria and Mongolia as not contrary to the principle of the Open Door. He mentioned no treaties or conventions.

Philippe Berthelot, head of the Asiatic Division in the French Foreign Office, strongly favored continuing the French membership in the consortium, but Poincaré found it difficult to ignore Izvolsky's constant pressure for withdrawal. Although Grey was not willing to follow Berthelot's suggestion that he urge Poincaré to dissociate French policy from that of Russia, he did instruct Bertie to point out to Poincaré that the break-up of the consortium might precipitate China's collapse. China's political stability was the main concern for the British and for the French as well, since their chief interests had never lain north of the Great Wall. The consortium could not be preserved if Russia would not join, since

41. Davison and Schiff to Morgans, June 8, 1912, DS 893.51/931; Calhoun to Knox, June 19, 1912, DS 893.51/930.
42. Herrick to Knox, June 13, 1912, *FR, 1912,* 137; Knox to Herrick, June 14, 1912, DS 893.51/939.

France was extremely sensitive to Russian pressures and Britain only slightly less so. Grey was willing to acquiesce in Russia's demands on Mongolia and Manchuria to prevent the break-up of the consortium because working through the banks seemed to offer the only chance of preventing the disintegration of China proper.

And the Russians had to cooperate, since Russia's allies, Britain especially, considered it to their advantage not to permit the collapse of China but to have a government there strong enough to maintain order. In explaining St. Petersburg's policy to the Russian minister in Peking, Neratov pointed out that openly to oppose Anglo-French efforts would mean loss of possibly vital support for Russia's own plans in northern China. The Chinese border areas were much more important to Russia than the eighteen provinces of China proper. Therefore Russia chose to join the consortium.[43]

On June 19 the Russian Government notified the four governments that it would join the consortium, on the condition that its group would have the right to withdraw if Russia disapproved of any proposed undertaking. The Japanese then asked for the same concession. Since it was unlikely that the United States, Britain, and Germany could proceed without the cooperation of French financiers—who would retire with the Russians—and in the face of probable political opposition from Russia and Japan, accepting the Russian condition amounted virtually to granting Russia a veto power over the consortium's undertakings. The six groups signed the final agreement on June 20. Thus the Russians, however reluctantly, entered the consortium and on terms that they professed to find distinctly unsatisfactory. Sazanov complained that the failure to limit the consortium's operations to the reorganization of China's finances meant that any of the other groups could float a loan for a specific undertaking in northern China that Russia would view as objectionable. The only condition that limited such loans was the agreement that each group must offer the other consortium members the chance to participate in its projects. In order to prevent such undertakings, Russia needed the support promised by England and France.[44]

Negotiations for the reorganization loan, resumed in April, made no progress. Although the banks advanced funds in mid-May, the Chinese insisted that they needed more money—if not

43. Reid to Knox, June 13, 1912, DS 893.51/966; Langley to Jordan, July 8, 1912, Jordan Papers; Bertie to Grey, June 19, 1912, and Grey to Bertie, June 19, 1912, FO 405/208/730-31; Siebert, *Benckendorff*, II, 429-31.
44. DS 893.51/1024; *FR, 1912*, 141; Siebert, *Benckendorff*, II, 17-18.

from the consortium, then from another source—because on June 19 would fall one of China's three annual "settling days," when it is customary to pay all public and private debts. The emergency was so great that the ministers assumed the responsibility for authorizing an advance, which the bank representatives paid out on June 18. The State Department approved this payment, since it had been urging it for almost two weeks. The total amount advanced on account of the reorganization loan was now £1,-800,000.[45] The consortium paid the Chinese no additional funds until they signed the final loan contract ten months later on April 27, 1913.

On July 9 the consortium governments informed the Chinese that they would not approve loan contracts signed by their nationals (either within or outside the consortium) that did not provide for foreign supervision and control. The Chinese would not consent to such conditions, on the grounds that neither the National Council nor public opinion would permit such control. Observers in Peking concurred that China would not accept these terms, and Calhoun warned that the government's submission to foreign control would arouse violent and widespread opposition throughout the country.[46]

Finally, Knox suggested that if the impasse could not be breached, China should be left free to make other arrangements for meeting her immediate requirements. Even before the confrontation of July 9, the American Group had reached the same conclusion, having advised its London agent on July 5 that if China would not accept the consortium's condition she should be permitted to borrow where she could. The group's attitude convinced Addis that the Americans were "dead sick" of the whole business and anxious to drop it as soon as possible. But for the moment the German Government blocked the group's escape; the Germans raised strong objections that killed Knox's proposal.[47]

It was during this comparative lull in negotiations that the department asked for the Powers' views on the question of recognizing the government in Peking. Expecting "entirely negative" results, Knox candidly admitted that public opinion had forced his hand; if the executive branch did not act soon, Americans would demand that Congress do so. "While we may get no credit if we

45. *FR, 1912,* 137-40; DS 893.51/928A, 946, 1218.
46. *FR, 1912,* 144.
47. Knox to Paris, London, and Berlin, *FR, 1912,* 147; DS 893.51/987; Langley to Jordan, August 9, 1912, Jordan Papers.

send [the note]," one member of the department remarked, "we may get a lot of blame if we do not." Of the seven governments circularized, not one approved. The Russians went so far as to ridicule (in a diplomatic way) even the mention of recognition and called to the department's attention the fact that the Chinese themselves always referred to the "provisional" government of China.[48] The department later found this a convenient argument against domestic advocates of immediate recognition of the Republic of China.

After July 9 China tried desperately to get money from nonconsortium bankers, but not until the end of August was she successful. On September 11 Calhoun reported the rumor that China had signed a £10,000,000 loan contract with an English syndicate headed by Charles B. Crisp. The security was the salt gabelle—the same guarantee offered for the reorganization loan—and the terms did not include foreign control over expenditures. The British Foreign Office instructed Jordan to protest, but, as he pointed out to Langley, protest was a meaningless gesture, since China had broken no engagements. Its only effect was to stir up a fierce campaign in the Chinese press against the British Government and Jordan personally.

London was indeed in an embarrassing position. "We are all very mortified at the Crisp loan having got through . . . ," confessed B. Alston of the Far Eastern Division. Unlike the French Foreign Office, the British could not close the market to undesired loans, and mere notification to negotiators of its disapproval was not always effective. London's embarrassment was due not only to the unhappiness of other governments over the Crisp loan but also to the circumstance that, since the consortium was making no progress, other British firms were certain to put more pressure on the Foreign Office to let them into the Chinese field. The French, German, and American groups were all combinations of large banking interests in their respective countries, but the British interest was represented solely by the Hongkong and Shanghai Bank. This bank was very large and powerful in China but comparatively small and ineffectual in London. The many really influential London banks, which could easily form an effective combination, resented the Hongkong and Shanghai Bank's practical monopoly, and their antagonism had shown in their reaction to the Crisp loan. The British Foreign Office was sharply attacked

48. Miller to Knox, July 19, 1912, DS 893.00/1398; *FR, 1912,* 81-86.

for supporting only one bank, and Grey eventually tried to expand the British Group.[49]

Anxious to resume negotiations because of its vulnerable position, the Hongkong and Shanghai Bank asked the Americans to accept less stringent contract terms for the reorganization loan. Since they believed that China had taken up the Crisp loan for just one reason—to force concessions from the banks—the American Group did not respond enthusiastically. Even if they had favored changes, they thought the moment ill-chosen. Although approving of the group's position as a "present expedient," the department wanted it to keep an open mind about future developments.[50]

On September 21 China handed the Peking bank representatives her terms for concluding the reorganization loan, and when the representatives rejected them, China broke off negotiations. Three days later the Crisp syndicate paid China the first advance. The consensus in Peking was that if Crisp could float the entire loan his operation would exhaust all possible revenue securities and make continued existence of the consortium pointless.[51]

When Yuan refused to cancel the Crisp loan, Grey proposed that the six groups promptly try to come to terms with China by easing their demands. If the two sides could not agree forthwith, the only alternative, in Grey's mind, was to abandon the negotiations. Should that happen, Britain would make no effort to stop China from getting money outside the consortium. Not only would the Foreign Office have difficulty in defending such a prohibition in theory; the Crisp loan demonstrated that in practice it was ineffective. Grey did not consider the bankers' demands unreasonable, and he was anxious to prevent China's indiscriminate borrowing for nonproductive expenditures. For that reason, even though he thought the consortium should dissolve, he wanted it to sign the reorganization loan contract before being liquidated.[52]

But the opinions expressed by China's recently appointed political adviser, Dr. George Morrison, offered little hope for a quick settlement. The influential "China" Morrison, former correspondent of the *London Times*, was at the moment traveling in

49. *FR, 1912,* 150, 157-59; Jordan to Langley, October 5, 1912, Alston to Jordan, October 4, 1912, Jordan Papers; DS 893.51/1115, 1120; *GP,* 32, 351-52.
50. DS 893.51/1055.
51. DS 893.51/1218; *FR, 1912,* 152-54.
52. Grey Circular, FO 405/209/236; *FR, 1912,* 153-54; Grey to Jordan, October 31, 1912, Jordan Papers.

Europe. There, he was declaring quite openly that China would not deal with the consortium so long as Russia and Japan were members. Yuan, too, said as much to Jordan, remarking that he had no confidence in the six-Power group, although he trusted in the four banks. What money did Russia and Japan have to lend to anybody? They had joined the consortium, Yuan asserted, merely to further their political aims and to prevent China from strengthening herself through foreign capital.[53]

To Huntington-Wilson, Grey's suggestion implied immediate dissolution of the consortium, which would wreck what remained of the department's China policy—the salvation of China proper. When Addis informally sounded the other groups to see if they thought China's refusal to negotiate meant the end of the six-Power arrangement, the situation appeared even blacker. After the American Group had indicated to the department that it was willing to continue in the syndicate, Huntington-Wilson wrote the English a long letter, intended to encourage them with the optimistic report that the United States saw "in the present situation no reason whatever why the international understanding should not continue quite as strong and effective as hitherto." He professed not to be discouraged over the protracted negotiations, which were only natural for such a complicated subject. As for the loan conditions, the department was ready to take up the subject again with China. Only the Americans and the Germans were amenable to Grey's proposal that the groups ease their demands on China. The others felt no need to offer better terms; China had nowhere else to go.[54]

While the groups were reassessing their position, China shocked them by granting a railroad contract to a Belgian firm with Franco-Russian backing. This deal represented a return to the old policy of granting industrial concessions instead of making purely financial loans. The bank representatives now feared that outsiders were about to start a general campaign for concessions against which the consortium groups would be powerless. The deadlock on the reorganization loan prevented the consortium banks from competing jointly for industrial contracts, while the interbank agreement bound them not to act independently. The British, especially perturbed, deemed it imperative to revise

53. Urbig to Addis, October 1, 1912, Jordan to Grey, September 21, 1912, FO 405/209/249, 265; Alston to Jordan, October 4, 1912, Jordan Papers.
54. *FR, 1912,* 152, 154-57; FO 405/209/300, 309; JFO, MT Series, Reel 224; *GP,* 32, 357.

the six-bank agreement, since British manufacturing interests were dependent upon the freedom of British capitalists to make industrial loans. And to make matters worse, Crisp's flotation of the first half of his loan was, contrary to expectations, comparatively successful.[55]

The Hongkong and Shanghai Bank, dependent almost entirely on business in China, finally proposed at the end of October that each group be free to negotiate industrial contracts in its own name. At a conference on January 10 and 11, 1913, the bankers accepted this suggestion and formally revised the agreement of 1912. Since the groups were no longer obliged to offer each other participation in industrial loans for which they contracted with the Chinese Government, the amendment in effect dissolved the six-Power consortium except for the reorganization loan. The four original members reverted to the interbank agreement of November 10, 1910, which bound each group to offer the other participation in all loans contracted. The negotiating group could then carry out the contract even if no others were interested.[56]

China meanwhile jockeyed back and forth between Crisp and the consortium but failed to get money from either. Crisp was unable to furnish the cash; the groups were unwilling so long as Crisp stayed in the picture. When the Chinese finally agreed to end their association with Crisp, the bankers on December 21 offered to advance £2,000,000 in the second half of January if by that time China had canceled the Crisp loan and had signed the reorganization loan agreement for £25,000,000. The Chinese raised objections to a number of points in the draft loan contract presented by the bankers. The six ministers themselves did not agree on the terms, the French being particularly difficult and the Russians supporting them.[57]

On December 9 Odagiri had suggested to Frank McKnight that Russia and Japan share the currency as well as the reorganization loan and that at the bank conference called for January 10 the groups reach an informal understanding on the matter, subject to China's approval. There the matter would rest until China signified that she was ready to take up currency reform. The group favored such a course, although it realized that, once Russia and Japan were admitted to the currency loan, they would demand the

55. *FR, 1912*, 157-59; *FR, 1913*, 146; FO 405/209/252.
56. DS 893.51/1118-19, 1230; *GP*, 32, 389-90.
57. DS 893.51/1218, 1244.

elimination of its Manchurian features. However, the group also had good reason to believe that Japan at least would not try to tighten her grip on Manchuria if the other Powers assured her they would not threaten the *status quo* by trying to strengthen China's authority in the Three Provinces. Furthermore, Japan had intimated that, once she had received these assurances, she would be willing to cooperate in the practical neutralization of the eighteen provinces of China proper, with a view to their development under the consortium's auspices. On the other hand, the group did not believe that keeping Russia and Japan out of the currency loan would save Manchuria; it might even precipitate further aggression.[58]

As Miller pointed out to Huntington-Wilson, the Japanese proposal was in line with the conclusions already reached by the department, both on Russian and Japanese participation in the currency loan and on the advisability of letting currency reform take its natural course as far as possible for the present. Therefore, with the department's blessing, the American bankers submitted the Japanese suggestion to the four-Power syndicate, telling the group's London agent that it felt early currency reform was essential to effective reorganization of the Chinese administration. Since it would be difficult to issue the currency and reorganization loans simultaneously, the group suggested combining the two and eliminating the industrial (Manchurian) enterprises of the currency loan as not germane to the general purposes of the reorganization loan. Such a course should secure Russian and Japanese approval for the currency loan.[59]

Although nothing ever came of the idea, the discussion was interesting as a clear articulation of the policy of withdrawal that the department had been pursuing toward northern China for many months. The Manchurian projects were abandoned; instead, the department now wanted the consortium to further the administrative reorganization of China and to work for tariff reform and the abolition of likin. Conceding that equality of investment opportunity was unattainable in Manchuria, the department hoped that by withdrawing the consortium it might yet save equality of commercial opportunity in that region and also win Russian and Japanese support for a six-Power guarantee of the integrity of China proper.

58. DS 893.51/1202.
59. DS 893.51/1376.

Motivated by political considerations, the French and Russians continued to obstruct the final settlement of the reorganization loan contract, and Knox would have been willing to accept any arrangement agreeable to the other Powers and China to get the matter settled. But the financial rather than the political complications disturbed the American bankers. On January 30, 1913, Ambassador Myron T. Herrick reported from Paris that, despite their commitment of June 1912, the French now objected to the internationalization of the loan. The French were not now acting against the Americans, however. The European situation had so deteriorated that after a brief relaxation of the ban the French Government reverted to its old policy of refusing to permit the quotation of German securities on the Bourse. The Americans were prepared to issue their entire share of the loan if England alone would agree to internationalization within a reasonable period of time, since only this knowledge would induce American investors to buy the bonds. The British, however, refused to promise even future quotation, explaining that if the London market remained open, it might have to absorb large amounts not only of the American issue but of the German and Russian as well.[60]

The American Group tried to find a way around the dilemma, but the conditions on the domestic exchange were not favorable. The market was reflecting the usual apprehension over the impending change in administrations, and investors were becoming increasingly edgy as they followed developments on the Mexican border. By February 20 the financial and political complications led the group to decide that before the Wilson Administration took office on March 4 the China loan must be settled either by signature of the reorganization loan contract or by definite withdrawal from the negotiations. The last thing Knox wanted was withdrawal, and his concern was not aroused solely by the plight of China; any change in the group's position could embarrass the Taft Administration. Davison reassured him that the group would postpone any decision that might embarrass the Government, but his statement plainly implied that the bankers intended to act soon after March 4.[61]

The six governments finally agreed on a loan contract, which the ministers presented to the Chinese Government on March 3

---

60. *FR, 1913,* 148, 154; Jordan to Grey, February 11, 1913, FO 405/211/174. H. Feis, *Europe, the World's Banker, 1870-1914;* DS 893.51/1279-81.
61. DS 893.51/1280, 1307, 1342.

and which China rejected on March 4. The next day Straight wrote William Jennings Bryan, Wilson's Secretary of State, to arrange a meeting between the Secretary and the bankers, and at the conference in Washington the group clearly indicated scant desire to continue on its present course. The Wilson Administration was no more eager than the bankers to continue Taft's Far Eastern policy, and on March 18 the President publicly disavowed it by announcing, without prior consultation with the other consortium governments, that the United States would no longer participate in the six-bank consortium.[62]

In July 1913, E. T. Williams, the American *chargé* in Peking, wrote home for instructions on the legation's attitude toward financial transactions between American capitalists and the Chinese Government, since he wanted to prevent any misunderstanding of the department's policy. The department's reply, sent on September 11 over Bryan's signature, was a combination of drafts by Miller and Adee. Williams was to take as his guide the instructions of Olney to Denby on December 19, 1896, and of Root to Rockhill on October 21, 1905, which the State Department considered still generally applicable. Adee noted of his own memorandum: "I think the Secretary may wish to sign it. I have attempted to get Oriental Dollar Diplomacy back to the Bayard-Olney ground."[63]

62. FO 405/211/326.
63. *FR, 1913,* 183-86; DS 893.51/1457.

14

Summary

Although the objectives of the United States were the same in China as in Latin America—stability, trade, and opportunities for American investment—the State Department discovered, belatedly, that the frame of reference in China was quite different from that in Latin America. In the Western Hemisphere no foreign power challenged American dominance. In Asia, however, the United States faced Japan and the various European nations, each jealously guarding its special privileges and immunities. The policy designed by Taft and Knox to make the United States a leading financial and commercial power in Asia could be consummated only by infringing upon established interests.

Since Taft and Knox believed that the country exercising the greatest financial influence in China would also exercise the greatest political influence, they planned to use American capital to create tangible United States interests that would serve as levers to limit the scope of the other Powers and increase that of the United States. At the same time that this policy increased the opportunities for American trade and investment, the projects executed by American capital would strengthen China, making her more capable not only of governing herself but also of defending herself against foreign encroachments. By deciding to strengthen China rather than to conciliate Japan, Taft and Knox reversed Roosevelt's policy and ignored his advice.

The Administration based its policy on two assumptions: that American capital was available for overseas investment and that the British would support American efforts to move into China. But the United States did not yet possess the degree of capital accumulation required to float large foreign loans, and American bankers were forced to rely upon the money markets of England

and France to carry through the operations demanded by the State Department. The Europeans, naturally enough, insisted that the United States play the game according to their rules. Knox himself said, with reference to China, that the borrower was the servant of the lender; he should have realized that this aphorism applied equally well to Americans seeking money in Europe.

The United States was also bitterly disappointed in its expectation of backing from England, particularly in the Manchurian projects. Although the lack of support from the British led the State Department to dally with the idea of seeking help from Germany or Russia, no serious attempt was made to carry it through. In any case Taft and Knox lacked Roosevelt's understanding of how world power was structured; in view of the European situation, England did not intend to alienate her allies to promote American policy in the Far East no matter how much she may have sympathized with certain of its objectives.

Despite these obstacles, Taft and Knox persisted in going ahead: They bullied their way into the Hukuang loan; they tried to neutralize the railroads in Manchuria; they proposed to build the Chinchou-Aigun railroad; and they secretly negotiated a preliminary contract for currency reform. Although it is doubtful that the aggressive policy of Taft and Knox would have succeeded, no matter how adroit the execution, the department's clumsy maneuvering incurred additional disadvantages: It alienated Japan and Russia and created among all the Powers a deep suspicion of American motives. Its grandiose design having collapsed, the Administration retreated in its last year to the Open Door Policy.

Bibliography

Manuscript Sources

Library of Congress identified as LC; Public Record Office as PRO.

Great Britain, Foreign Office, PRO
Microfilm of the Archives of the Japanese Ministry of Foreign Affairs, JFO
United States, Department of the Navy, National Archives
United States, Department of State, National Archives

Henry Adams, Massachusetts Historical Society
Nelson Aldrich, LC
Chandler P. Anderson, LC
Herbert Asquith, Bodleian Library
James Bryce, Bodleian Library
Andrew Carnegie, LC
Fred Dearing, University of Missouri Library
Henry Fletcher, LC
Edward Grey, PRO
Francis M. Huntington-Wilson, Ursinus College Library
John Jordan, PRO
Philander C. Knox, LC
Wilfrid Laurier, Public Archives of Canada
Henry Cabot Lodge, Massachusetts Historical Society
George von Lengerke Meyer, Massachusetts Historical Society
Charles Nagel, Yale University Library
Whitelaw Reid, LC
William W. Rockhill, Harvard University Library
Theodore Roosevelt, LC
Elihu Root, LC
Cecil Spring Rice, PRO
Henry L. Stimson, Yale University Library
Willard Straight, Cornell University Library
William Howard Taft, LC
James Harrison Wilson, LC
Leonard Wood, LC

Printed Materials

Aaron, D., *Men of Good Hope.* New York, 1951.

Adams, Henry, *Henry Adams and His Friends: A Collection of his Unpublished Letters,* H. E. Cater, ed. Boston, 1947.

——, *Letters of Henry Adams,* C. F. Worthington, ed., Boston, 1930.

Adler, C., *Jacob H. Schiff.* New York, 1928.

Allen, G. C., and A. G. Donnithorne, *Western Enterprise in Far Eastern Economic Development, China and Japan.* London, 1954.

Allen, H. C., *Great Britain and the United States.* New York, 1955.

Annals of the American Academy of Political and Social Science. November, 1916.

Arenas Guzmán, D., *La consumación del crimen.* Mexico, 1935.

Baker, R. S., *American Chronicle.* New York, 1945.

Barnes, W., and J. H. Morgan, *The Foreign Service of the United States.* Washington, 1961.

Bax, E., *Miss Bax of the Embassy.* Boston, 1939.

Beale, H. K., *Theodore Roosevelt and the Rise of America to World Power.* Baltimore, 1956.

Beard, Charles A., *The Idea of National Interest.* Chicago, 1966.

Bemis, S.F., *The Latin American Policy of the United States.* New York, 1943.

Bernstorff, Count Johann von, *Memoirs.* New York, 1936.

Blaisdell, L. L., "Was it revolution or filibustering?" *Pacific Historical Review,* May, 1954.

Blakeslee, G. H., ed., *China and the Far East.* New York, 1910.

Blunt, W. S., *My Diaries.* New York, 1923.

Borden, H., *Robert L. Borden: His Memoirs.* Toronto, 1938. 2 vols.

Braisted, W. R., *The United States Navy in the Pacific, 1897-1909.* Austin, Texas, 1958.

British Documents on the Origins of the World War, 1898-1914. London, 1926-1936, 11 vols. (Cited as *BD.*)

Burton, J. H., *The Life of Andrew Carnegie.* Garden City, N.Y., 1932.

Butt, A., *Taft and Roosevelt.* New York, 1930. 2 vols.

——, *The Letters of Archie Butt,* L. F. Abbott, ed. New York, 1924.

Calcott, W. H., *The Caribbean Policy of the United States, 1890-1920.* Baltimore, 1942.

Callahan, J. M., *American Foreign Policy in Canadian Relations.* New York, 1937.

Calvert, P. A. R., "Francis Stronge en la Décima Trágica." *Historia Mexicana,* Julio-Septiembre, 1965.

Campbell, A. E., *Great Britain and the United States, 1895-1903.* Glasgow, 1960.

Campbell, J. B., "Taft, Roosevelt and the Arbitration Treaties of 1911." *Journal of American History,* September, 1966.

Challener, R. D., "Montenegro and the United States: A Balkan Fantasy." *Journal of Central European Affairs,* October, 1957.

Chamberlain, A., *Politics from the Inside.* New Haven, 1927.

Chapman, C. E., *A History of the Cuban Republic.* New York, 1927.

Clinard, O. J., *Japan's Influence on American Naval Power, 1897-1917.* Berkeley, Calif., 1947.

Cline, H. F., *The United States and Mexico.* Cambridge, Mass., 1953.

Clubb, O. E., *Twentieth Century China.* New York, 1964.

Clyde, P. H., *International Rivalries in Manchuria.* Columbus, Ohio, 1926.

Cohen, N. W., "Ambassador Straus in Turkey, 1909-1910." *Journal of American History,* March, 1959.

Conant, C., "Putting China on the Gold Standard." *North American Review,* November, 1903.

Congressional Record. 1909-1913.

Corbett, P. E., *The Settlement of Canadian-American Disputes.* New Haven, 1937.

Cortissoz, R., *The Life of Whitelaw Reid.* New York, 1921. 2 vols.

Cosío Villegas, D., "Magdalene Bay: An Historical Lesson." (Mimeograph of paper presented at University of Nebraska, 1960.)

Cox, I. J., *Nicaragua and the United States, 1907-1927.* Boston, 1927.

Crane, K., *Mr. Carr of the State Department.* New York, 1960.

Croly, H., *Willard Straight.* New York, 1924.

Cumberland, C. C., *Mexican Revolution: Genesis Under Madero.* Austin, Texas, 1952.

Dafoe, J. W., *Laurier.* Toronto, 1963.

Davis, H. P., *Black Democracy.* New York, 1928.

Davis, O. K., *Released for Publication.* Boston, 1925.

Dawson, R. M., *William Lyon Mackenzie King: A Political Biography, 1874-1923.* Toronto, 1958.

Denny, H. N., *Dollars for Bullets.* New York, 1929.

DeNovo, J. A., "A Railroad for Turkey." *Business History, Autumn, 1959.*

————, *American Interests and Policies in the Middle East, 1900-1939.* Minneapolis, 1963.

Deutsch, H. B., *The Incredible Yanqui: The Career of Lee Christmas.* New York, 1931.

Dinwoodie, D. H., "Dollar Diplomacy in the Light of the Guatemalan Loan Project, 1909-1913." *Americas,* January, 1970.

Documents on British Foreign Policy, 1919-1939, R. Butler, et al., eds. London, 1946————. (Cited as *BF.*)

Documents diplomatiques français, 1871-1914. Paris, 1929————. (Cited as *DDF.*)

Dominican Custom Receivership, Annual Reports. Washington.

Dugdale, B. E. C., *Arthur James Balfour.* New York, 1937. 2 vols.

Ellis, L. E., *Reciprocity, 1911.* New Haven, 1939.

Esthus, R. A., "The Changing Concept of the Open Door, 1899-1910." *Journal of American History,* December, 1959.

————, *Theodore Roosevelt and Japan.* Seattle, 1966.

———, "The Taft-Katsura Agreement—Reality or Myth." *Journal of Modern History,* March, 1959.

Feis, H., *Europe, The World's Banker, 1870-1914.* New York, 1961.

Field, F. V., *American Participation in the China Consortium.* Chicago, 1931.

Fisher, H. A. L., *James Bryce.* New York, 1927. 2 vols.

Fitzgibbon, R. H., *Cuba and the United States, 1900-1935.* Menasha, Wis., 1935.

Garraty, J. A., *Henry Cabot Lodge.* New York, 1953.

Gérard, A., *Ma mission au Japon, 1907-1914.* Paris, 1919.

Gibb, G. S., and E. H. Knowlton, *The Resurgent Years, 1911-1927.* New York, 1956.

Gluek, A. C., "The Passamaquoddy Bay Treaty, 1910." *Canadian Historical Review,* March, 1966.

Gordon, D. C., *The Dominion Partnership in Imperial Defense, 1870-1914.* Baltimore, 1965.

Graebner, N. A., ed., *An Uncertain Tradition.* New York, 1961.

Great Britain, Accounts and Papers, China, No. 3, 1913, Cd 7054. London, 1914.

Greene, F., "The Military View of American National Policy, 1904-1940." *American Historical Review,* January, 1961.

Grew, Joseph C., *Turbulent Era.* London, 1953. 2 vols.

Grey, E., *Twenty Five Years, 1892-1916.* New York, 1925. 2 vols.

Grieb, K. J., *The United States and Huerta.* Lincoln, Nebr., 1969.

Griswold, A. W., *The Far Eastern Policy of the United States.* New York, 1938.

Grosse Politik der europäischen Kabinette, 1871-1914, Die. Berlin, 1922-1927. 40 vols. (Cited as *GP.*)

Hagedorn, H., *Leonard Wood.* New York, 1931. 2 vols.

Hamada, Kengi, *Prince Ito.* London, 1936.

Hammond, J. M., *Autobiography.* New York, 1935. 2 vols.

Hechler, K. W., *Insurgency and Personalities and Politics of the Taft Era.* New York, 1940.

Hidy, R. W., and M. E. Hidy, *Pioneering in Big Business, 1882-1911.* New York, 1955.

Hill, R. R., *Fiscal Intervention in Nicaragua.* New York, 1933.

Holt, W. S., *Treaties Defeated by the Senate.* Baltimore, 1933.

Hoover, I. H., *Forty-two Years in the White House.* New York, 1934.

Hou, C., *Foreign Investment and Economic Development in China, 1840-1937.* Cambridge, Mass., 1965.

Howe, M. A. D., *George von Lengerke Meyer.* New York, 1920.

Hsü, S., *China and her Political Entity.* New York, 1926.

Hulen, B. D., *Inside the Department of State.* New York, 1939.

Huntington-Wilson, Francis M., *Memoirs of an Ex-Diplomat.* Boston, 1945.

———, *The Peril of Hifalutin.* New York, 1918.

Ilchman, W. F., *Professional Diplomacy in the United States.* Chicago, 1961.

Jenkins, R., *Asquith.* New York, 1964.

Jessup, Philip C., *Elihu Root.* New York, 1938. 2 vols.

Jones, C. L., *The Caribbean Since 1900.* New York, 1936.

Jordan, D. S., *The Days of Man.* Yonkers-on-Hudson, N.Y., 1922. 2 vols.

Jusserand, J. J., *What Me Befell.* Boston, 1933.

Kahler, H. M., "Current Misconceptions of Trade with Latin America." *Annals of the American Academy of Political and Social Science,* May, 1911.

Kamikawa, H., ed., *Japan-American Diplomatic Relations in the Meiji-Taisho Era.* Tokyo, 1958.

Katz, F., *Deutschland, Diaz, und die mexikanische Revolution.* Berlin, 1964.

Kennan, G., *E. H. Harriman: A Biography.* Boston, 1922. 2 vols.

Kepner, C. D., and J. H. Soothill, *The Banana Empire.* New York, 1935.

Knight, M. M., *The Americans in Santo Domingo.* New York, 1928.

Lamont, T. W., *Henry P. Davison.* New York, 1933.

Leopold, R., *Elihu Root and the Conservative Tradition.* Boston, 1954.

Leuchtenburg, W. E., "Progressivism and Imperialism: The Progressive Movement and American Foreign Policy, 1898-1916." *Journal of American History,* December, 1952.

Levi, W., *Modern China's Foreign Policy.* Minneapolis, 1953.

Lewis, C., *America's Stake in International Investments.* Washington, 1938.

Livermore, S. W., "American Naval Base Policy in the Far East, 1850-1914." *Pacific Historical Review,* June, 1944.

———, "Battleship Diplomacy in South America, 1905-1925." *Journal of Modern History,* March, 1944.

———, "The American Navy as a Factor in World Politics, 1903-1913." *American Historical Review,* July, 1958.

Livezey, W. E., *Mahan on Sea Power.* Norman, Okla., 1947.

Lodge, H. C., ed., *Selections from the Correspondence of Roosevelt and Lodge.* New York, 1925. 2 vols.

Longworth, Alice Roosevelt, *Crowded Hours.* New York, 1933.

Lowe, C. J., *The Reluctant Imperialists: British Foreign Policy, 1878-1902.* London, 1967.

McCain, W. D., *The United States and the Republic of Panama.* Durham, N.C., 1937.

McCormick, T. J., *China Market. America's Quest for Informal Empire, 1893-1901.* Chicago, 1967.

McGann, T. F., *Argentina, the United States and the Inter American System, 1880-1914.* Cambridge, Mass., 1957.

MacMurray, J. V. A., ed., *Treaties and Agreements With and Concerning China, 1894-1912.* New York, 1921. 2 vols.

Marder, A. J., *From Dreadnought to Scapa Flow.* London, 1961.

Millard, T. F., *America and the Far Eastern Question.* New York,- 1909.

Minger, R. E., "Taft's Missions to Japan." *Pacific Historical Review,* August, 1961.

Monger, G. W., *The End of Isolation: British Foreign Policy, 1900-1907.* London, 1963.
Montague, L. L., *Haiti and the United States.* Durham, N.C., 1940.
Morison, E. E., *Admiral Sims and the Modern American Navy.* Boston, 1942.
Mott, T. B., *Myron T. Herrick.* Garden City, N.Y., 1929.
———, *Twenty Years as Military Attaché.* New York, 1937.
Mowry, G. E., *The Era of Theodore Roosevelt, 1900-1912.* New York, 1958.
Munro, Dana G., *Intervention and Dollar Diplomacy in the Caribbean, 1900-1921.* Princeton, 1964.
———, *The Five Republics of Central America.* New York, 1918.
Nearing, S., and J. Freeman, *Dollar Diplomacy.* New York, 1926.
Neu, C. E., *An Uncertain Friendship: Roosevelt and Japan, 1906-1909.* Cambridge, Mass., 1967.
———, "Theodore Roosevelt and American Involvement in the Far East, 1901–1909." *Pacific Historical Review,* November, 1966.
Neumann, W. L., *America Encounters Japan.* Baltimore, 1963.
Nevins, A., *Henry White.* New York, 1930.
Nish, I. H., *The Anglo-Japanese Alliance: The Diplomacy of Two Island Empires, 1894-1907.* London, 1966.
Palmer, F., *Central America and its Problems.* New York, 1910.
———, *With My Own Eyes.* Indianapolis, 1933.
Parlett, H., *A Brief Account of Diplomatic Events in Manchuria.* London, 1929.
Perkins, B., *The Great Rapprochement: England and the United States, 1895-1914.* New York, 1968.
Perkins, D., *Hands Off: A History of the Monroe Doctrine.* Boston, 1963.
Pike, P. B., *Chile and the United States, 1880-1962.* Notre Dame, Ind., 1963.
Pratt, J. T., *War and Politics in China.* London, 1943.
Pratt, J. W., *America's Colonial Experiment.* New York, 1950.
Price, E. B., *The Russo-Japanese Treaties of 1907-1916 Concerning Manchuria and Mongolia.* Baltimore, 1933.
Pringle, Henry F., *The Life and Times of William Howard Taft: A Biography.* New York, 1939. 2 vols.
———, *Theodore Roosevelt: A Biography.* New York, 1931.
Reid, J. G., *The Manchu Abdication and the Powers, 1909-1912.* Berkeley, Calif., 1935.
Remer, C. F., *Foreign Investments in China.* New York, 1933.
Rippy, J. F., *The Caribbean Danger Zone.* New York, 1940.
Romero Flores, Jesús, *Del porfirismo a la revolución constitucionalista.* Mexico, 1960.
Roosevelt, Theodore, *The Letters of Theodore Roosevelt,* E. E. Morison, ed. Cambridge, Mass., 1951-1954. 8 vols.
Ross, S. R., *Francisco I. Madero.* New York, 1955.
Sands, W. F., *Our Jungle Diplomacy.* Chapel Hill, N.C., 1944.
Scholes, W., "Sir Lionel Carden's proposed agreement on Central America, 1912." *Americas,* January, 1959.

Schull, J., *Laurier, the First Canadian.* New York, 1965.

Siebert, Baron von, ed., *Graf Benckendorffs diplomatischer Schriftwechsel.* Berlin, 1928. 3 vols.

Simon, M., and D. E. Novocak, "Some dimensions of the American commercial invasion of Europe, 1871-1914." *Journal of Economic History,* December, 1964.

Skelton, O. D., *Life and Letters of Sir Wilfrid Laurier.* London, 1922. 2 vols.

Solvick, S. D., "William Howard Taft and the Payne-Aldrich Tariff." *Journal of American History,* December, 1963.

Speeches Incident to the Visit of Philander Chase Knox to the Countries of the Caribbean. Washington, 1913.

Spring-Rice, Sir Cecil, *The Letters and Friendships of Sir Cecil Spring-Rice,* S. Gwynn, ed. Boston, 1929. 2 vols.

Sprout, H., and M. Sprout, *The Rise of American Naval Power, 1776-1918.* Princeton, 1939.

Stephenson, N. W., *Nelson W. Aldrich.* New York, 1930.

Stieve, F., *Der diplomatische Schriftwechsel Iswolskis 1911-1914.* Berlin, 1924. 3 vols.

Straus, O. S., *Under Four Administrations.* Boston, 1922.

Stuart, G. H., *The Department of State.* New York, 1949.

Sullivan, Mark, *Our Times.* New York, 1926-1935. 6 vols.

Sun, E-tu, *Chinese Railways and British Interests, 1898-1911.* New York, 1954.

Taft, H. H., *Recollections of Full Years.* New York, 1914.

Taft, W. H., *Present Day Problems.* New York, 1908.

——, *The Presidency.* New York, 1916.

Tansill, C. C., *Canadian-American Relations, 1875-1911.* New Haven, 1943.

Tompkins, P., *American-Russian Relations in the Far East.* New York, 1949.

Treat, P. J., *Japan and the United States,* 1853-1928. Stanford, Calif., 1928.

Trevelyan, G. M., *Grey of Fallodon.* Boston, 1937.

Trubetzkoi, G. N., *Russland als Grossmacht.* Berlin, 1917.

Turner, F. C., "Anti-Americanism in Mexico, 1910-1913." *Hispanic American Historical Review,* November, 1967.

Uloa, B., "Las relaciones México-Norteamericanas, 1910-1911." *Historia Mexicana,* Julio-Septiembre, 1965.

U. S., Bureau of the Census, *Historical Statistics of the United States, Colonial Times to 1957.* Washington, 1960.

U. S., Congress, Senate, *Hearings Before the Subcommittee of the Committee on Foreign Relations.* 69th Cong. 2d sess., 1927.

U. S., *Naval Institute Proceedings.*

U. S., *Papers Relating to the Foreign Relations of the United States 1909-1913.* Washington, 1914-1920.

Vagts, A., *Deutschland und die Vereinigten Staaten in der Weltpolitik.* New York, 1935. 2 vols.

Varg, P. A., *Missionaries, Chinese and Diplomats.* Princeton, 1958.
———, *Open Door Diplomat. The Life of W. W. Rockhill.* Urbana, Ill., 1952.
———, *The Making of a Myth: The United States and China, 1897-1912.* East Lansing, Mich., 1968.
———, "The Myth of the China Market, 1890-1940." *American Historical Review,* February, 1968.
Vevier, C., *The United States and China, 1906-1913.* New Brunswick, N.J., 1955.
Weitzel, G. T., "The United States and Central America." *Annals of the American Academy of Political and Social Science.* July, 1927.
Welles, S., *Naboth's Vineyard.* New York, 1928. 2 vols.
Wheeler, P., and H. E. Rives, *Dome of Many-Coloured Glass.* New York, 1955.
Wilson, H. L., *Diplomatic Episodes in Mexico, Belgium and Chile.* New York, 1927.
Wilson, Hugh, *The Education of a Diplomat.* New York, 1938.
Wright, A. R., "German Interest in Panama's Piñas Bay, 1910-1938." *Journal of Modern History,* March 1955.
Yeselson, A., *United States–Persian Diplomatic Relations, 1883–1921.* New Brunswick, N.J., 1956.
Zabriskie, E. H., *American-Russian Rivalry in the Far East: A Study in Diplomacy and Power Politics, 1895-1914.* Philadelphia, 1946.
Zook, D. H., "The Spanish Arbitration of the Ecuador–Peru Dispute." *Americas,* April, 1964.

Newspapers and Magazines

London Times
New York Times
New York Tribune

Bankers Magazine
Fortune
Literary Digest
Nation
Review of Reviews

Index